كبرياء بغداد

مستوحاة من قصة واقعية

VERTIGO
DC COMICS

بغداد

مستوحاة من قصة واقعية

للكاتب : بريان فوقان

رسوم : نايكو هينريكون

طباعة : تود كلين

كبرياء

PRIDE OF BAGHDAD

INSPIRED BY A TRUE STORY

WRITTEN BY BRIAN K. VAUGHAN

ART BY NIKO HENRICHON

LETTERING BY TODD KLEIN

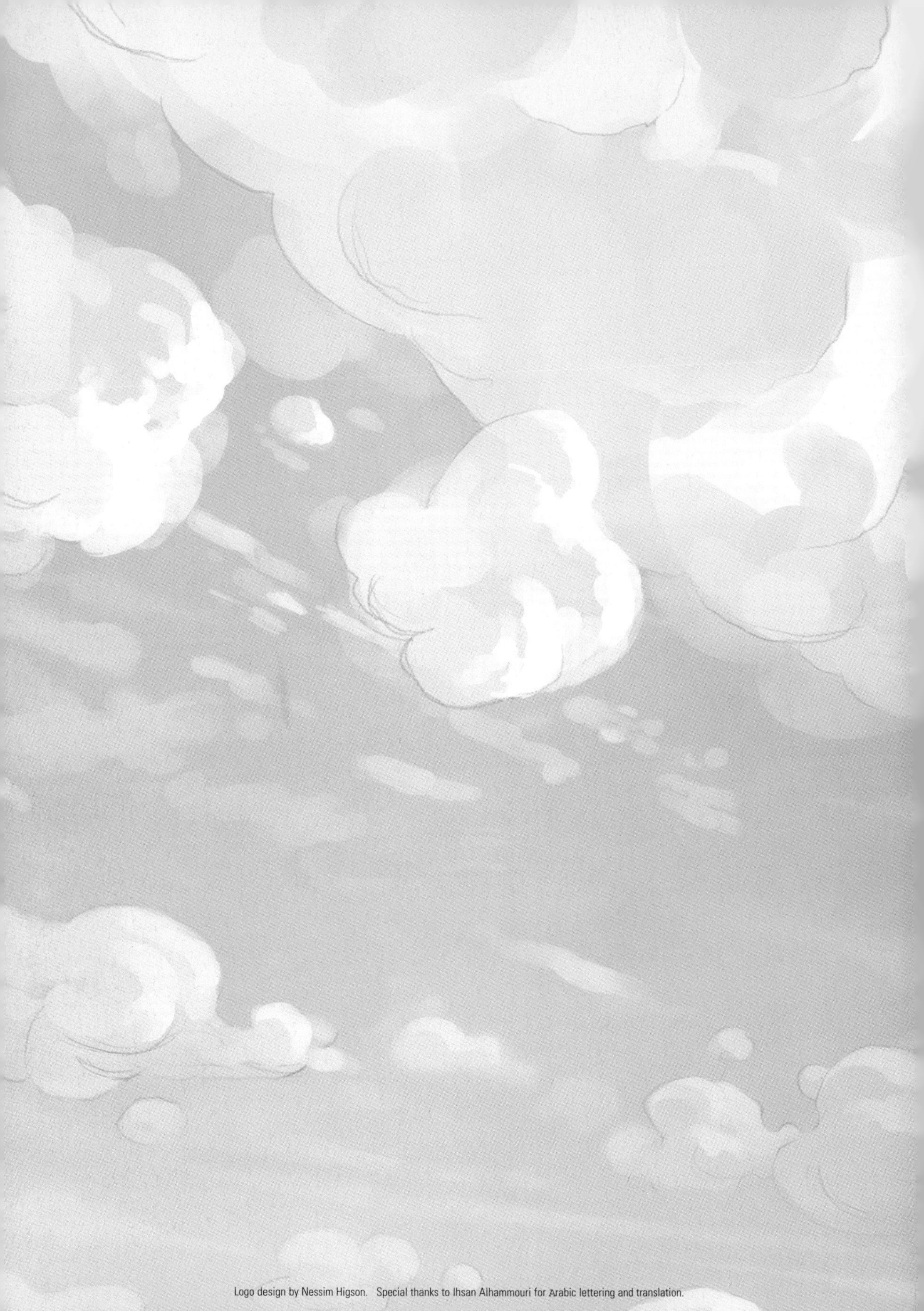

Logo design by Nessim Higson. Special thanks to Ihsan Alhammouri for Arabic lettering and translation.

PRIDE OF BAGHDAD Published by DC Comics, 1700 Broadway, New York, NY 10019.
HC ISBN: 1-4012-0314-0 ISBN13: 978-1-4012-0314-6 SC ISBN: 1-4012-0315-9 ISBN13: 978-1-4012-0315-3
Printed in Canada. DC Comics, a Warner Bros. Entertainment Company.

FOR DANIEL M. KANEMOTO
-BRIAN K. VAUGHAN

FOR LAËTITIA CASSAN
-NIKO HENRICHON

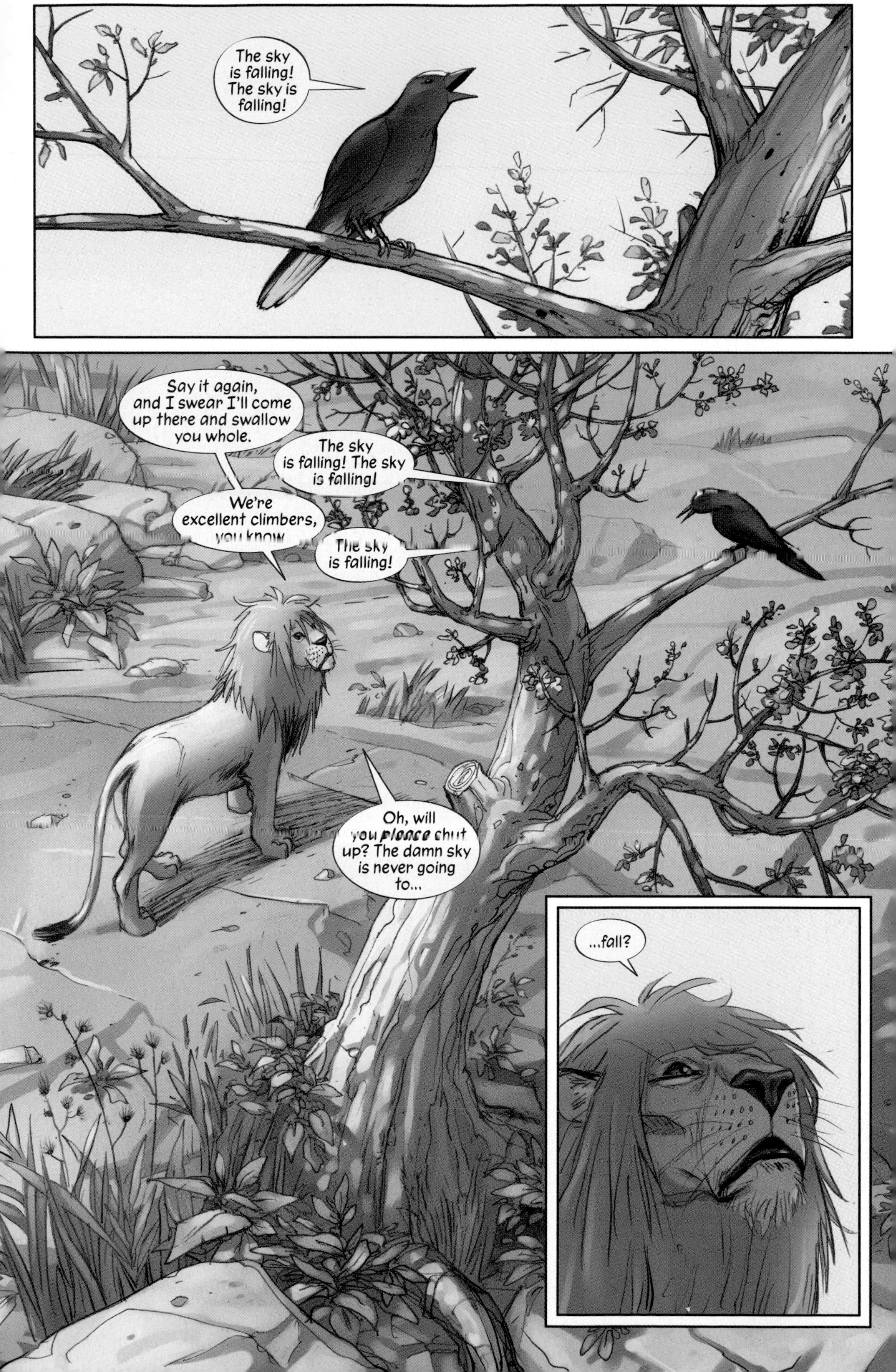
The sky is falling! The sky is falling!
Say it again, and I swear I'll come up there and swallow you whole.
The sky is falling! The sky is falling!
We're excellent climbers, you know.
The sky is falling!
Oh, will you please shut up? The damn sky is never going to...
...fall?

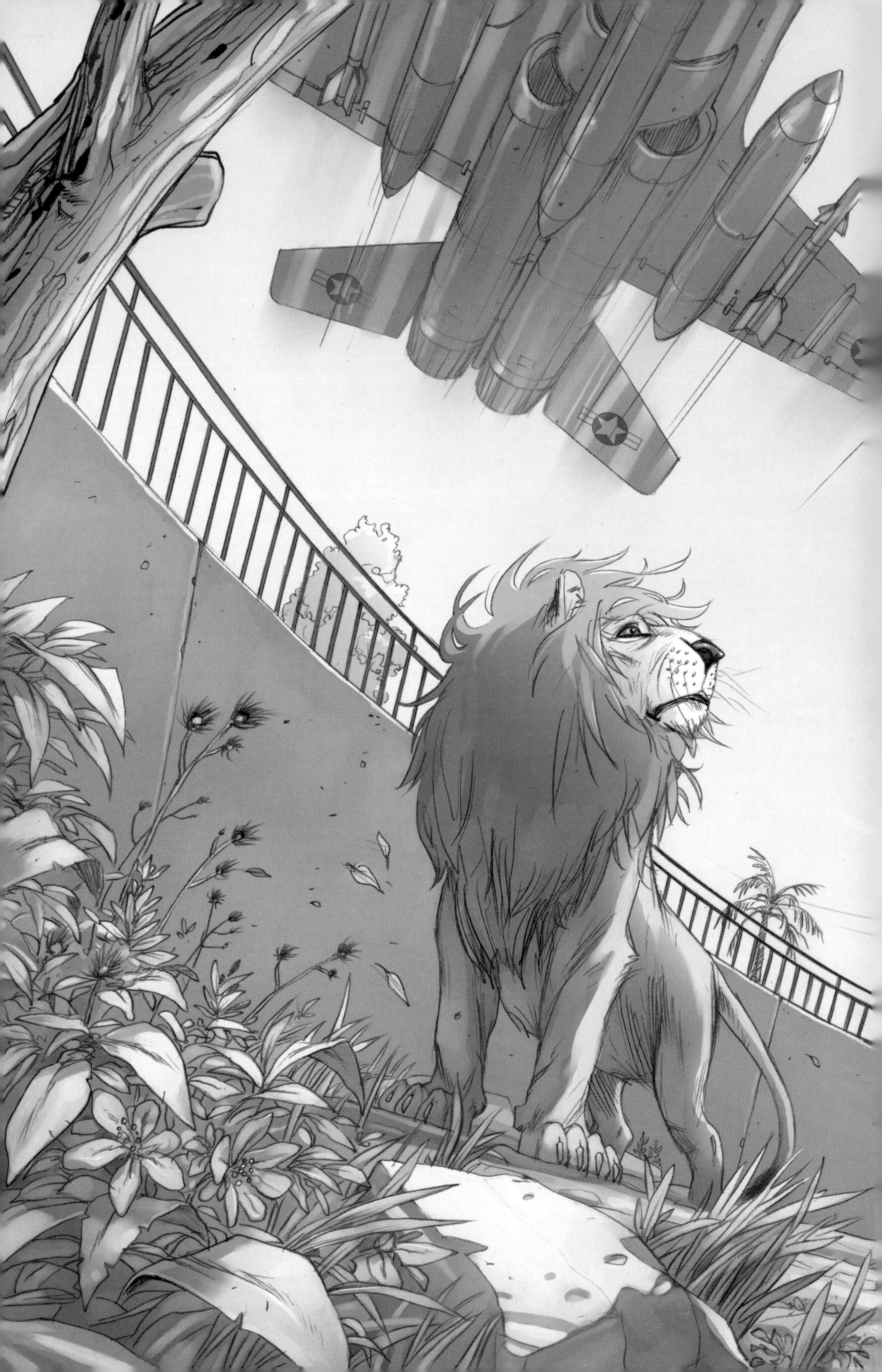

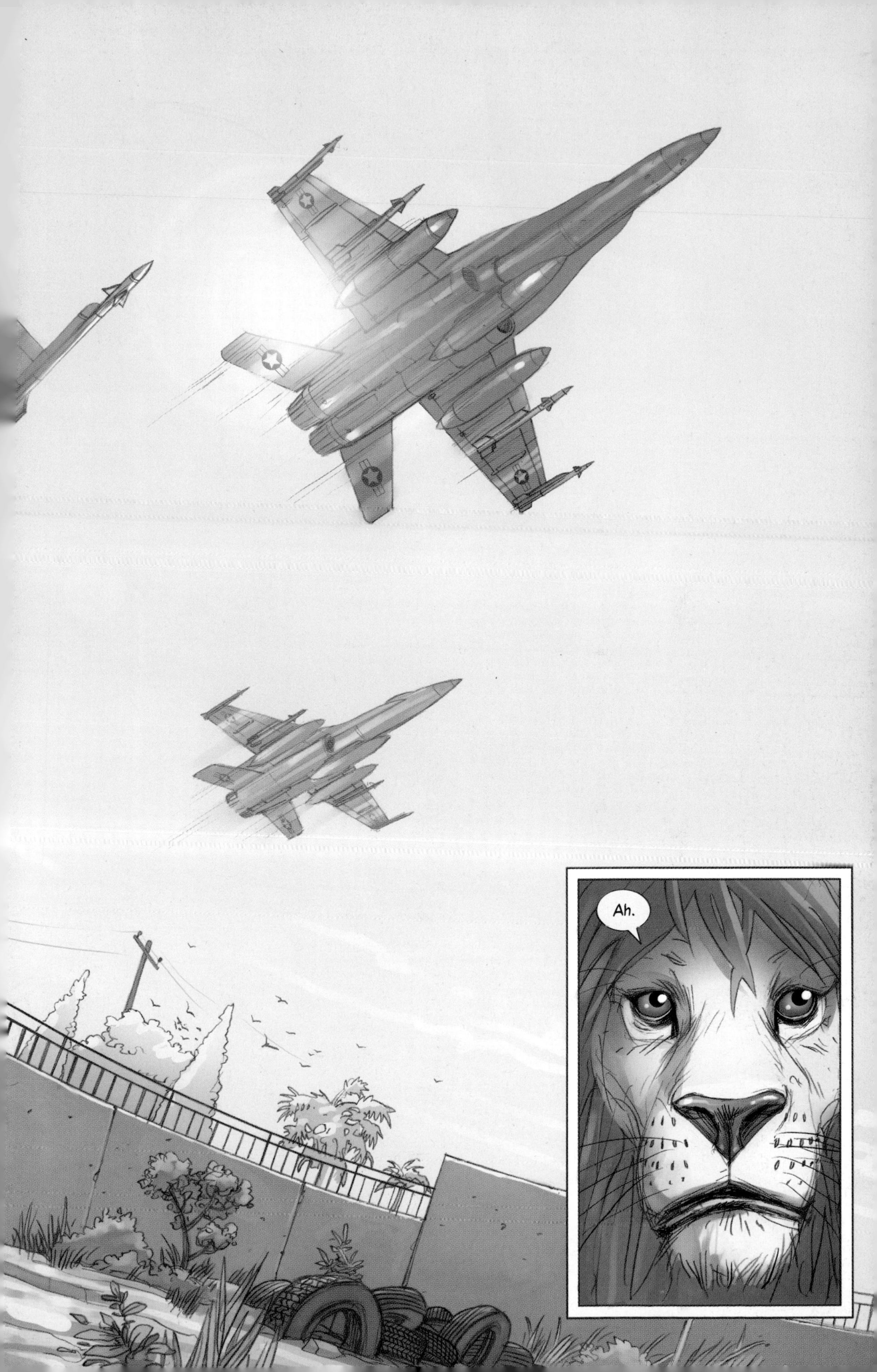
Ah.

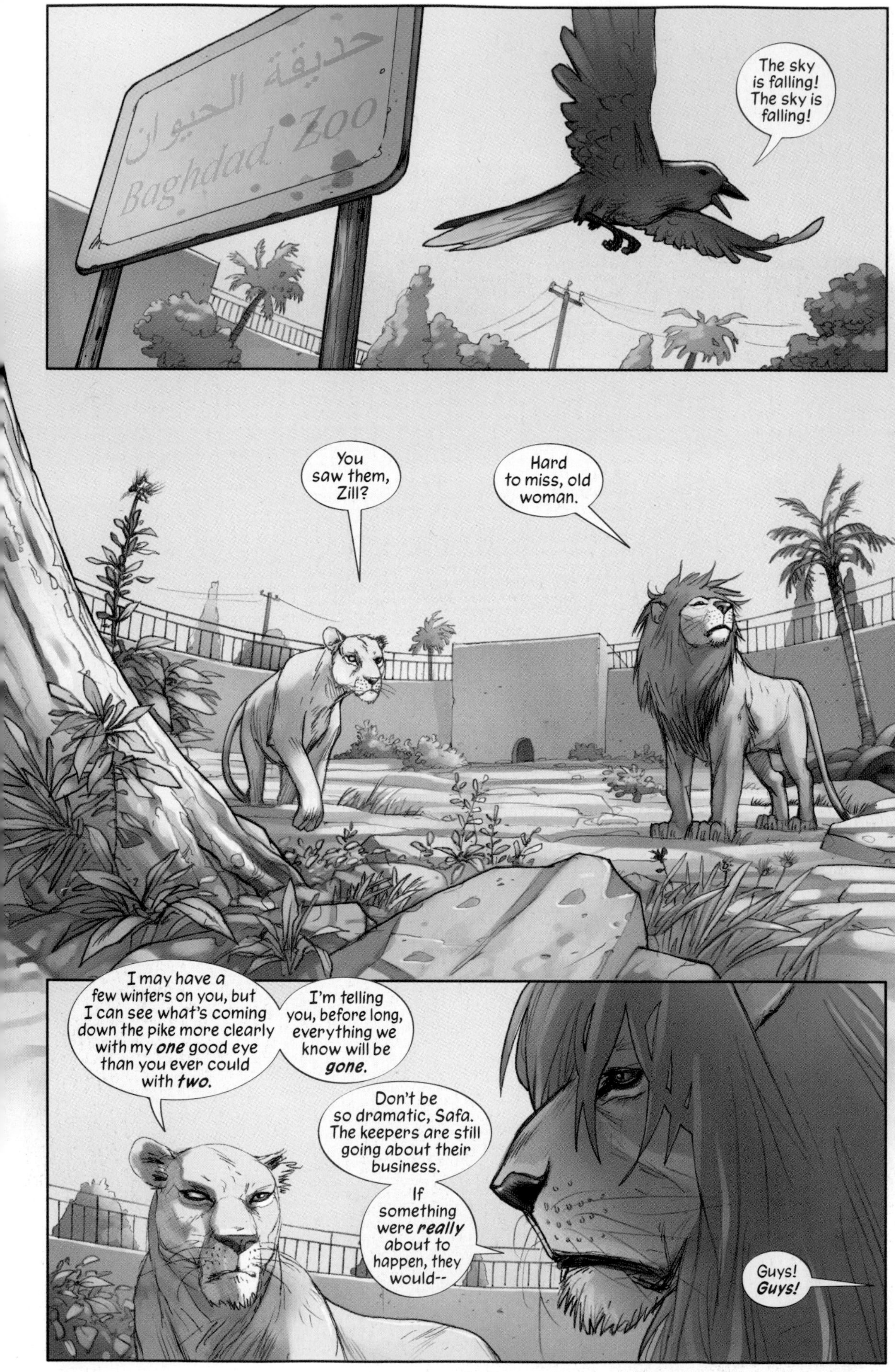
حديقة الحيوان
Baghdad Zoo
The sky is falling! The sky is falling!
You saw them, Zill?
Hard to miss, old woman.
I may have a few winters on you, but I can see what's coming down the pike more clearly with my *one* good eye than you ever could with *two*.
I'm telling you, before long, everything we know will be *gone*.
Don't be so dramatic, Safa. The keepers are still going about their business.
If something were *really* about to happen, they would--
Guys! *Guys!*

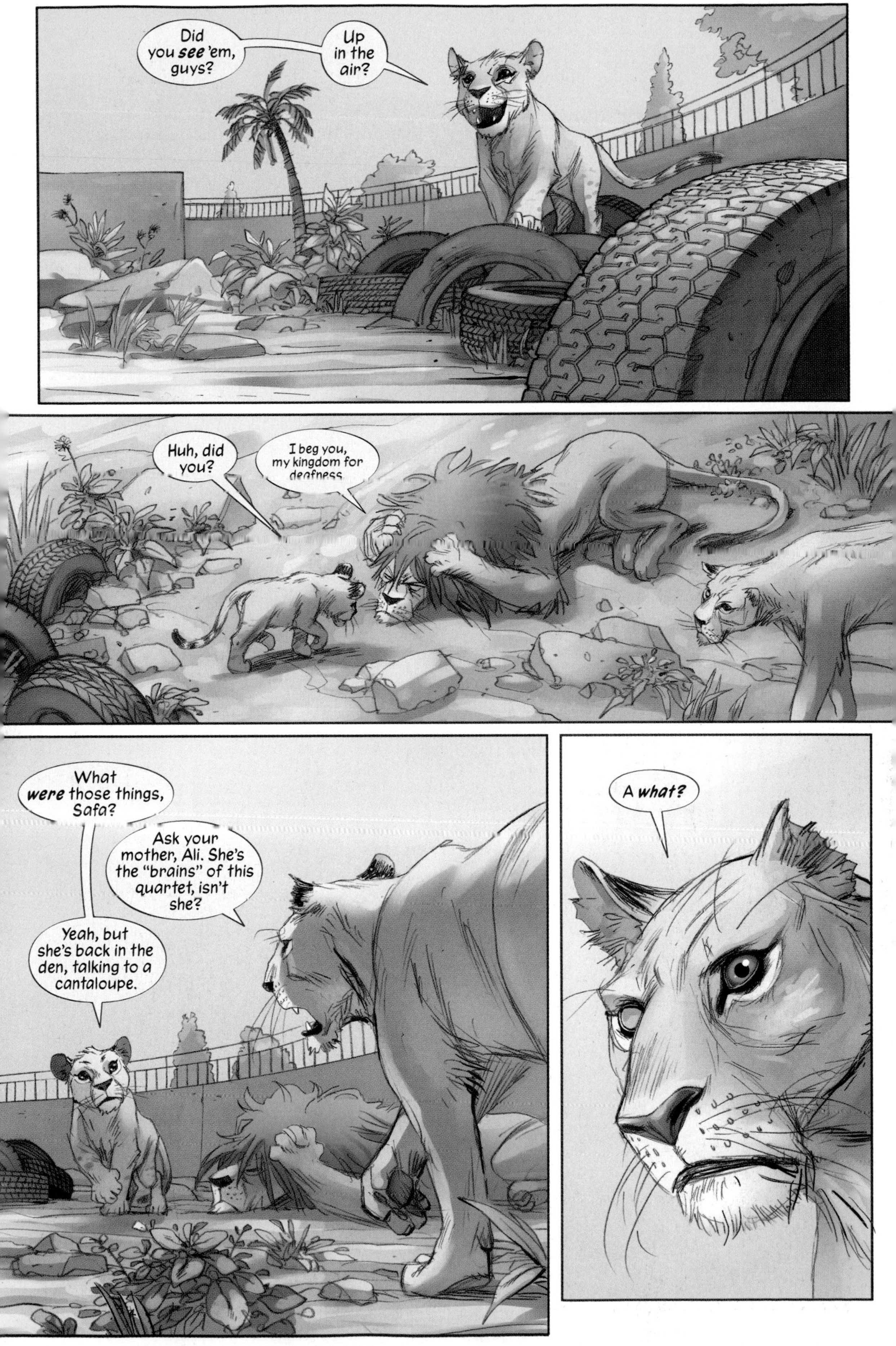
Did you *see* 'em, guys?
Up in the air?
Huh, did you?
I beg you, my kingdom for deafness.
What *were* those things, Safa?
Ask your mother, Ali. She's the "brains" of this quartet, isn't she?
Yeah, but she's back in the den, talking to a cantaloupe.
A *what?*

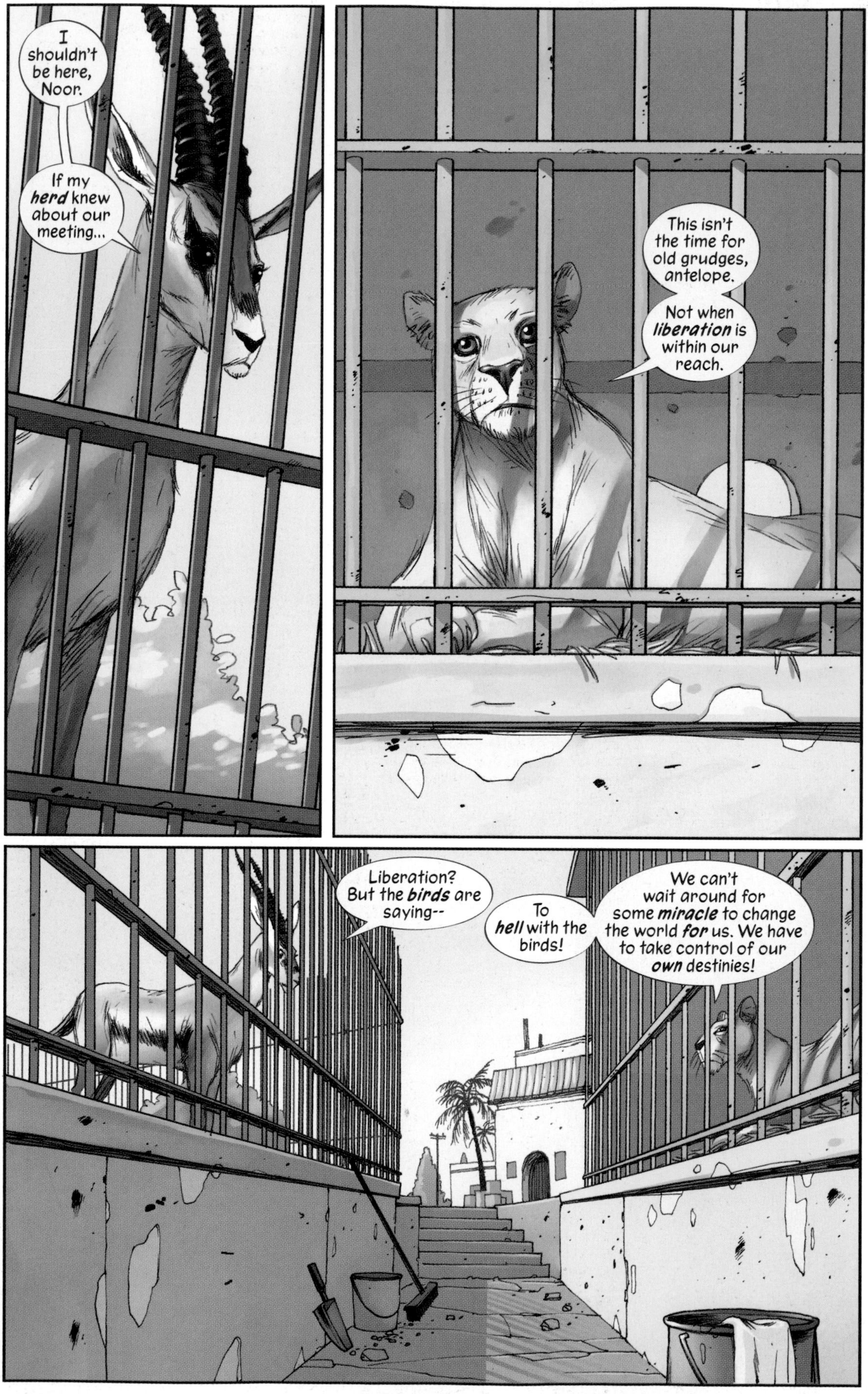
I shouldn't be here, Noor.
If my *herd* knew about our meeting...
This isn't the time for old grudges, antelope.
Not when *liberation* is within our reach.
Liberation? But the *birds* are saying--
To *hell* with the birds!
We can't wait around for some *miracle* to change the world *for* us. We have to take control of our *own* destinies!

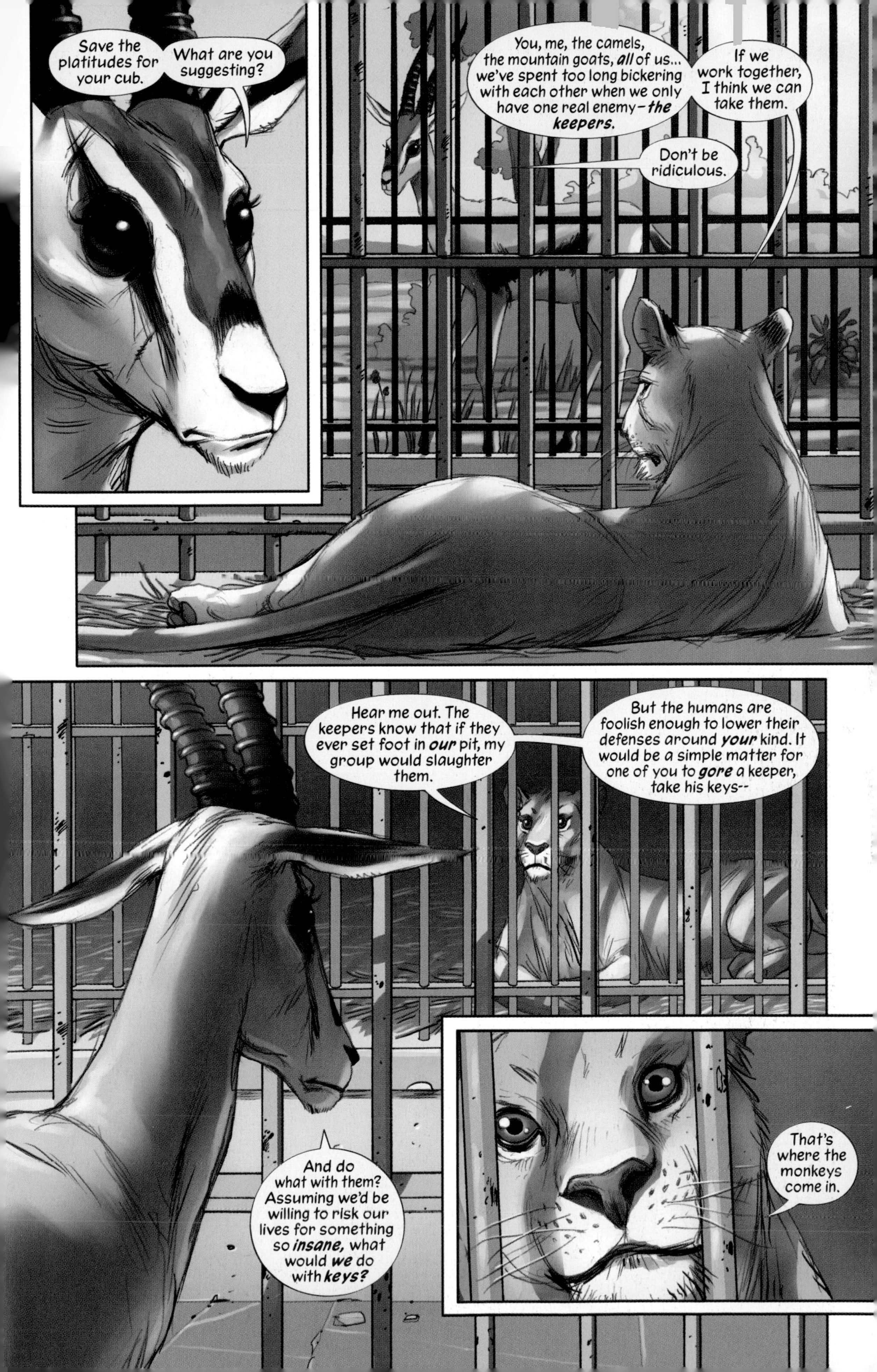

Save the platitudes for your cub.
What are you suggesting?
You, me, the camels, the mountain goats, *all* of us... we've spent too long bickering with each other when we only have one real enemy—*the keepers*.
If we work together, I think we can take them.
Don't be ridiculous.
Hear me out. The keepers know that if they ever set foot in *our* pit, my group would slaughter them.
But the humans are foolish enough to lower their defenses around *your* kind. It would be a simple matter for one of you to *gore* a keeper, take his keys--
And do what with them? Assuming we'd be willing to risk our lives for something so *insane,* what would *we* do with *keys?*
That's where the monkeys come in.

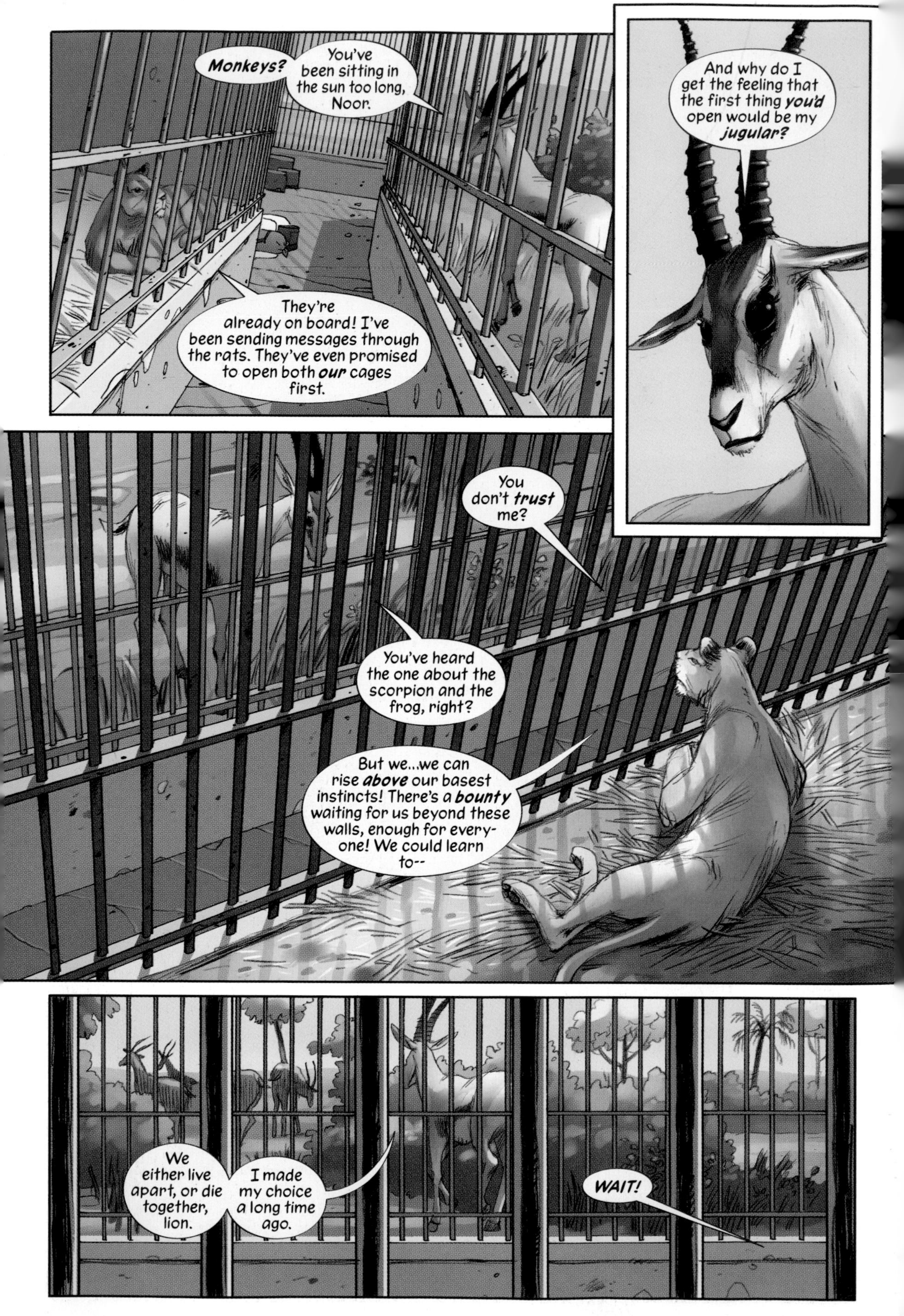

Monkeys?
You've been sitting in the sun too long, Noor.
They're already on board! I've been sending messages through the rats. They've even promised to open both our cages first.
And why do I get the feeling that the first thing you'd open would be my jugular?
You don't trust me?
You've heard the one about the scorpion and the frog, right?
But we...we can rise above our basest instincts! There's a bounty waiting for us beyond these walls, enough for every-one! We could learn to--
We either live apart, or die together, lion.
I made my choice a long time ago.
WAIT!

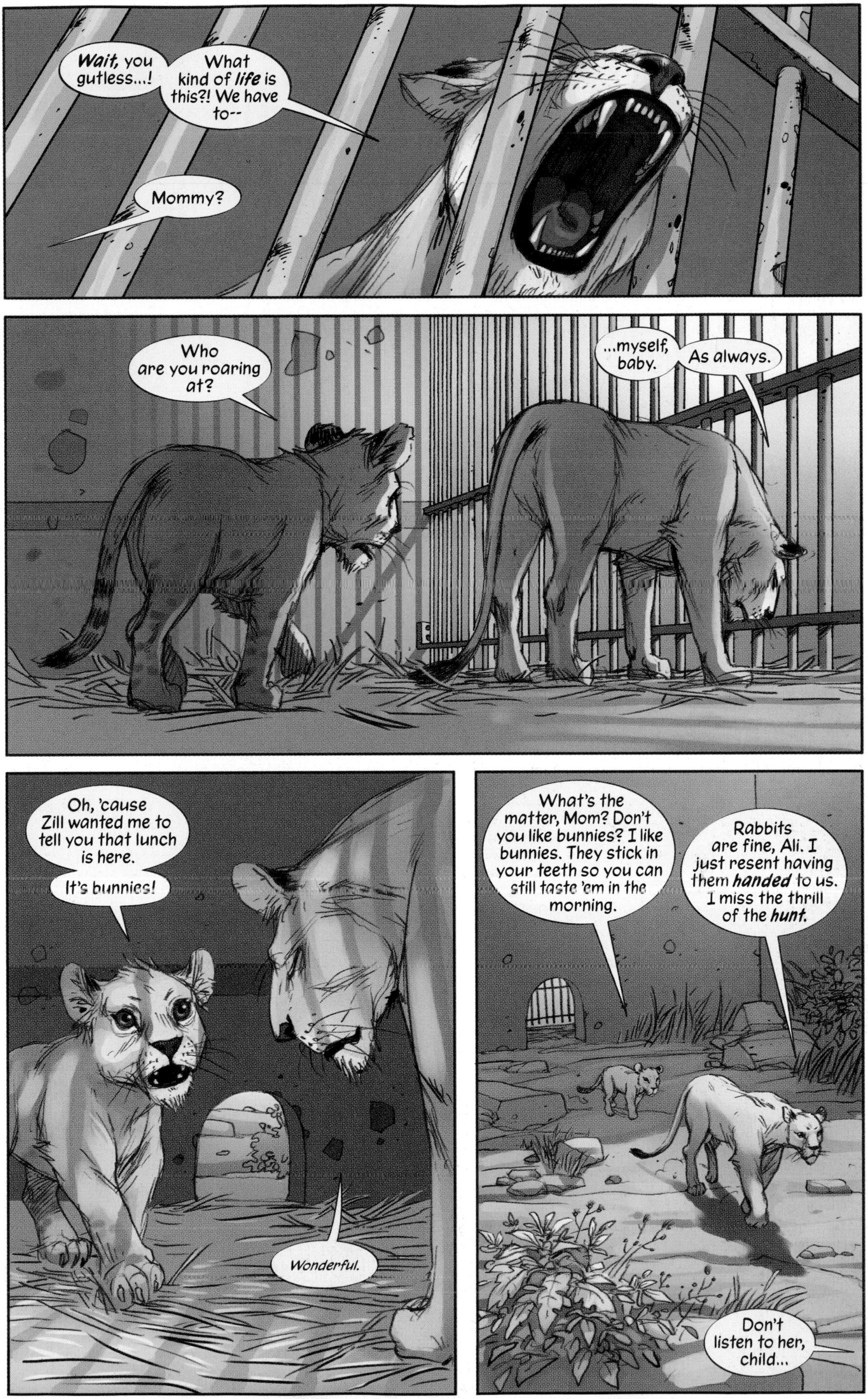
Wait, you gutless...!
What kind of ***life*** is this?! We have to--
Mommy?
Who are you roaring at?
...myself, baby.
As always.
Oh, 'cause Zill wanted me to tell you that lunch is here.
It's bunnies!
Wonderful.
What's the matter, Mom? Don't you like bunnies? I like bunnies. They stick in your teeth so you can still taste 'em in the morning.
Rabbits are fine, Ali. I just resent having them ***handed*** to us. I miss the thrill of the ***hunt.***
Don't listen to her, child...

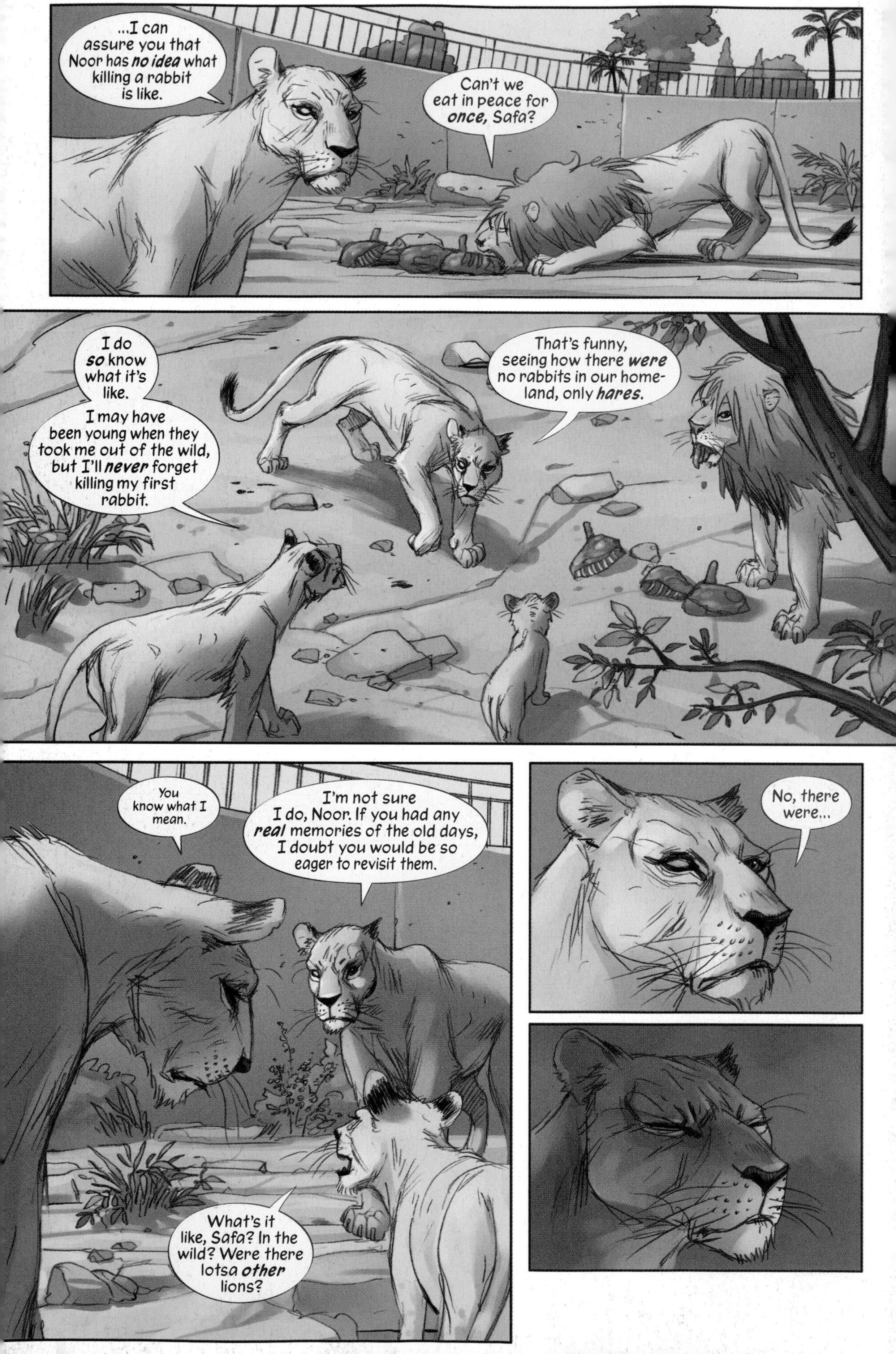
...I can assure you that Noor has *no idea* what killing a rabbit is like.
Can't we eat in peace for *once,* Safa?
I do *so* know what it's like.
I may have been young when they took me out of the wild, but I'll *never* forget killing my first rabbit.
That's funny, seeing how there *were* no rabbits in our homeland, only *hares*.
You know what I mean.
I'm not sure I do, Noor. If you had any *real* memories of the old days, I doubt you would be so eager to revisit them.
What's it like, Safa? In the wild? Were there lotsa *other* lions?
No, there were...

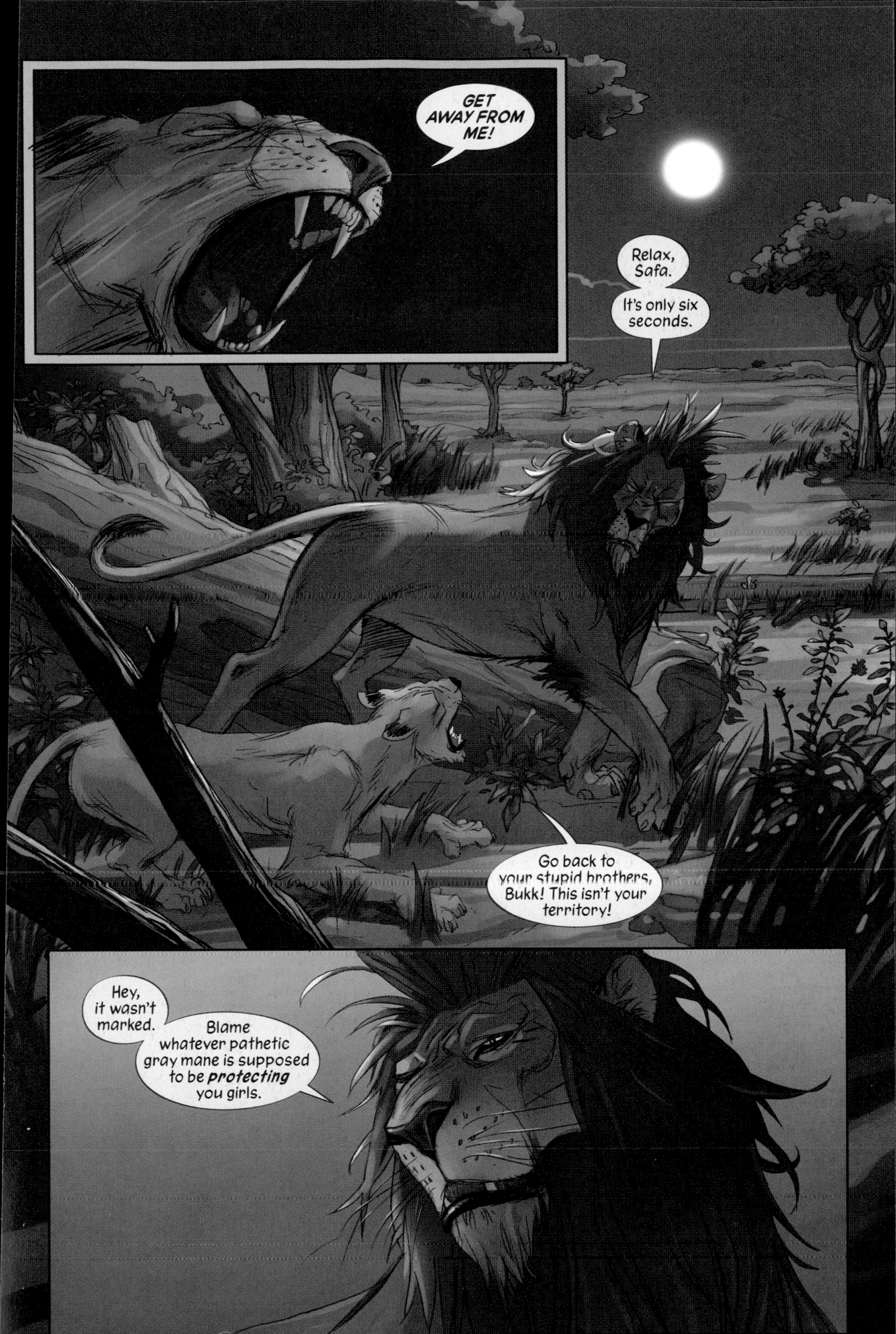
GET AWAY FROM ME!
Relax, Safa.
It's only six seconds.
Go back to your stupid brothers, Bukk! This isn't your territory!
Hey, it wasn't marked.
Blame whatever pathetic gray mane is supposed to be *protecting* you girls.

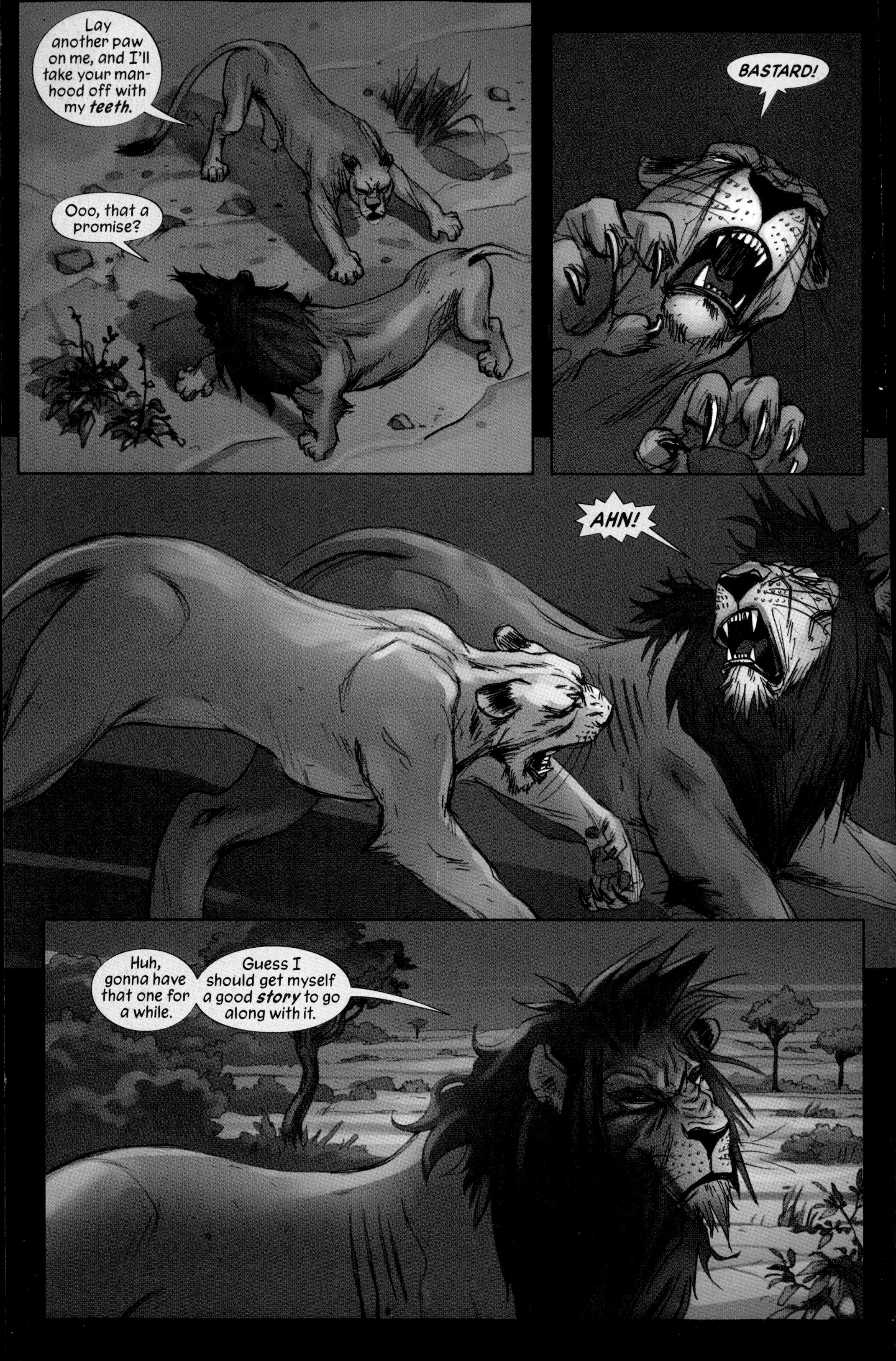
Lay another paw on me, and I'll take your manhood off with my *teeth*.
Ooo, that a promise?
BASTARD!
AHN!
Huh, gonna have that one for a while.
Guess I should get myself a good *story* to go along with it.

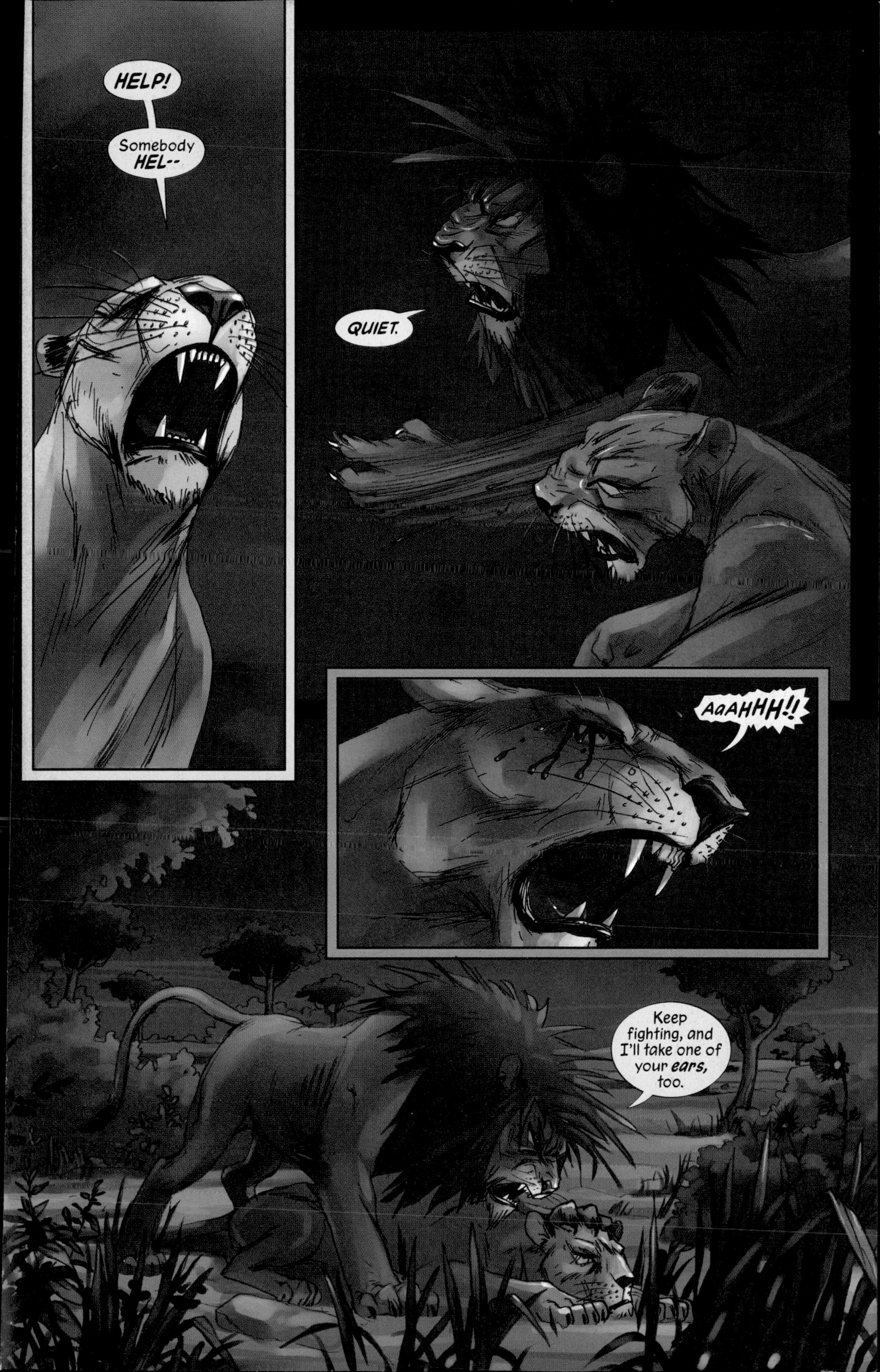
HELP!
Somebody HEL--
QUIET.
AaAHHH!!
Keep fighting, and I'll take one of your ears, too.

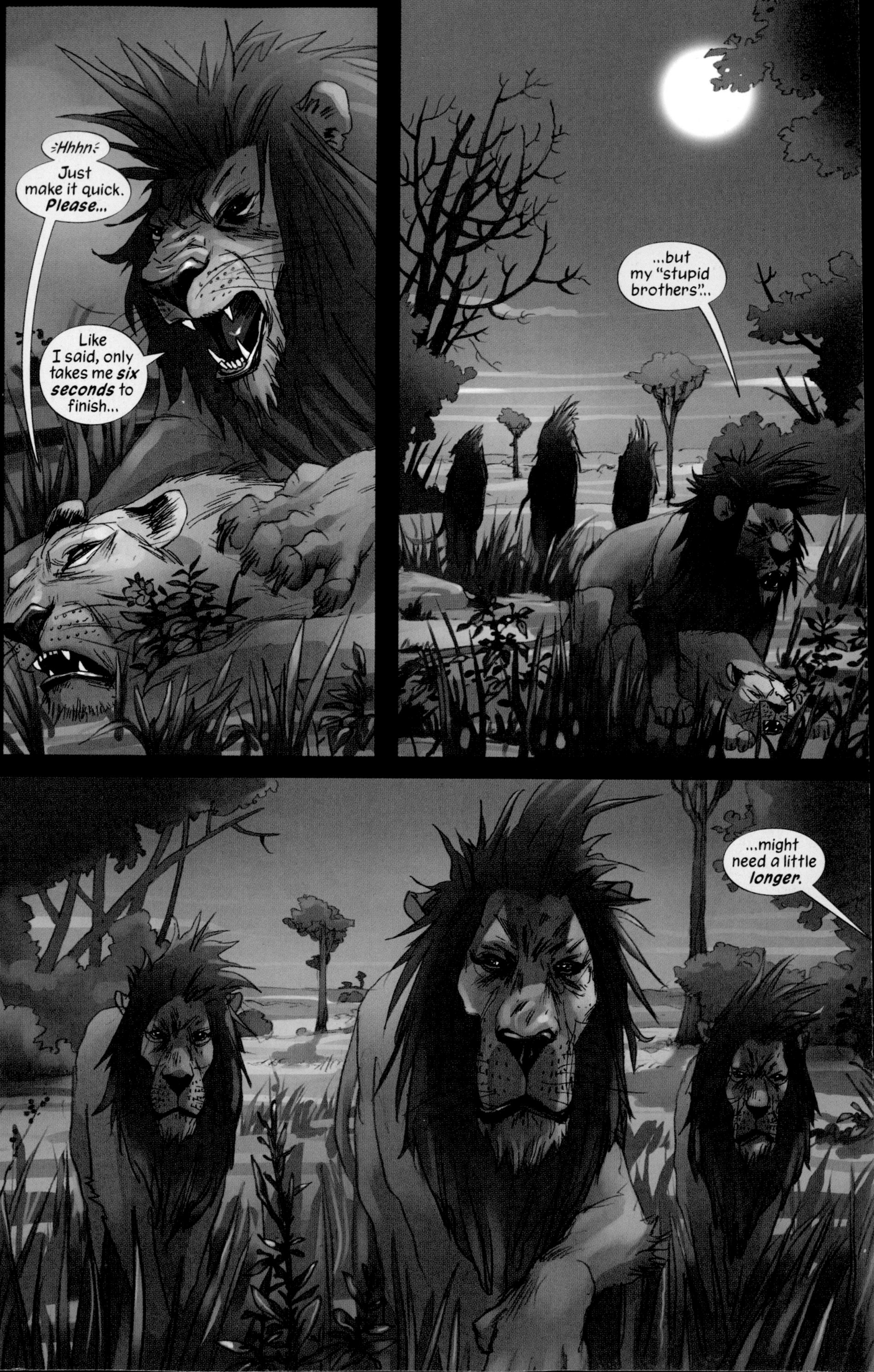
Hhhn
Just make it quick. **Please...**
Like I said, only takes me ***six seconds*** to finish...
...but my "stupid brothers"...
...might need a little ***longer.***

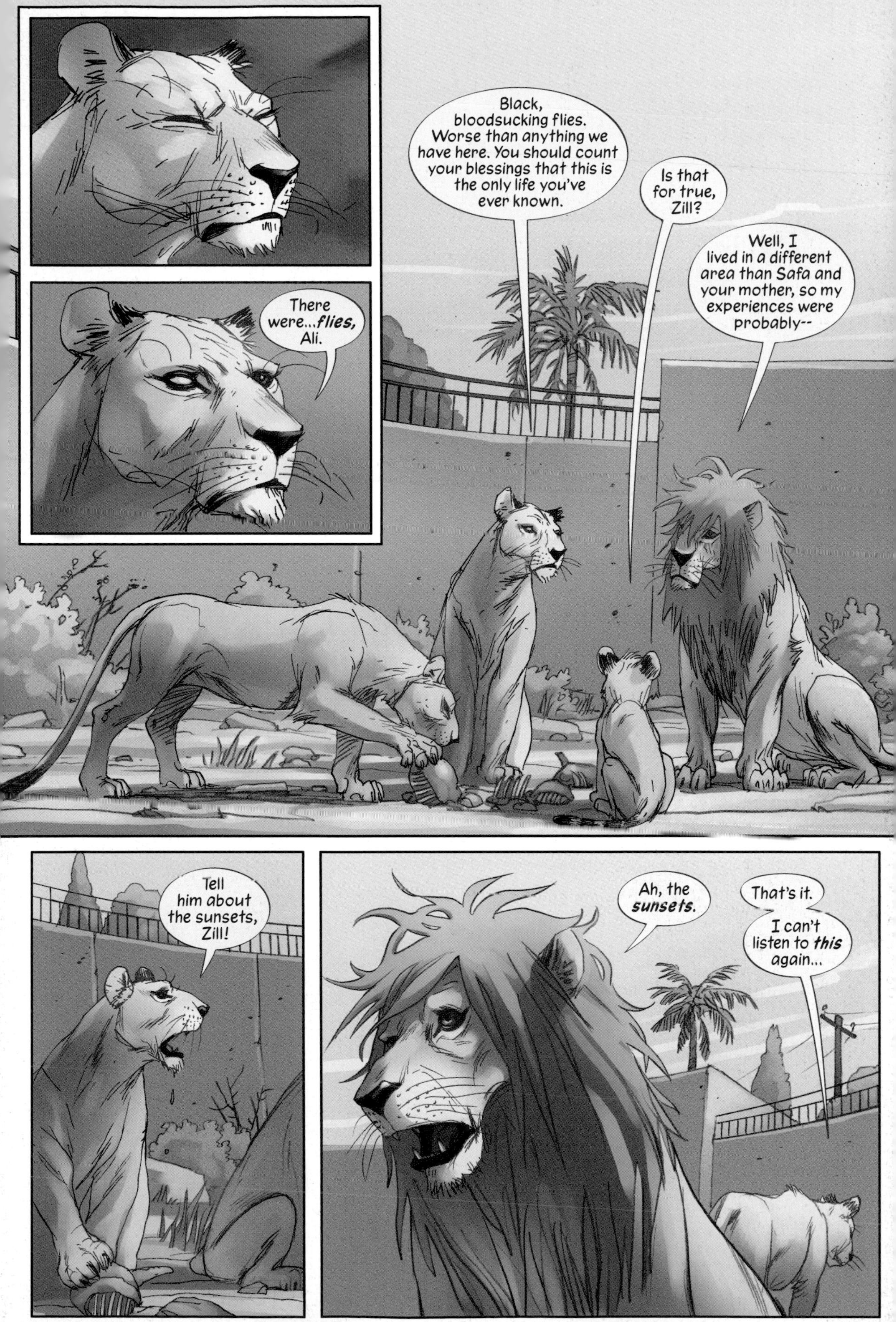

There were...*flies,* Ali.
Black, bloodsucking flies. Worse than anything we have here. You should count your blessings that this is the only life you've ever known.
Is that for true, Zill?
Well, I lived in a different area than Safa and your mother, so my experiences were probably--
Tell him about the sunsets, Zill!
Ah, the *sunsets.*
That's it.
I can't listen to *this* again...

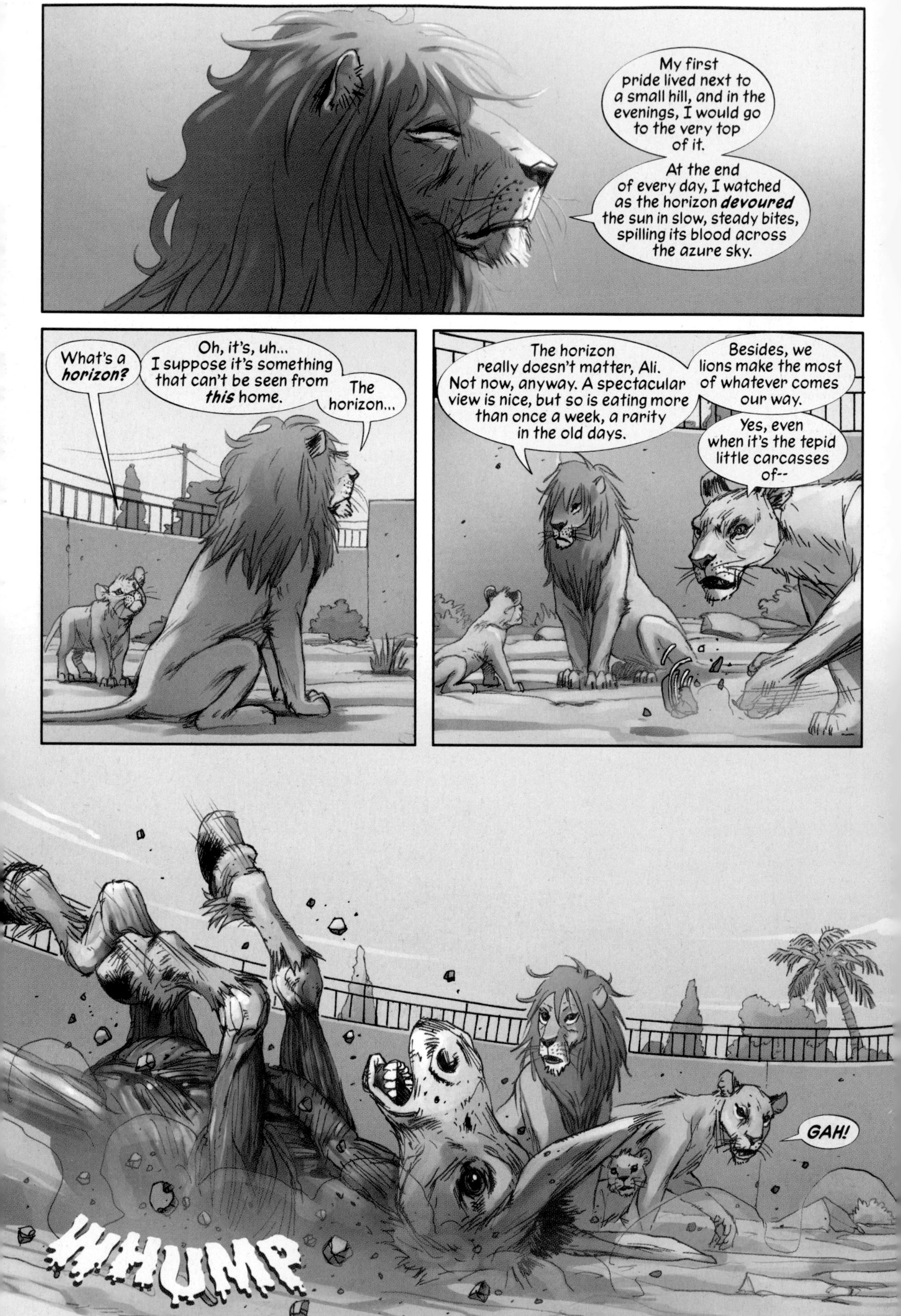

My first pride lived next to a small hill, and in the evenings, I would go to the very top of it.
At the end of every day, I watched as the horizon ***devoured*** the sun in slow, steady bites, spilling its blood across the azure sky.
What's a ***horizon?***
Oh, it's, uh... I suppose it's something that can't be seen from ***this*** home.
The horizon...
The horizon really doesn't matter, Ali. Not now, anyway. A spectacular view is nice, but so is eating more than once a week, a rarity in the old days.
Besides, we lions make the most of whatever comes our way.
Yes, even when it's the tepid little carcasses of--
WHUMP
GAH!

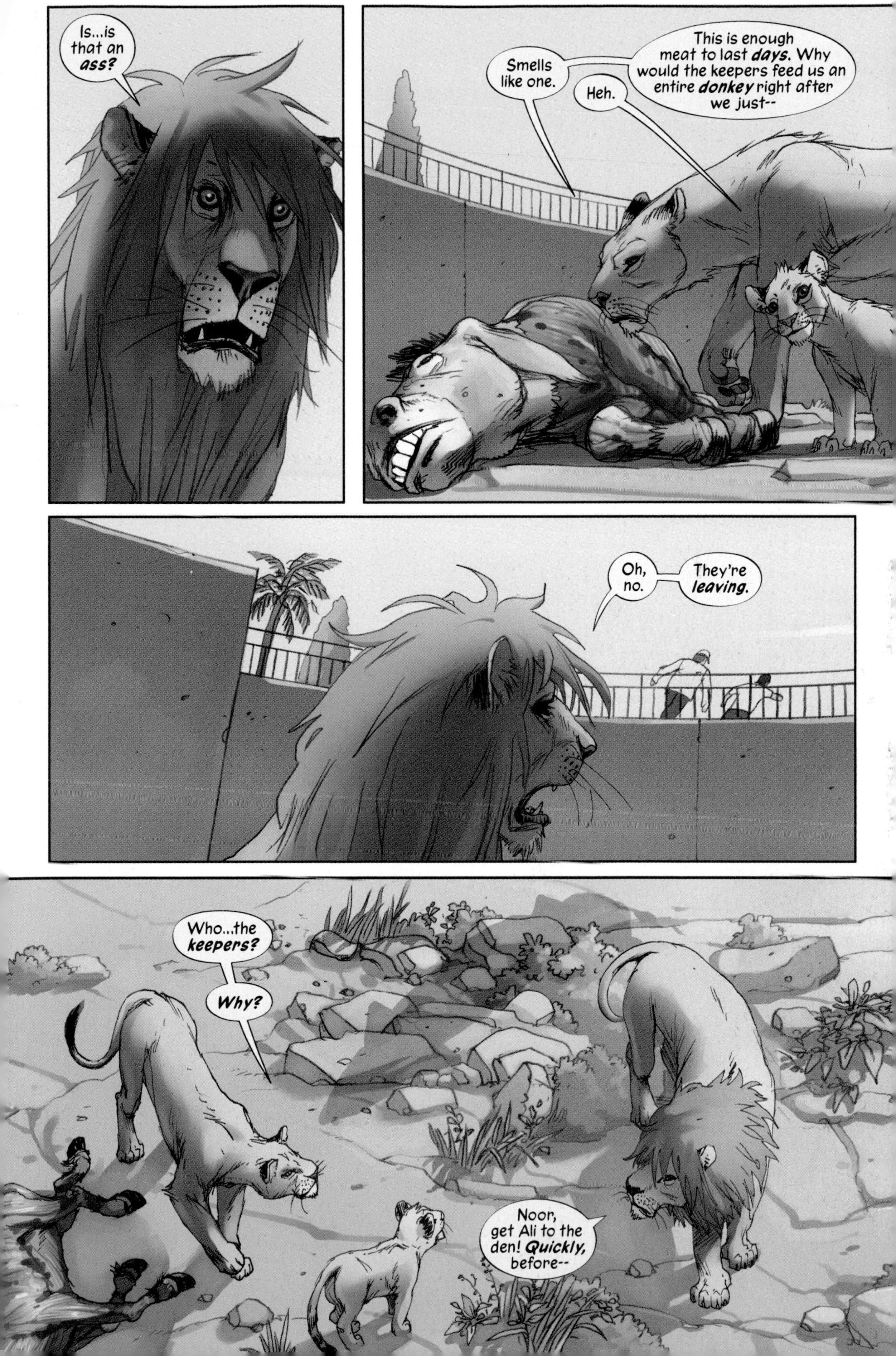

Is...is that an *ass?*
Smells like one.
This is enough meat to last *days.* Why would the keepers feed us an entire *donkey* right after we just--
Heh.
Oh, no.
They're *leaving.*
Who...the *keepers?*
Why?
Noor, get Ali to the den! *Quickly,* before--

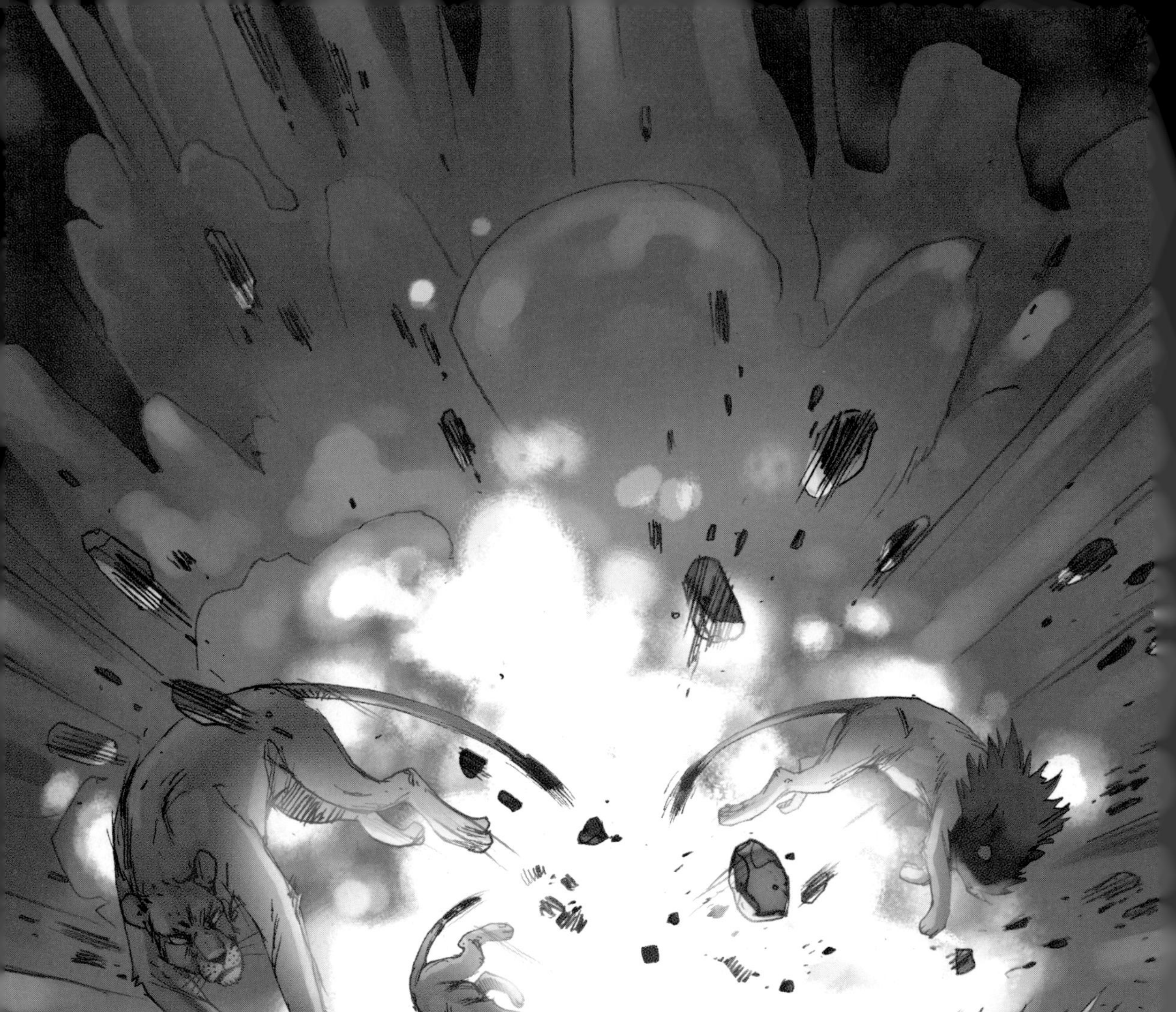

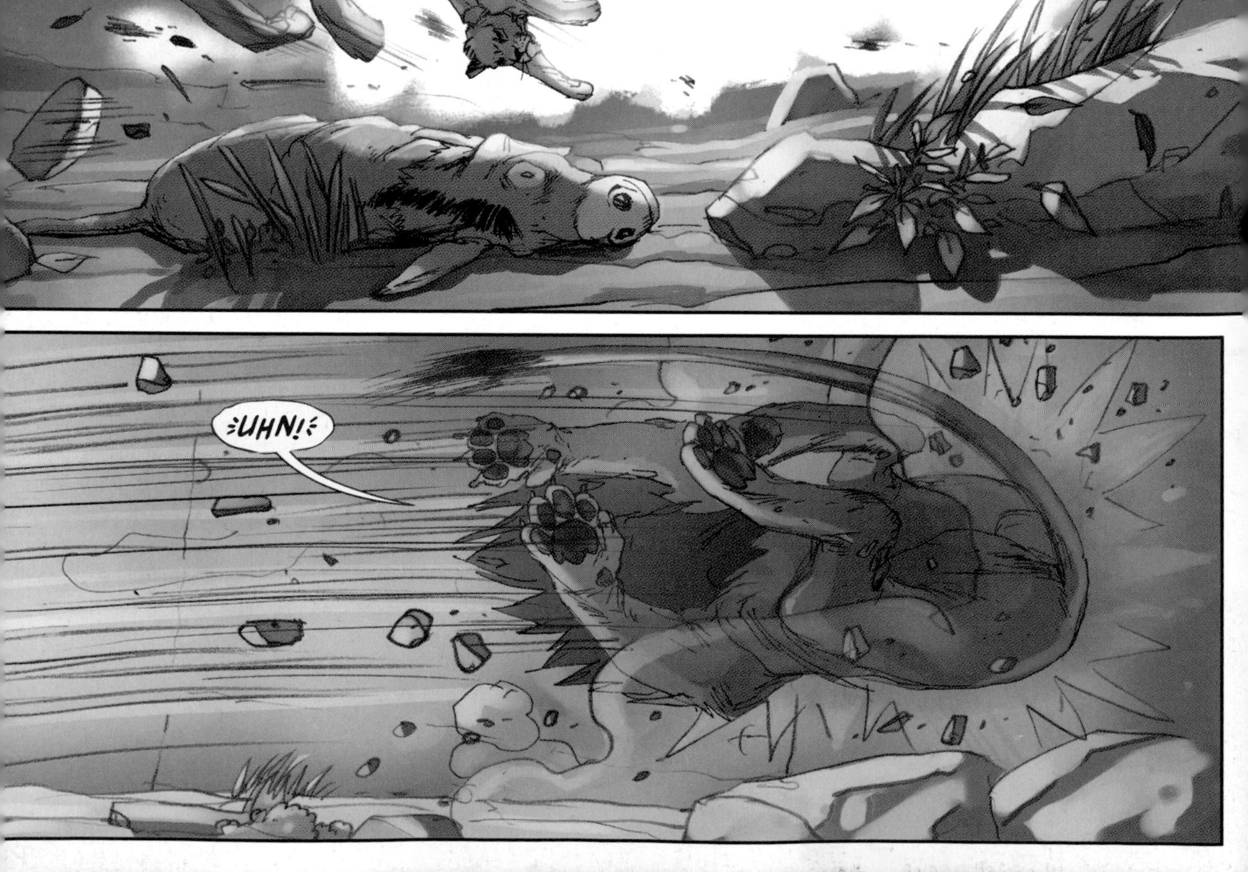
UHN!

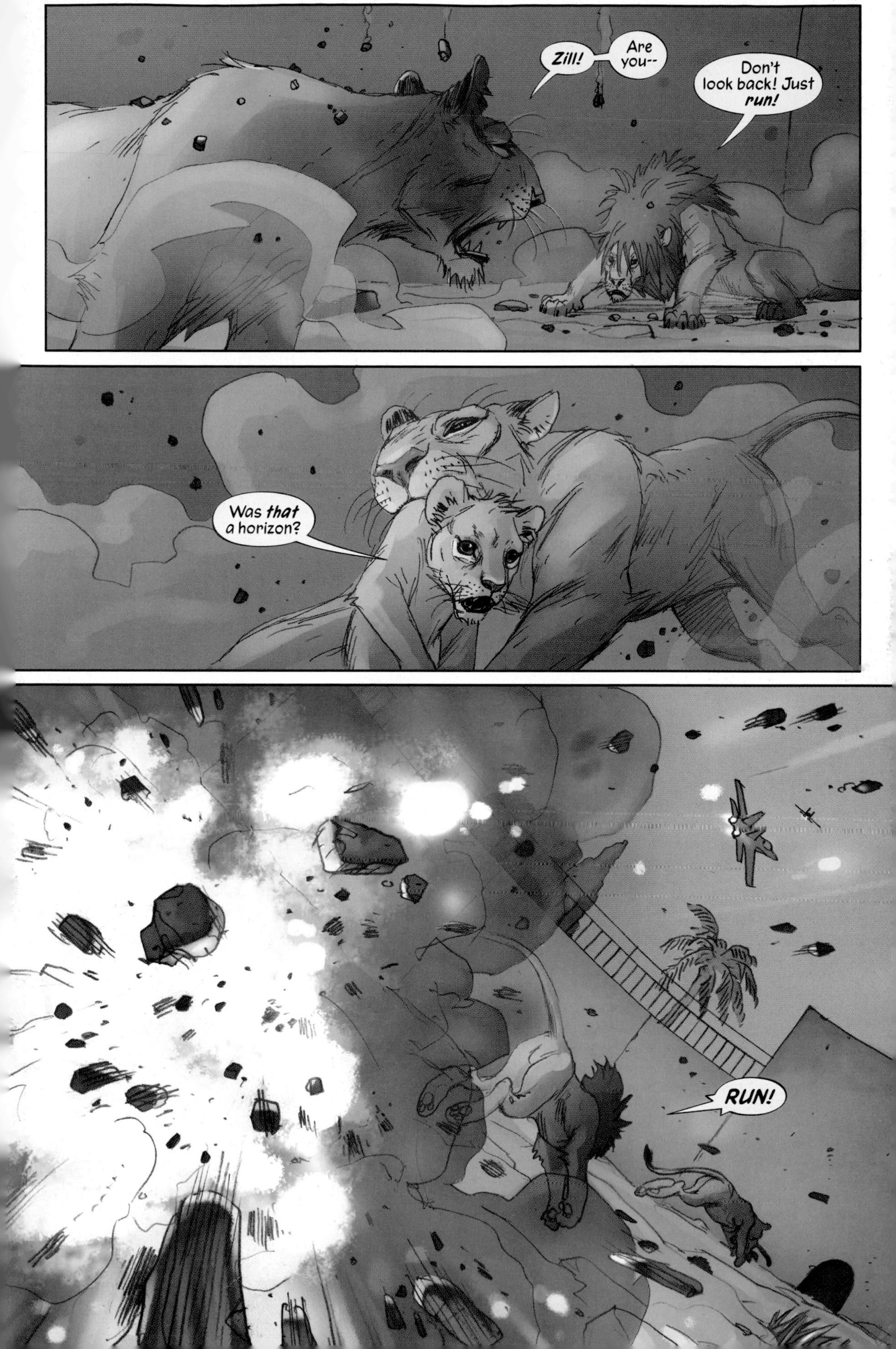
Zill!
Are you--
Don't look back! Just run!
Was that a horizon?
RUN!

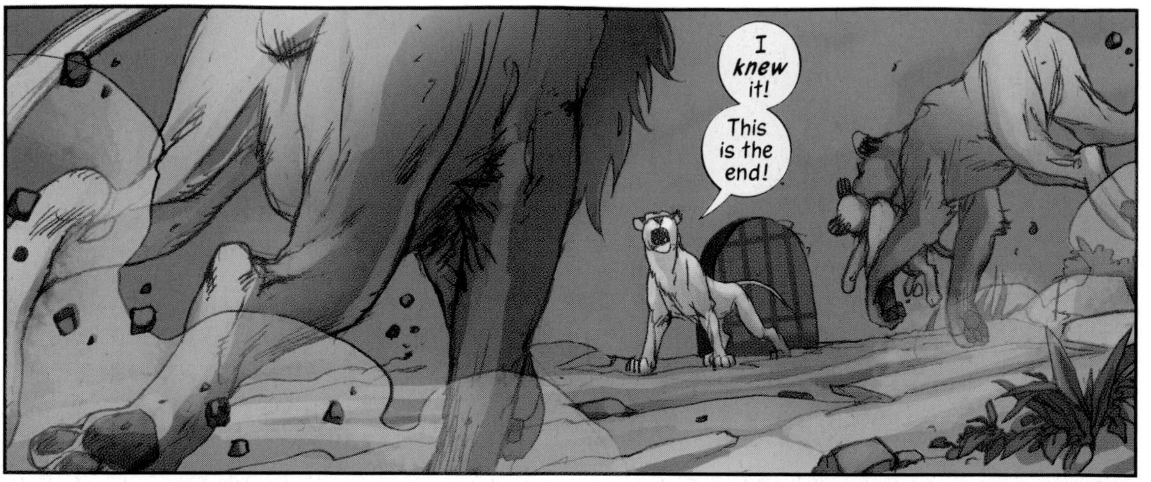
I *knew* it!
This is the end!

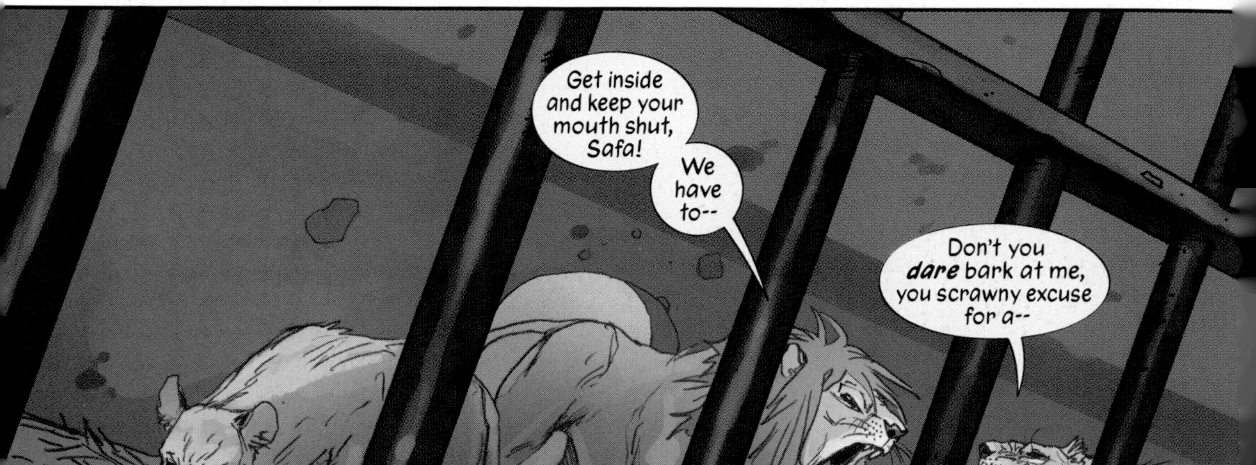
Get inside and keep your mouth shut, Safa!
We have to--
Don't you *dare* bark at me, you scrawny excuse for a--

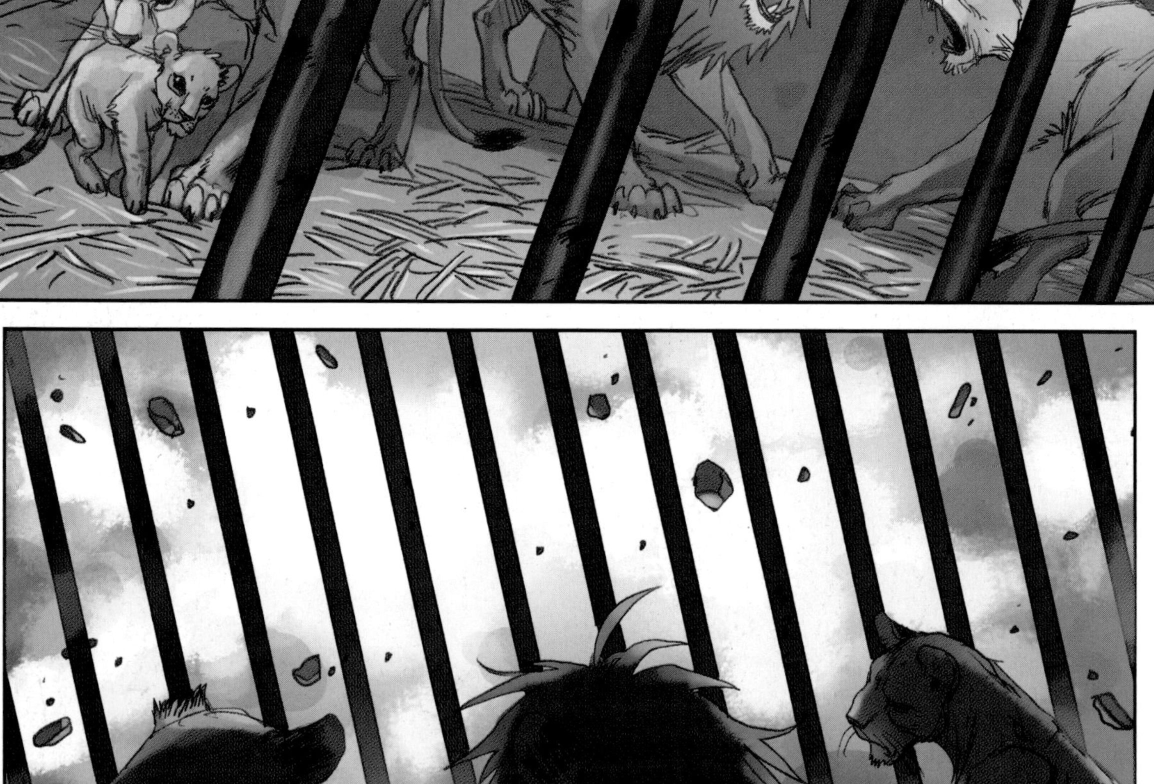

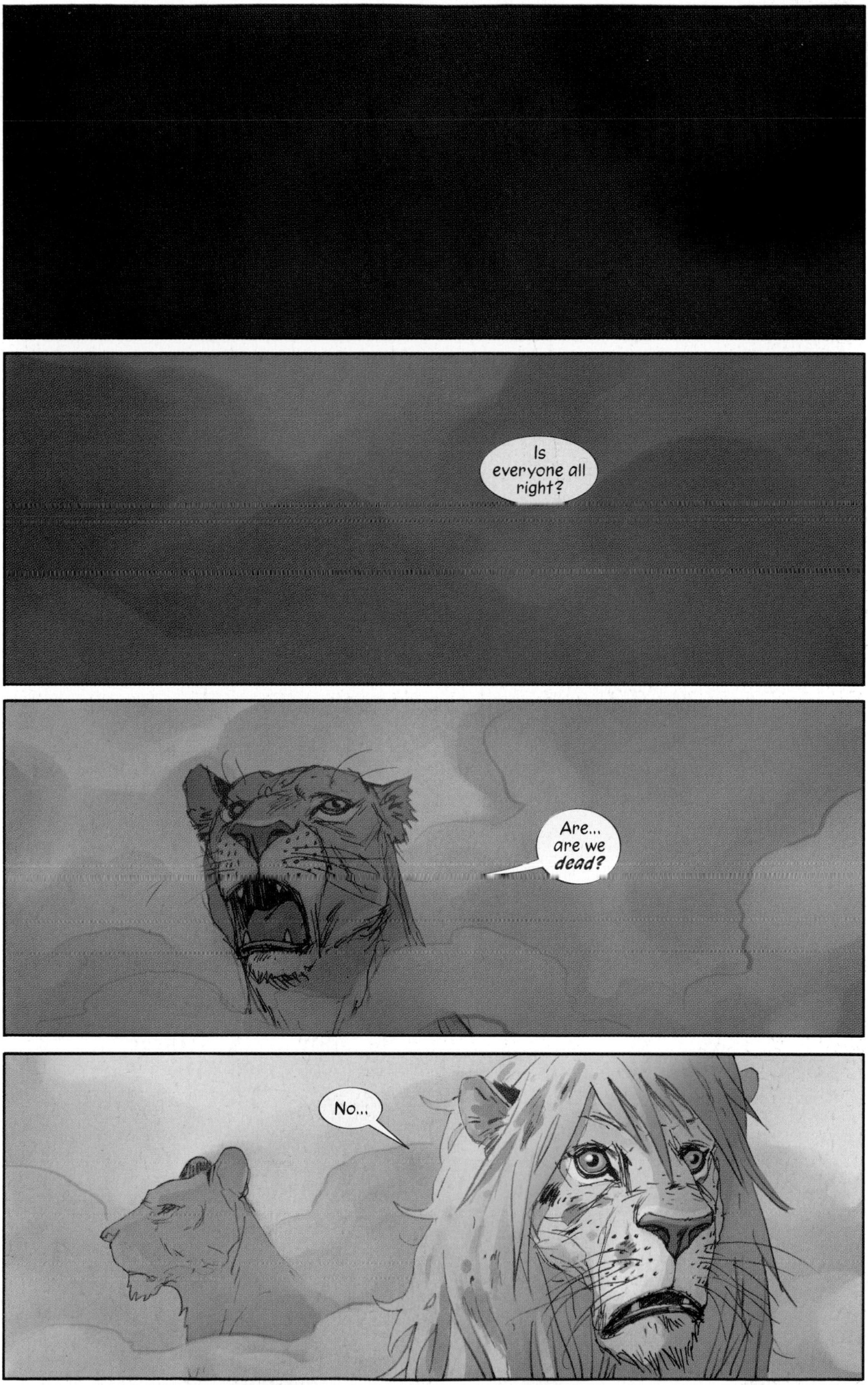
Is everyone all right?
Are... are we *dead?*
No...

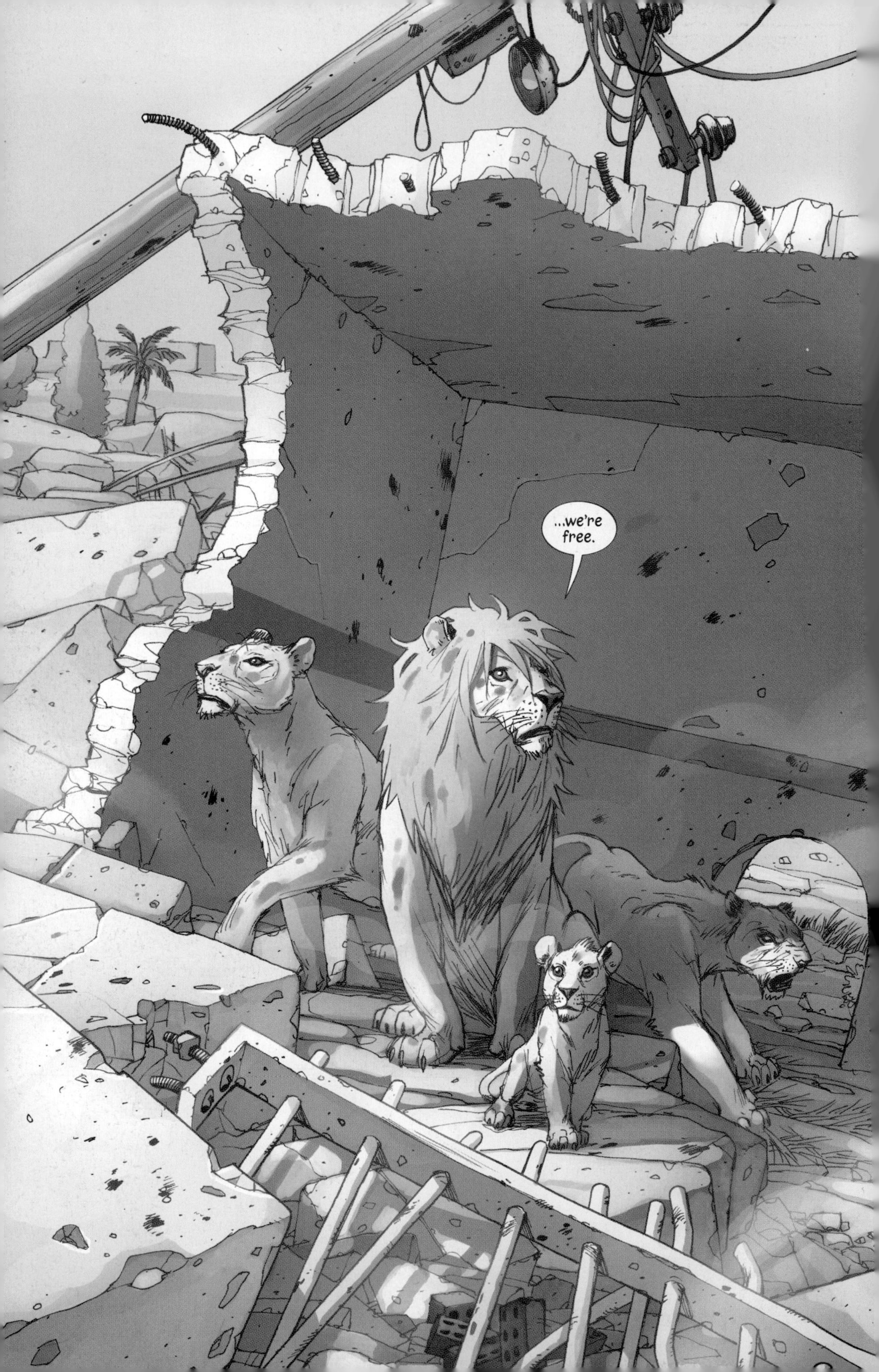
...we're free.

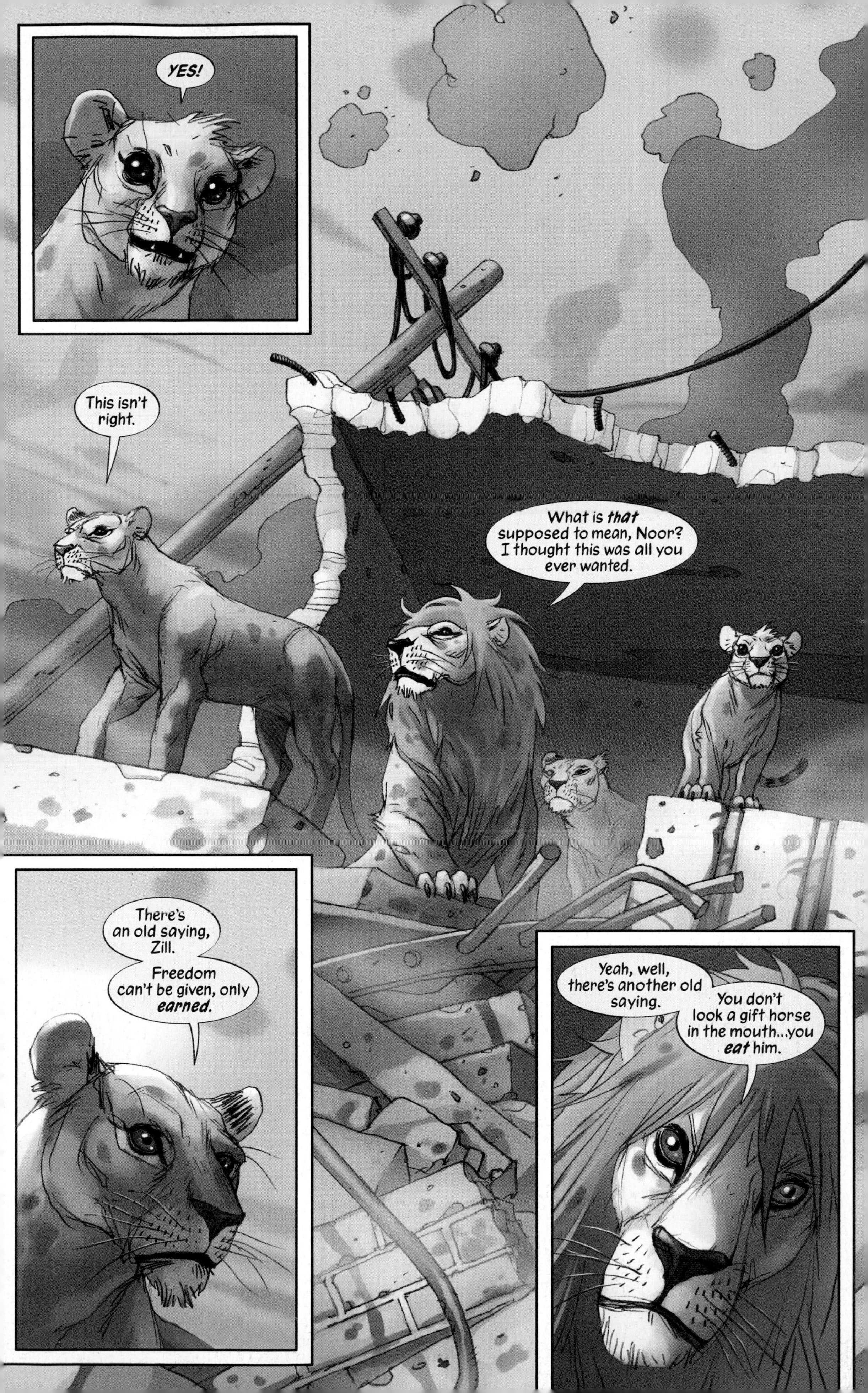
YES!
This isn't right.
What is *that* supposed to mean, Noor? I thought this was all you ever wanted.
There's an old saying, Zill.
Freedom can't be given, only *earned*.
Yeah, well, there's another old saying.
You don't look a gift horse in the mouth...you *eat* him.

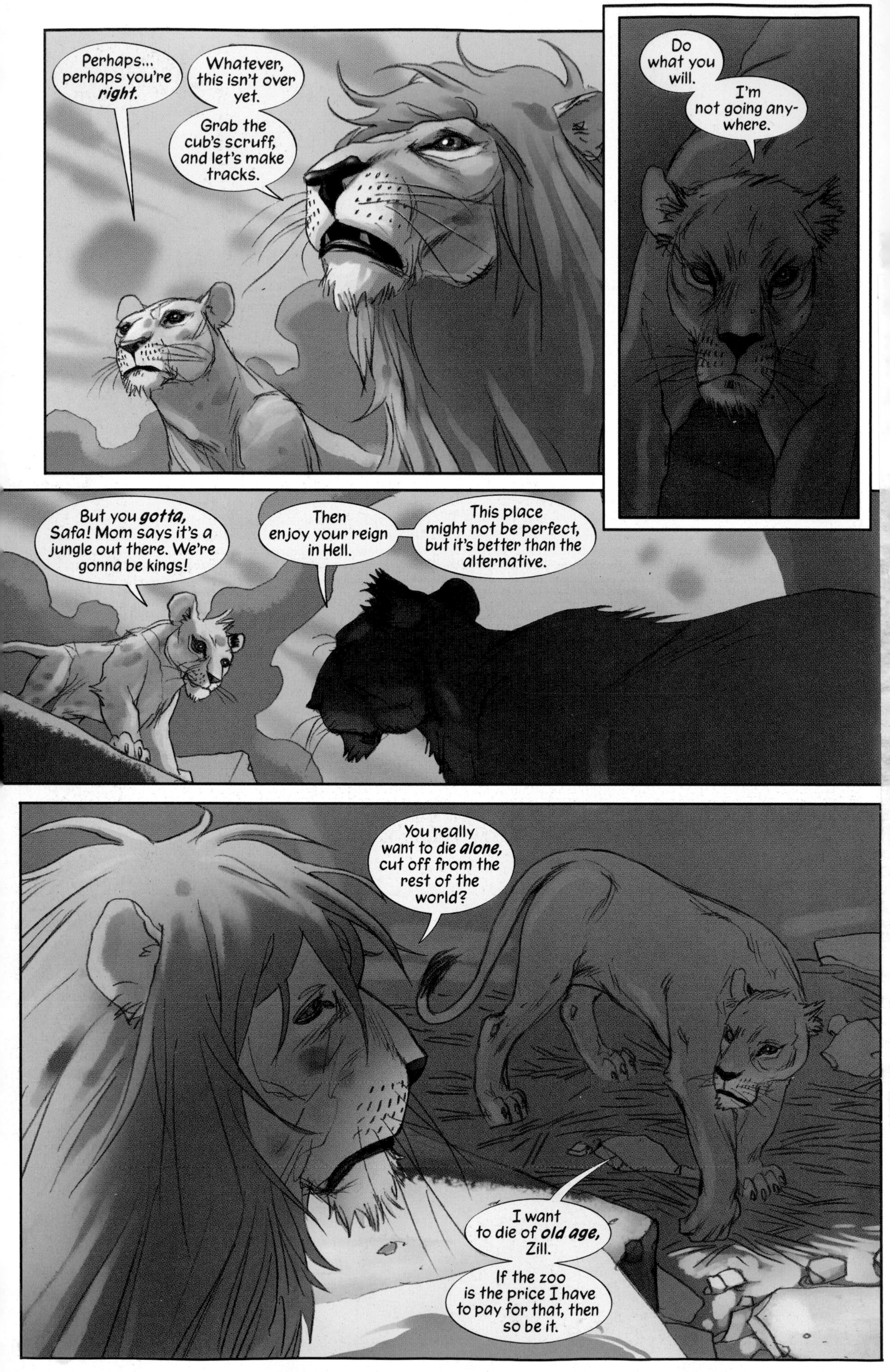

Perhaps... perhaps you're ***right.***
Whatever, this isn't over yet.
Grab the cub's scruff, and let's make tracks.
Do what you will.
I'm not going any-where.
But you ***gotta,*** Safa! Mom says it's a jungle out there. We're gonna be kings!
Then enjoy your reign in Hell.
This place might not be perfect, but it's better than the alternative.
You really want to die ***alone,*** cut off from the rest of the world?
I want to die of ***old age,*** Zill.
If the zoo is the price I have to pay for that, then so be it.

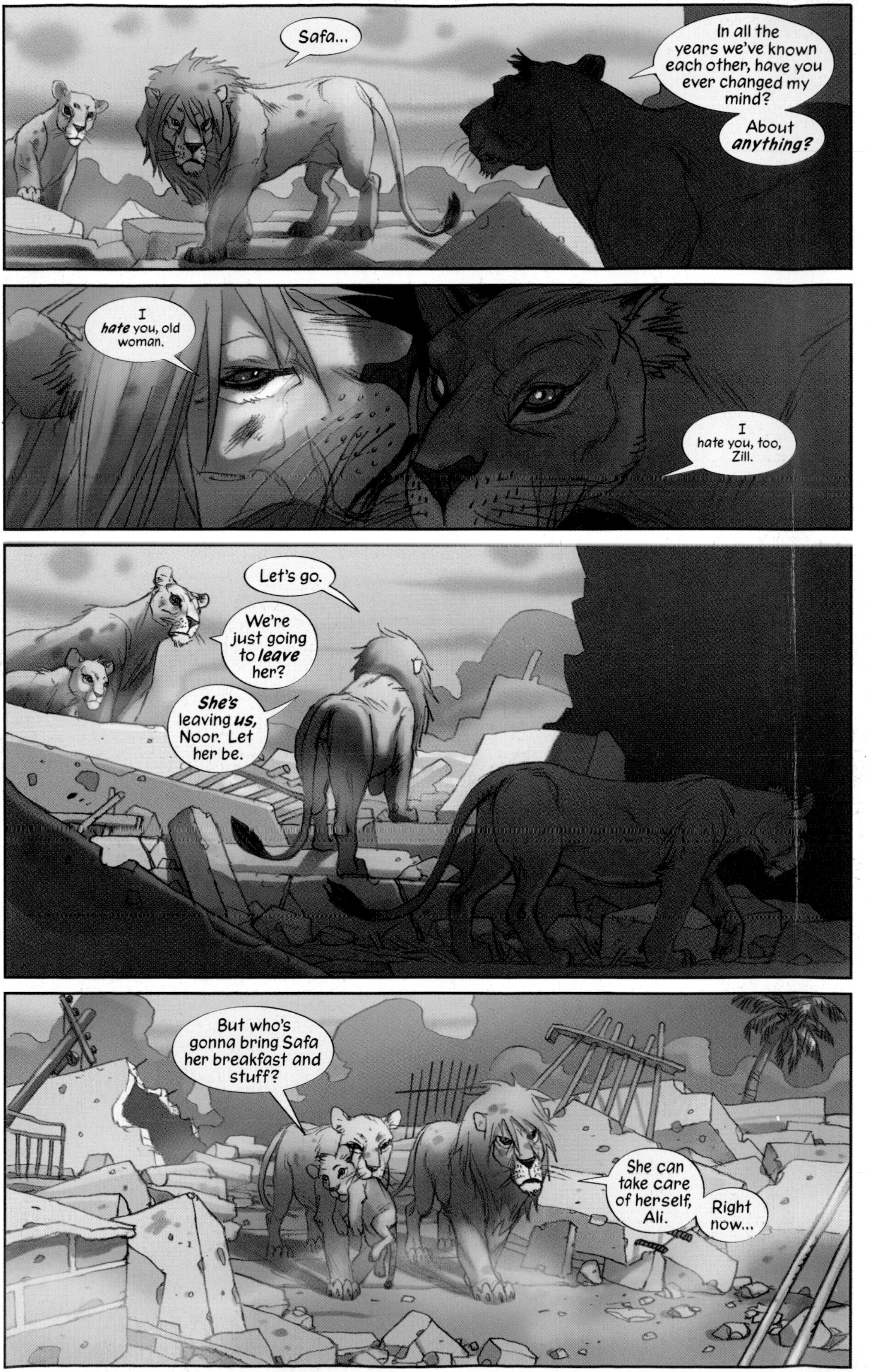
Safa...
In all the years we've known each other, have you ever changed my mind?
About *anything?*
I *hate* you, old woman.
I hate you, too, Zill.
Let's go.
We're just going to *leave* her?
She's leaving *us,* Noor. Let her be.
But who's gonna bring Safa her breakfast and stuff?
She can take care of herself, Ali.
Right now...

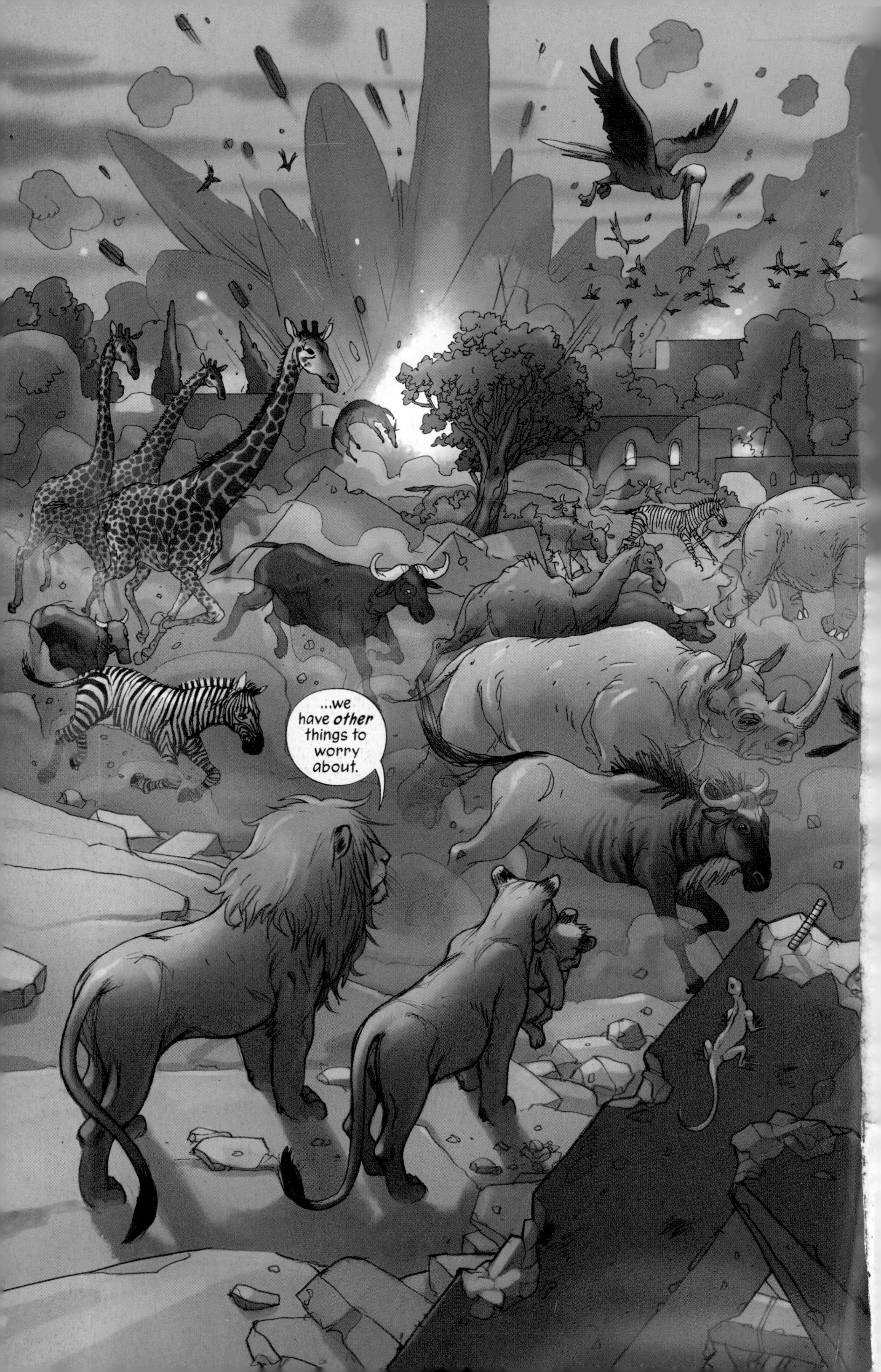
...we have *other* things to worry about.

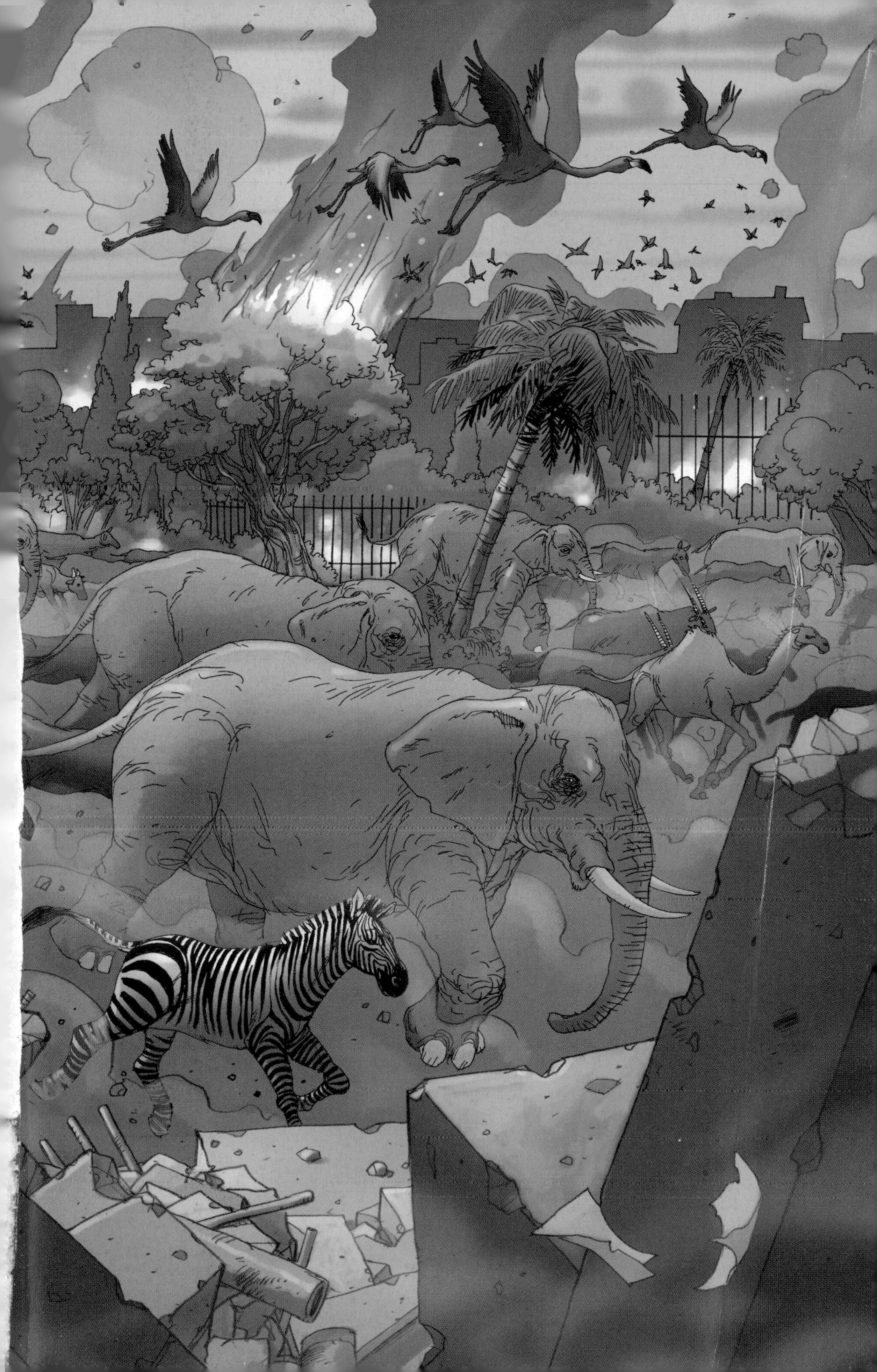

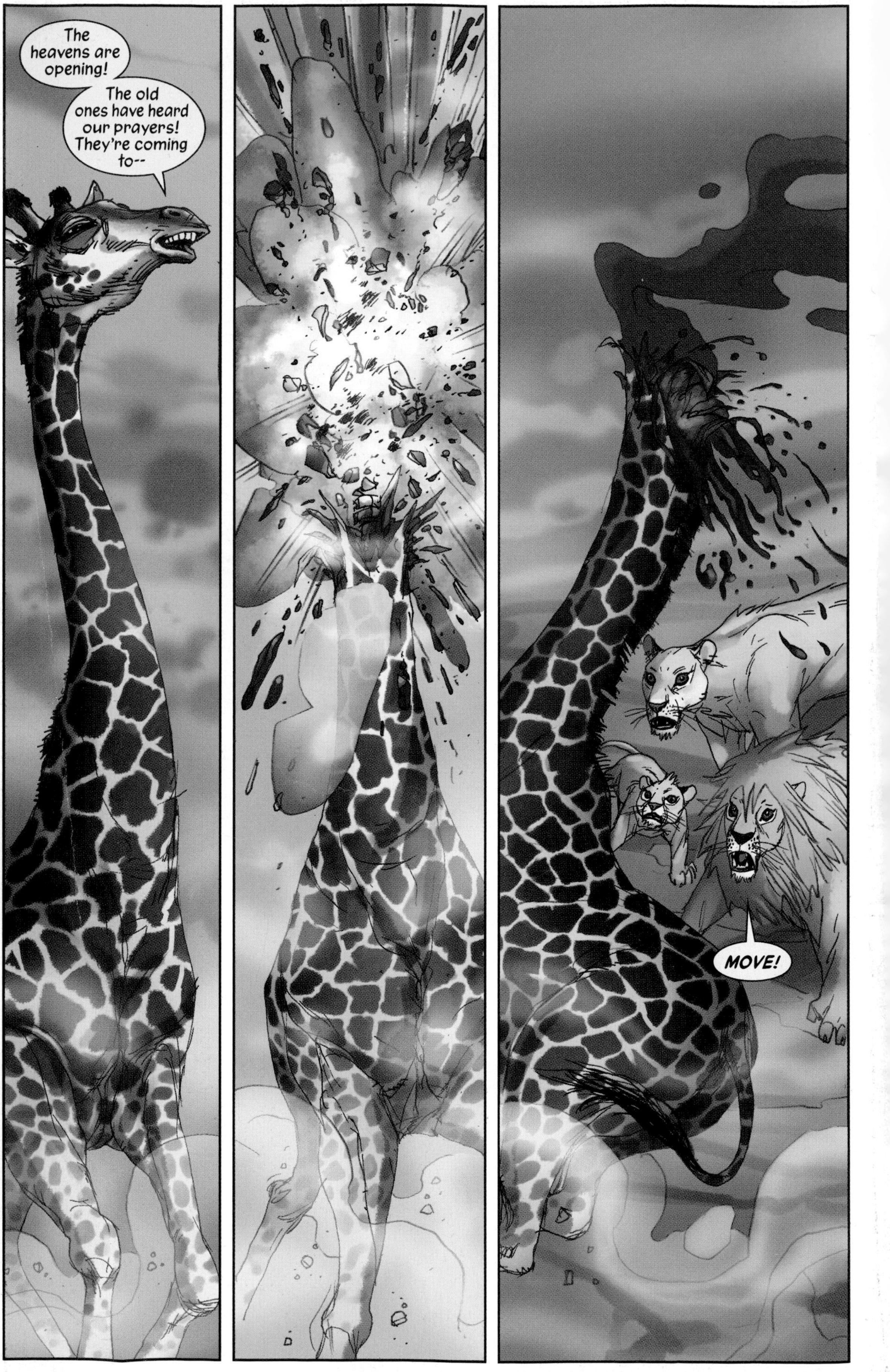
The heavens are opening!
The old ones have heard our prayers! They're coming to--
MOVE!

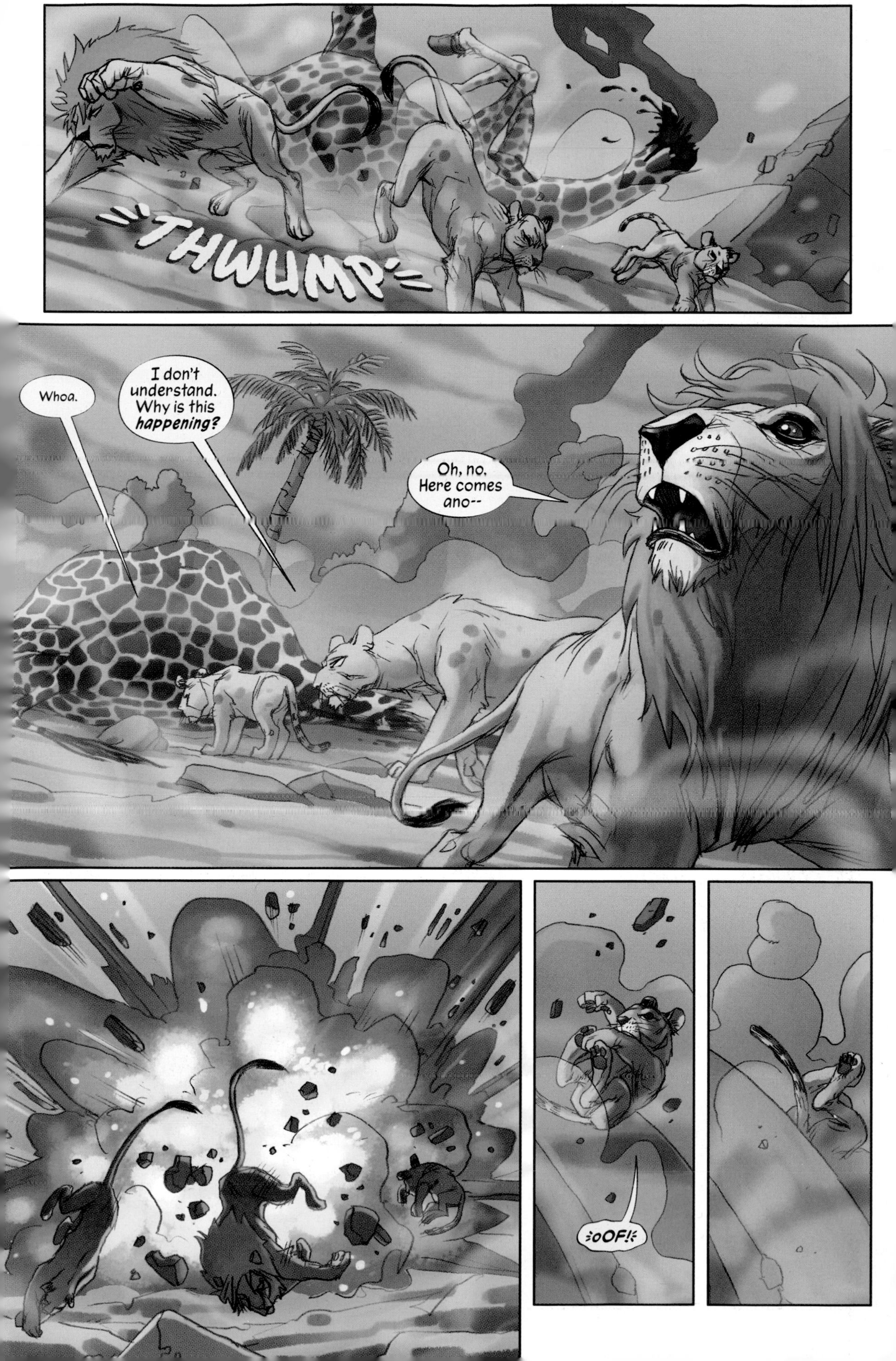
THWUMP
Whoa.
I don't understand. Why is this *happening?*
Oh, no. Here comes ano--
OOF!

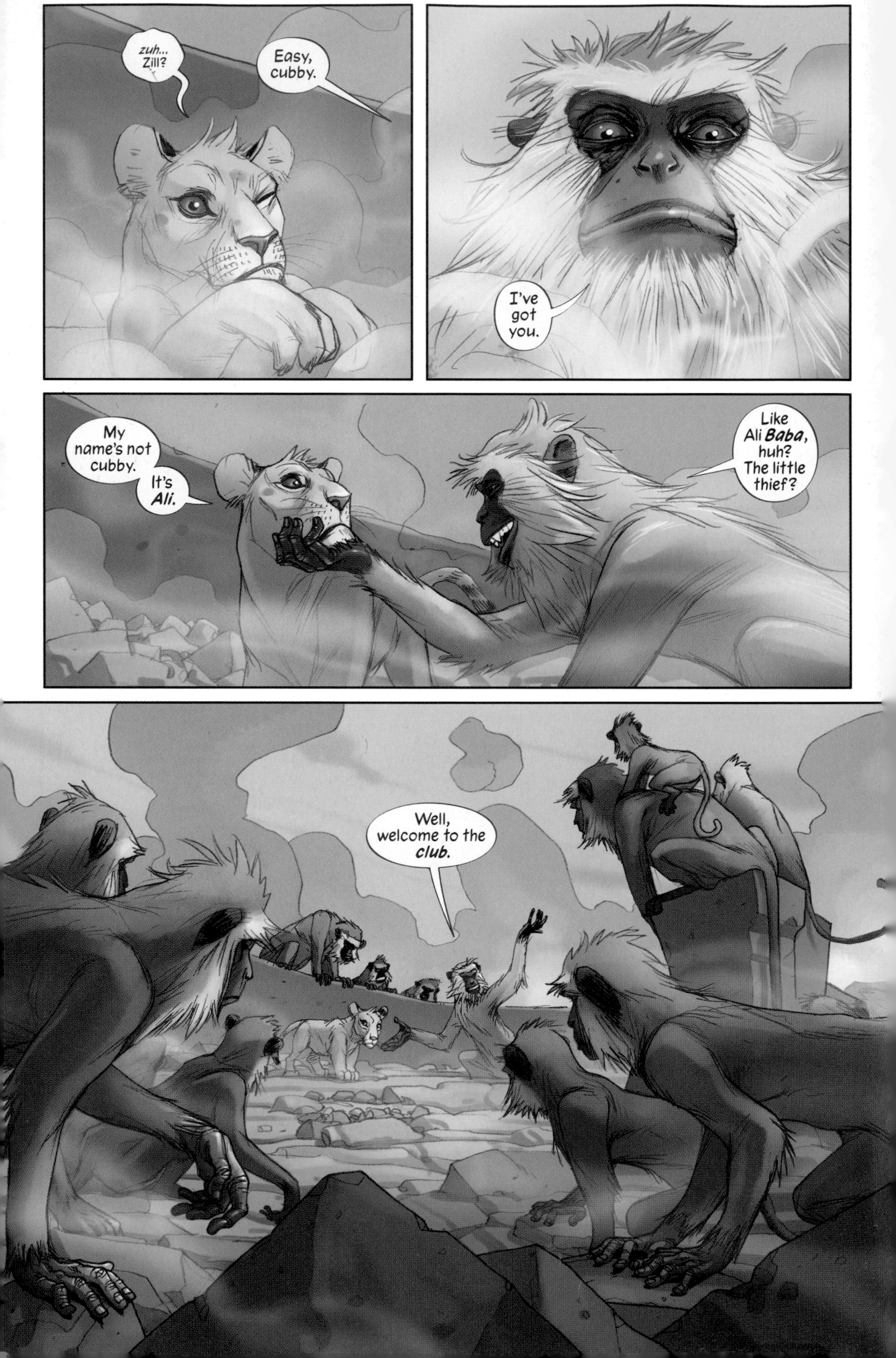
zuh... Zill?
Easy, cubby.
I've got you.
My name's not cubby.
It's Ali.
Like Ali Baba, huh? The little thief?
Well, welcome to the club.

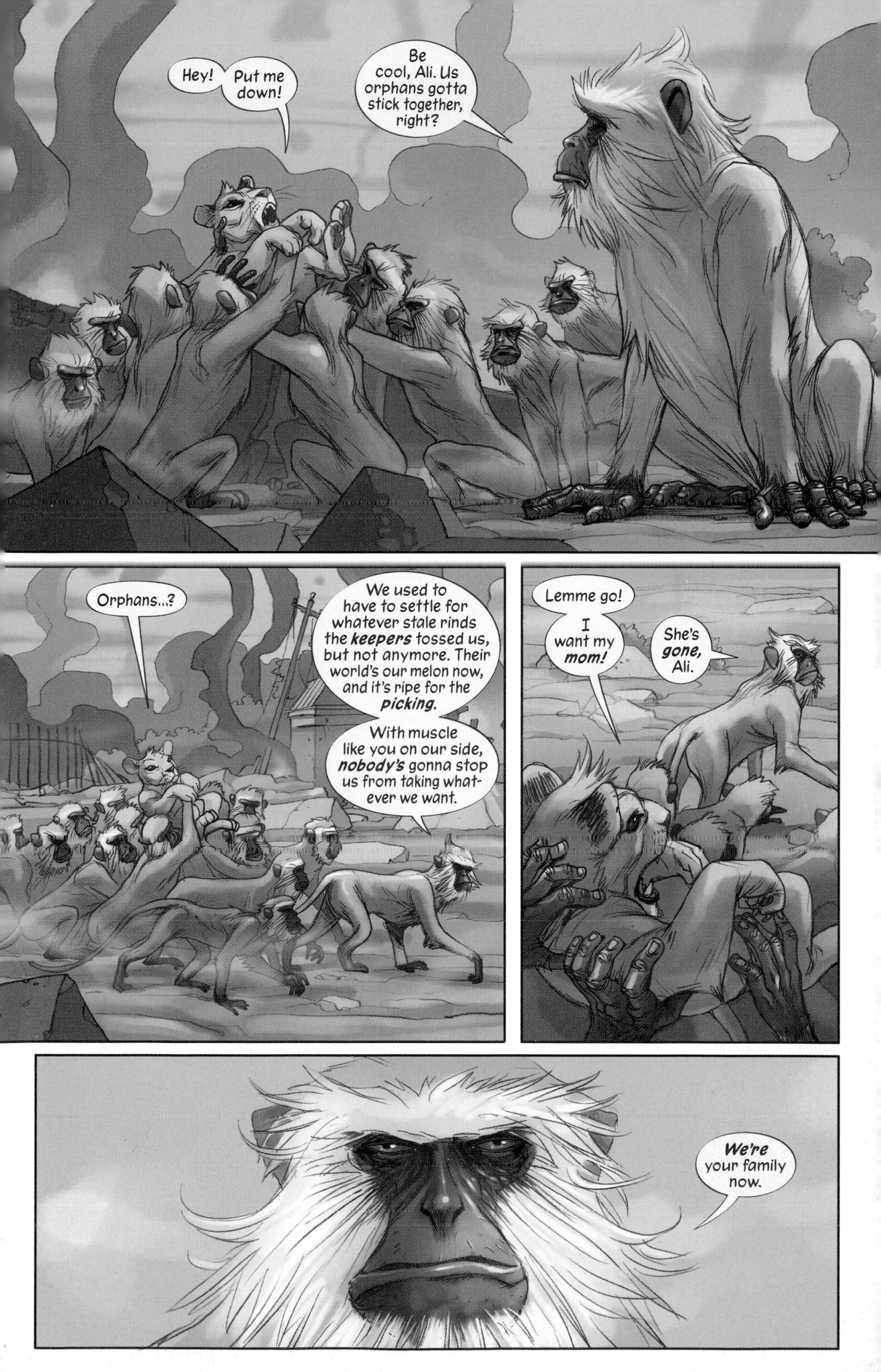
Hey!
Put me down!
Be cool, Ali. Us orphans gotta stick together, right?
Orphans...?
We used to have to settle for whatever stale rinds the ***keepers*** tossed us, but not anymore. Their world's our melon now, and it's ripe for the ***picking***.
With muscle like you on our side, ***nobody's*** gonna stop us from taking whatever we want.
Lemme go!
I want my ***mom!***
She's ***gone,*** Ali.
We're your family now.

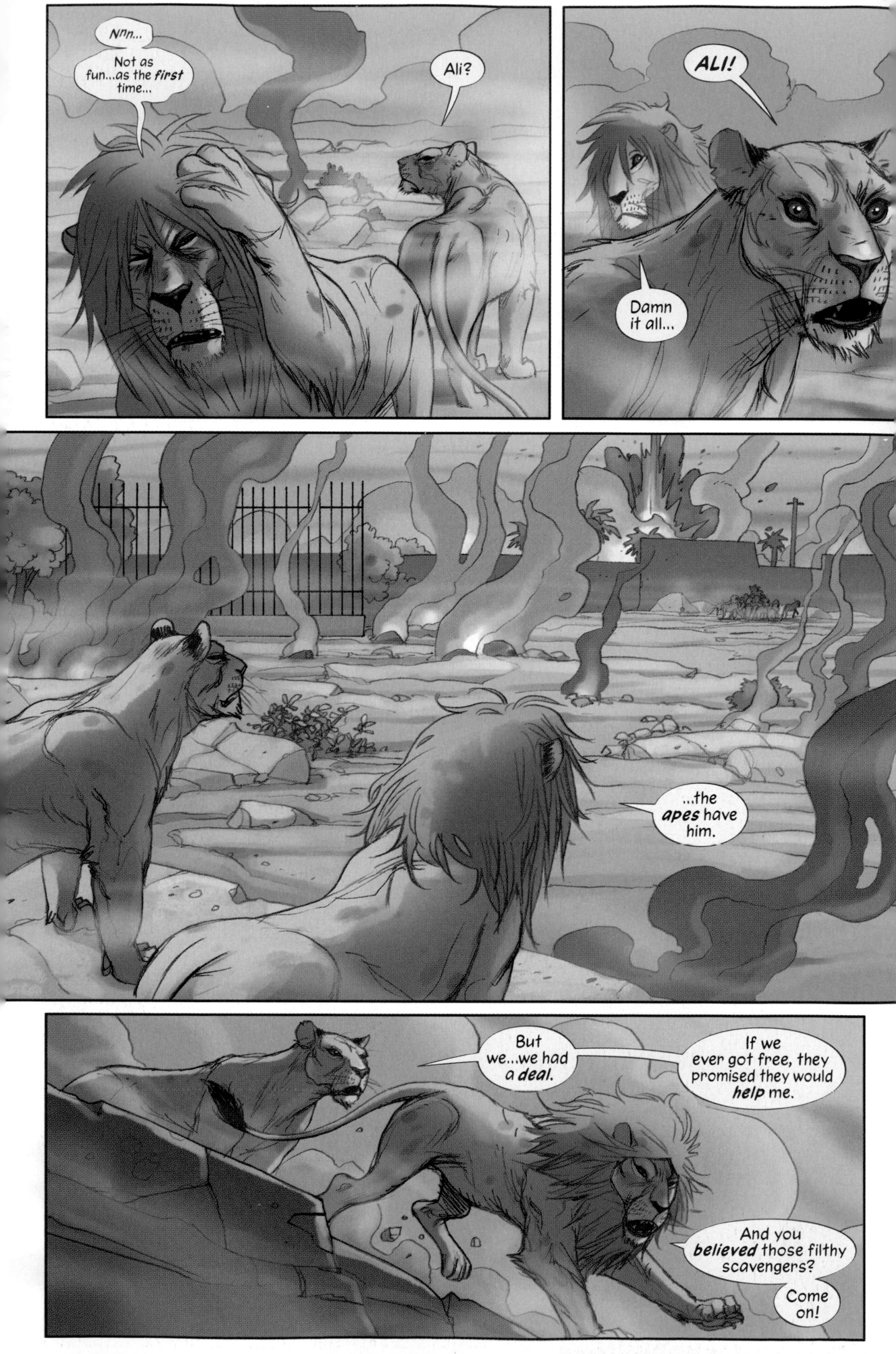
Nnn...
Not as fun...as the *first* time...
Ali?
ALI!
Damn it all...
...the *apes* have him.
But we...we had a *deal*.
If we ever got free, they promised they would *help* me.
And you *believed* those filthy scavengers?
Come on!

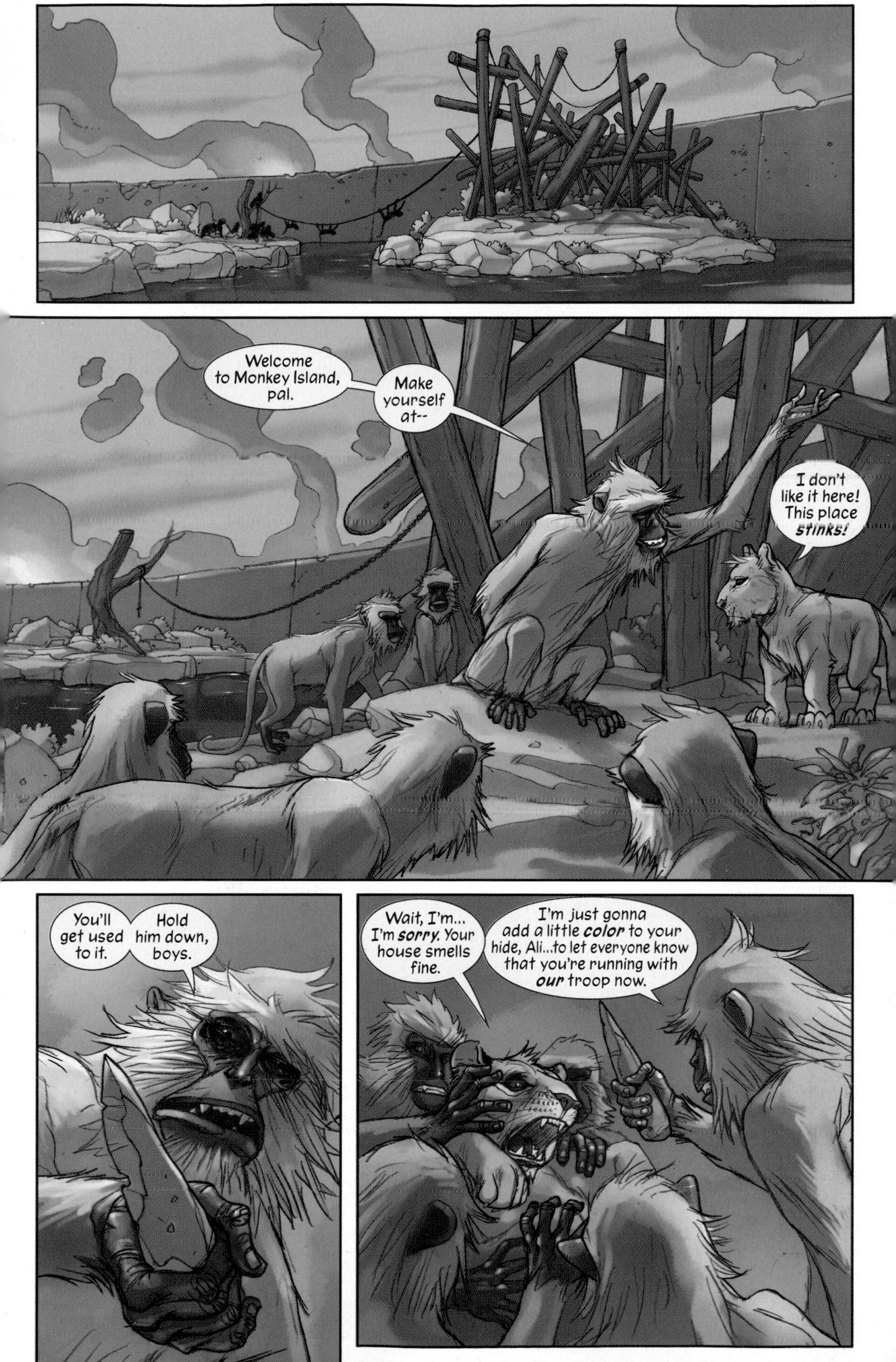
Welcome to Monkey Island, pal.
Make yourself at--
I don't like it here! This place *stinks!*
You'll get used to it.
Hold him down, boys.
Wait, I'm... I'm *sorry*. Your house smells fine.
I'm just gonna add a little *color* to your hide, Ali...to let everyone know that you're running with *our* troop now.

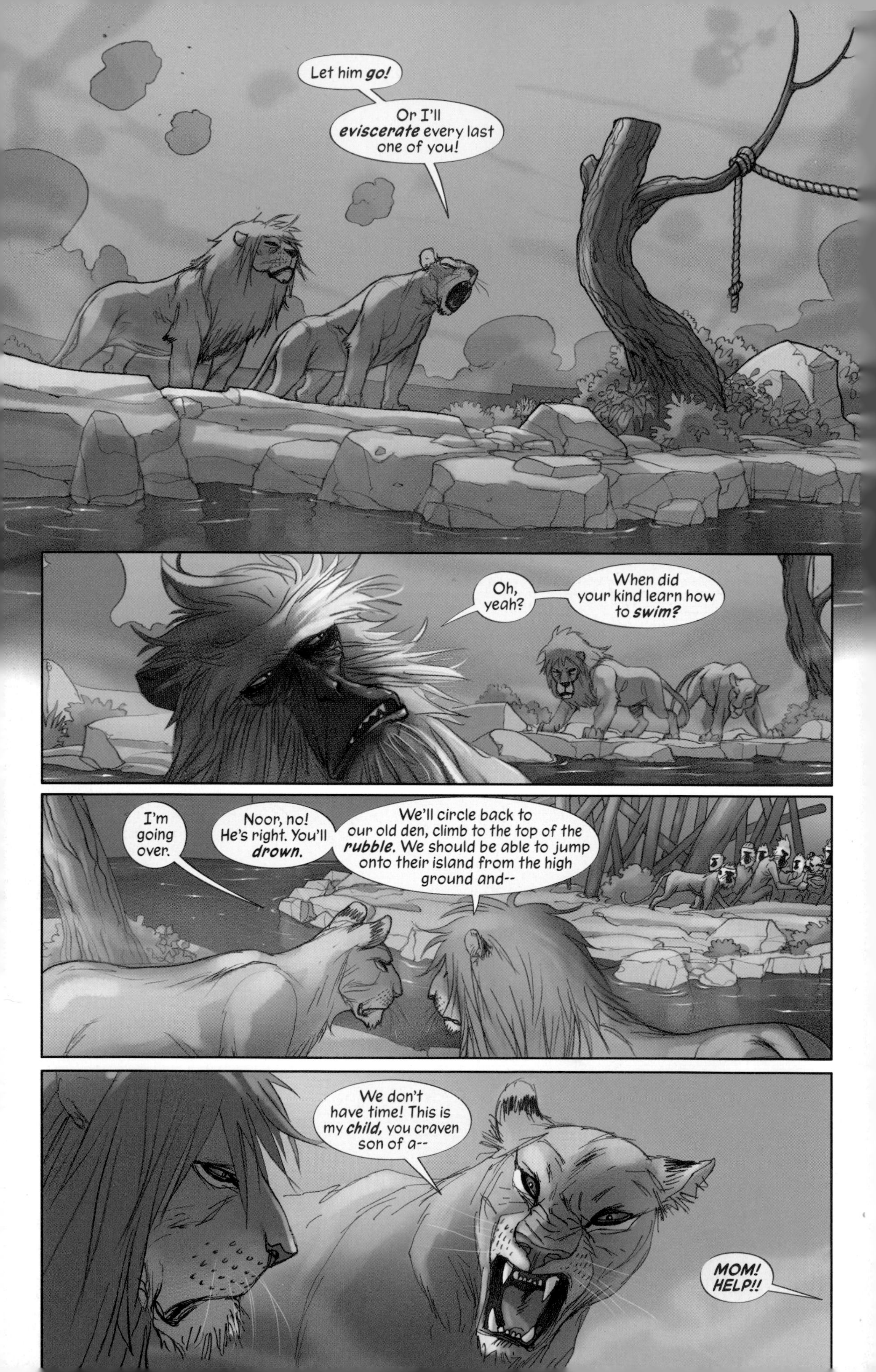
Let him go!
Or I'll eviscerate every last one of you!
Oh, yeah?
When did your kind learn how to swim?
I'm going over.
Noor, no! He's right. You'll drown.
We'll circle back to our old den, climb to the top of the rubble. We should be able to jump onto their island from the high ground and--
We don't have time! This is my child, you craven son of a--
MOM! HELP!!

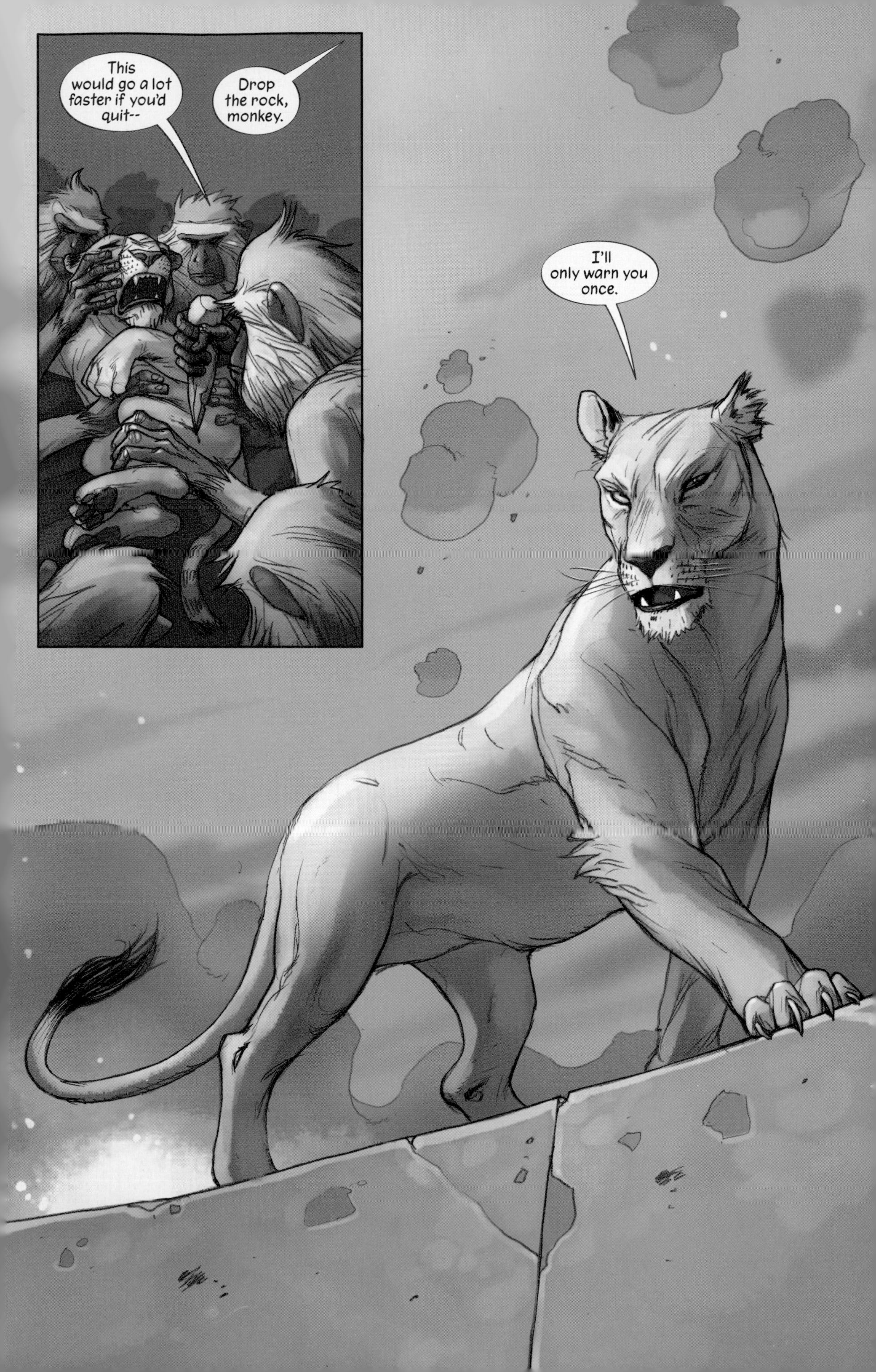
This would go a lot faster if you'd quit--
Drop the rock, monkey.
I'll only warn you once.

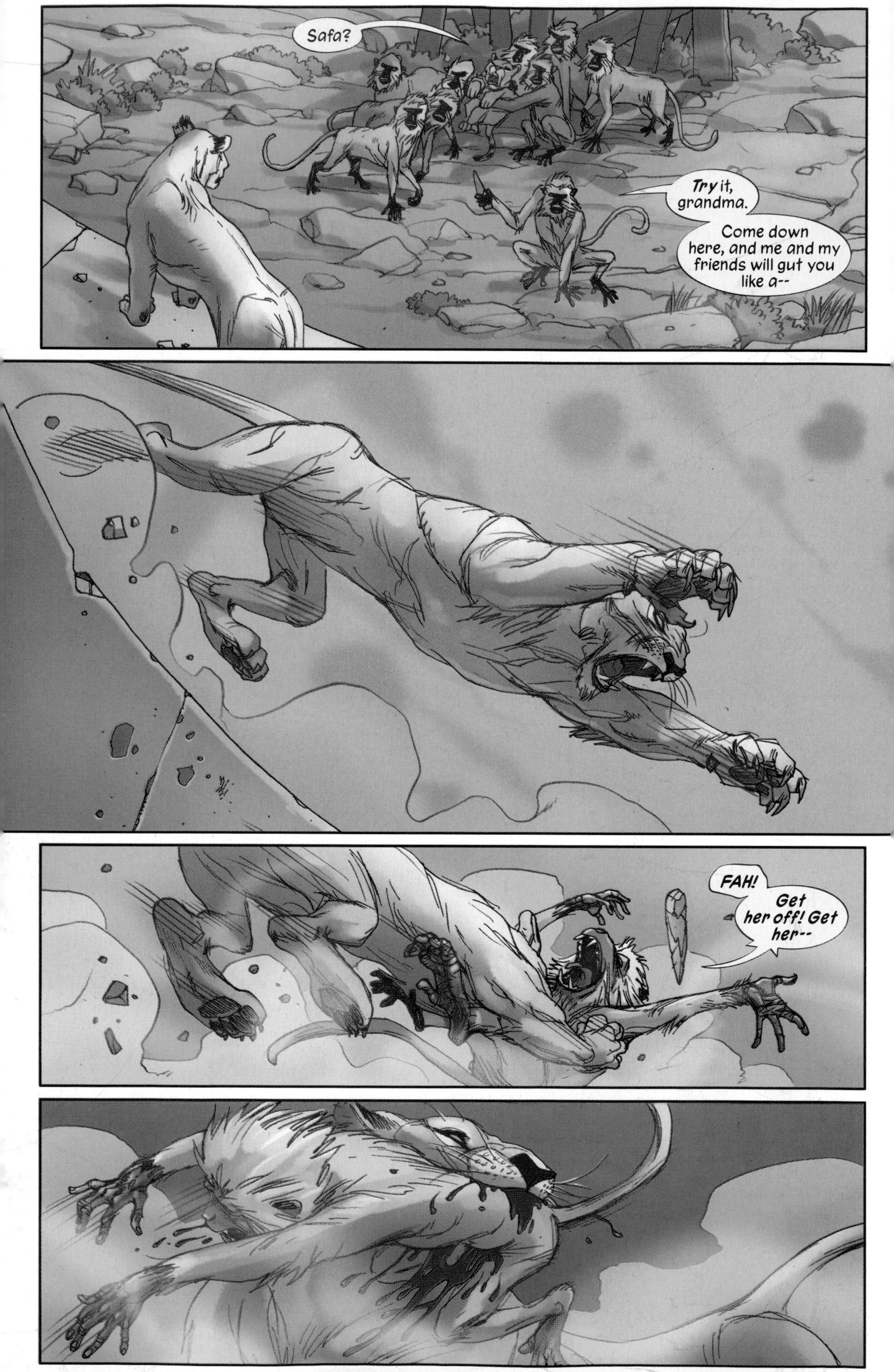
Safa?
Try it, grandma.
Come down here, and me and my friends will gut you like a--
FAH!
Get her off! Get her--

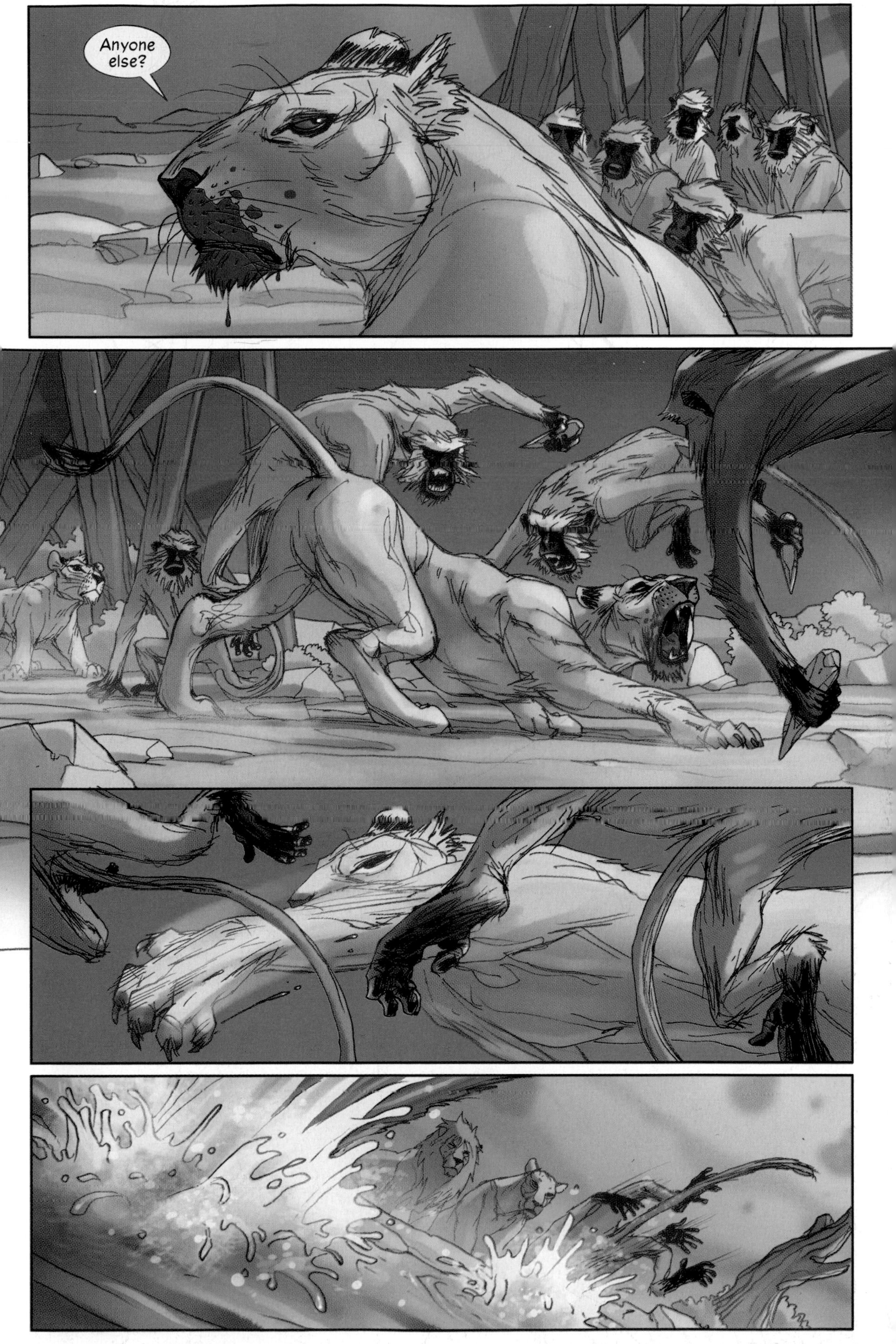
Anyone else?

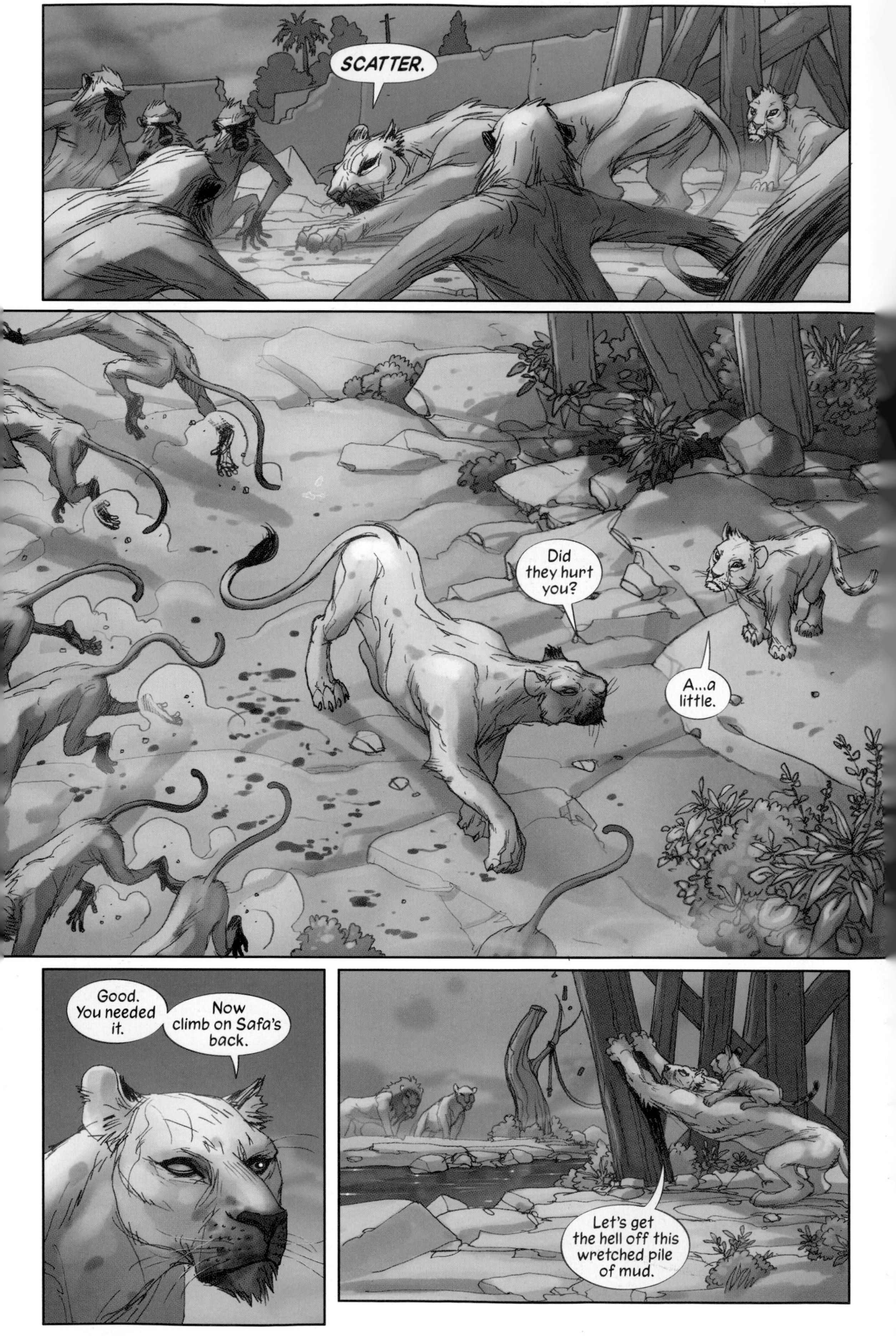
SCATTER.
Did they hurt you?
A...a little.
Good. You needed it.
Now climb on Safa's back.
Let's get the hell off this wretched pile of mud.

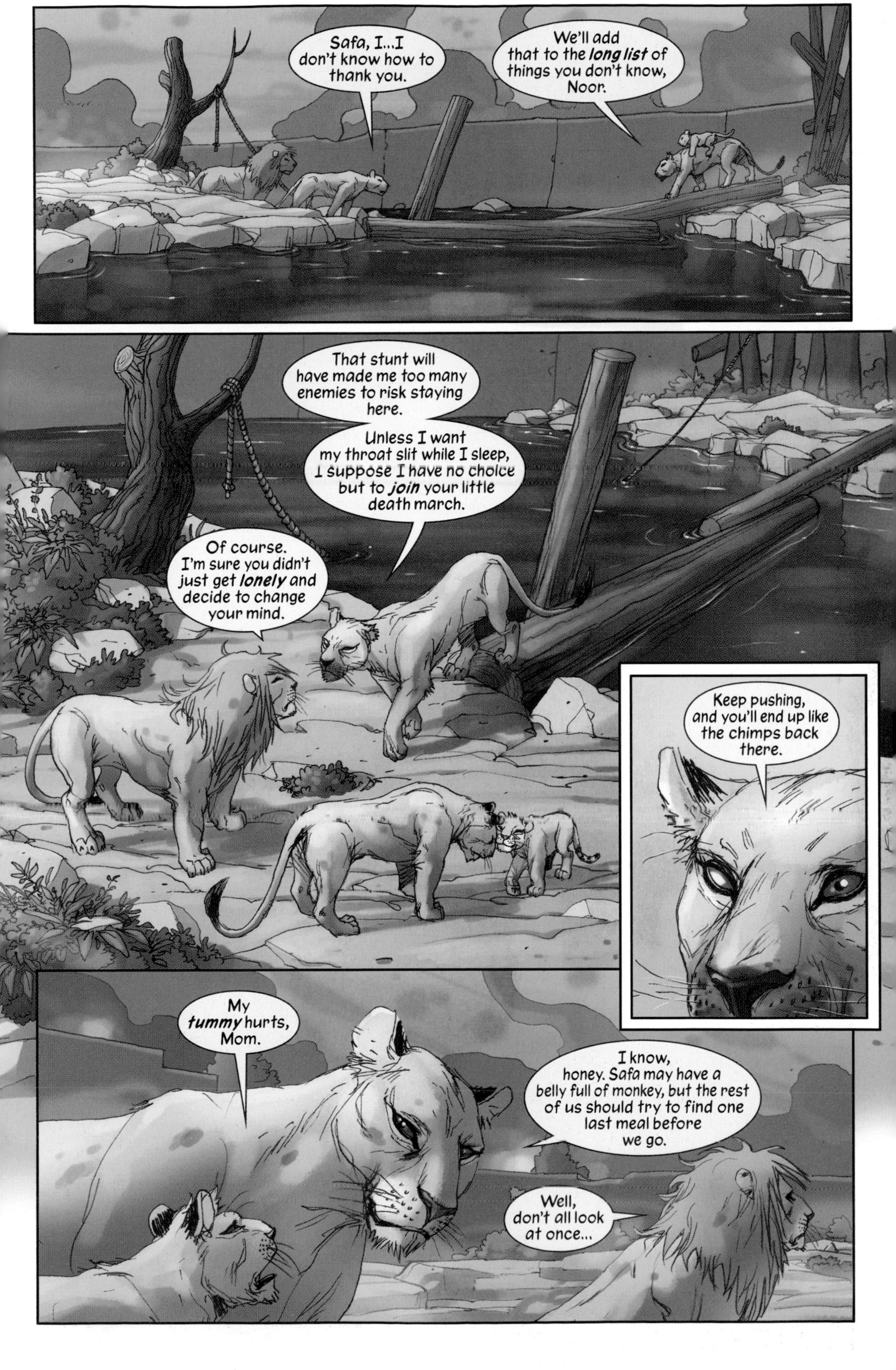

Safa, I...I don't know how to thank you.
We'll add that to the ***long list*** of things you don't know, Noor.
That stunt will have made me too many enemies to risk staying here.
Unless I want my throat slit while I sleep, I suppose I have no choice but to ***join*** your little death march.
Of course. I'm sure you didn't just get ***lonely*** and decide to change your mind.
Keep pushing, and you'll end up like the chimps back there.
My ***tummy*** hurts, Mom.
I know, honey. Safa may have a belly full of monkey, but the rest of us should try to find one last meal before we go.
Well, don't all look at once...

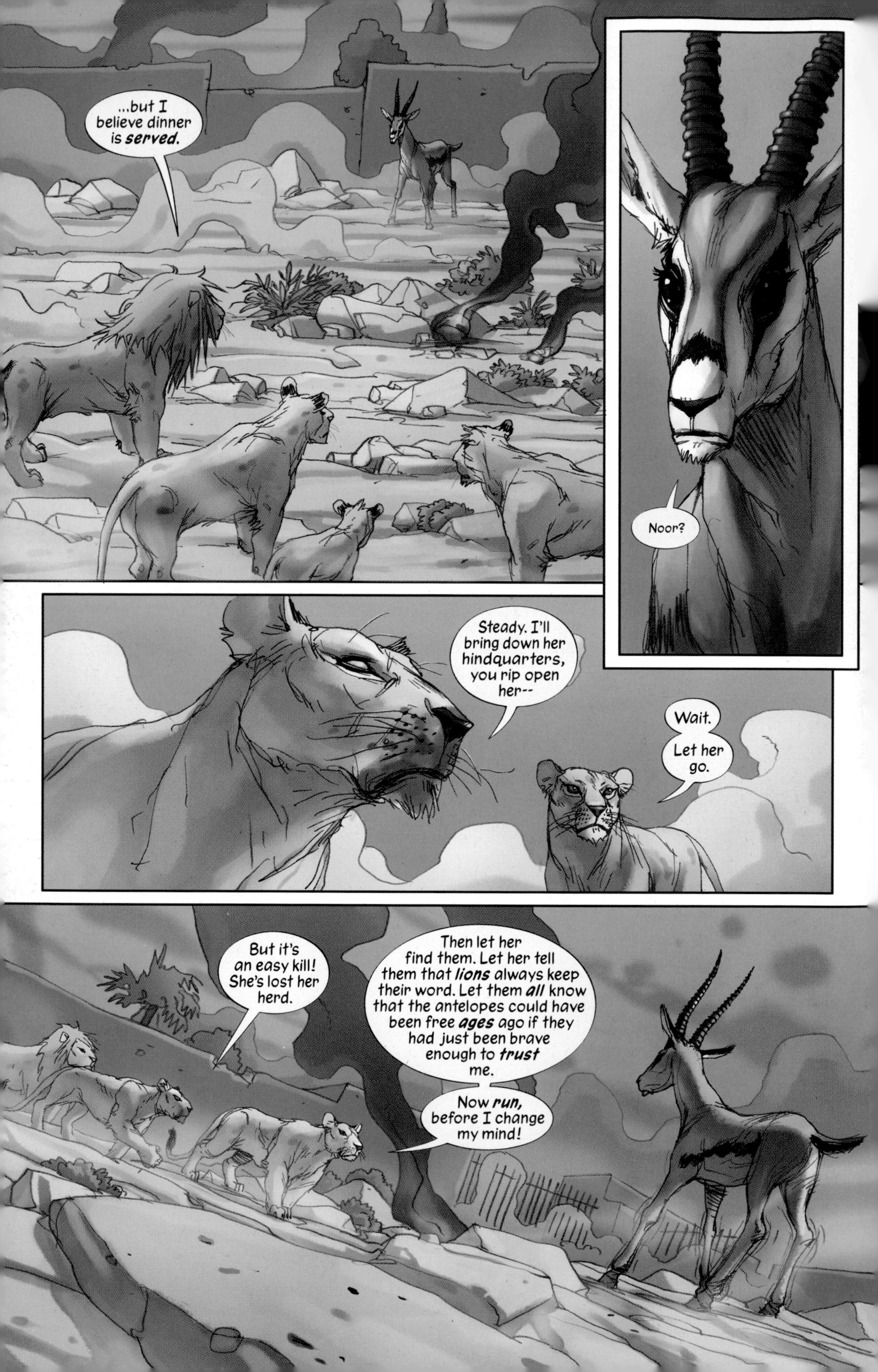

...but I believe dinner is *served.*
Noor?
Steady. I'll bring down her hindquarters, you rip open her--
Wait.
Let her go.
But it's an easy kill! She's lost her herd.
Then let her find them. Let her tell them that *lions* always keep their word. Let them *all* know that the antelopes could have been free *ages* ago if they had just been brave enough to *trust* me.
Now *run,* before I change my mind!

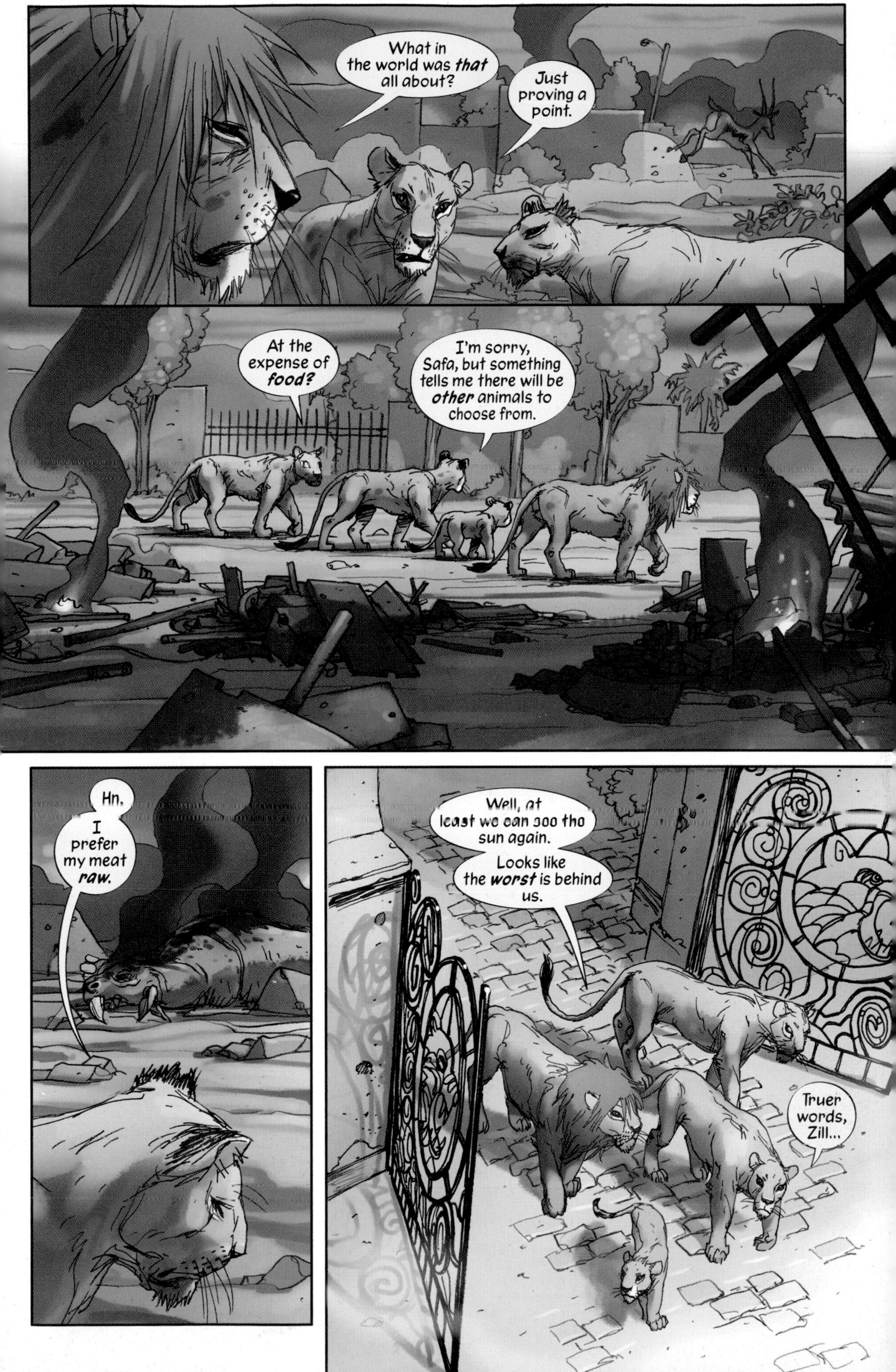
What in the world was *that* all about?
Just proving a point.
At the expense of *food?*
I'm sorry, Safa, but something tells me there will be *other* animals to choose from.
Hn.
I prefer my meat *raw.*
Well, at least we can see the sun again.
Looks like the *worst* is behind us.
Truer words, Zill...

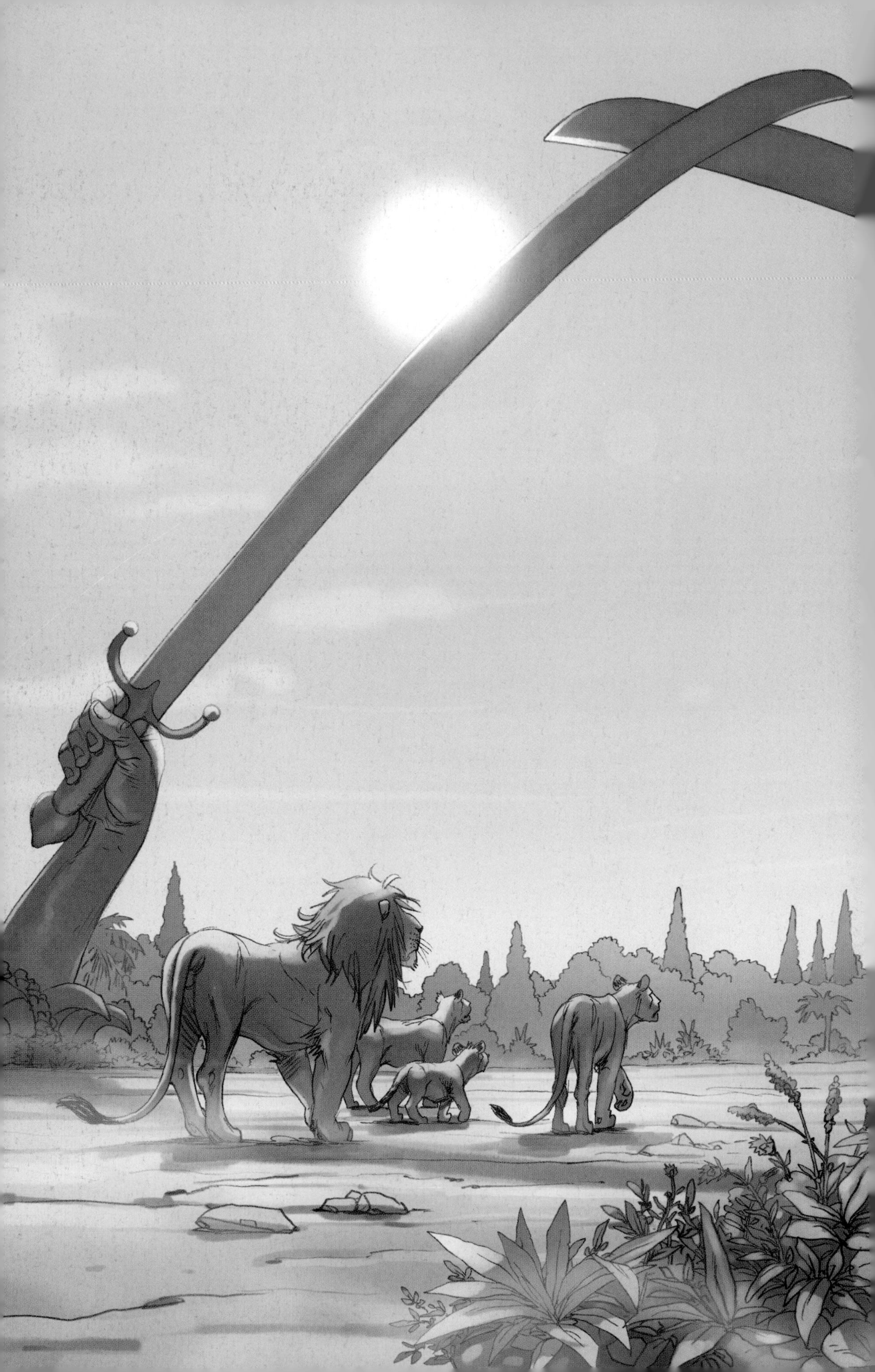

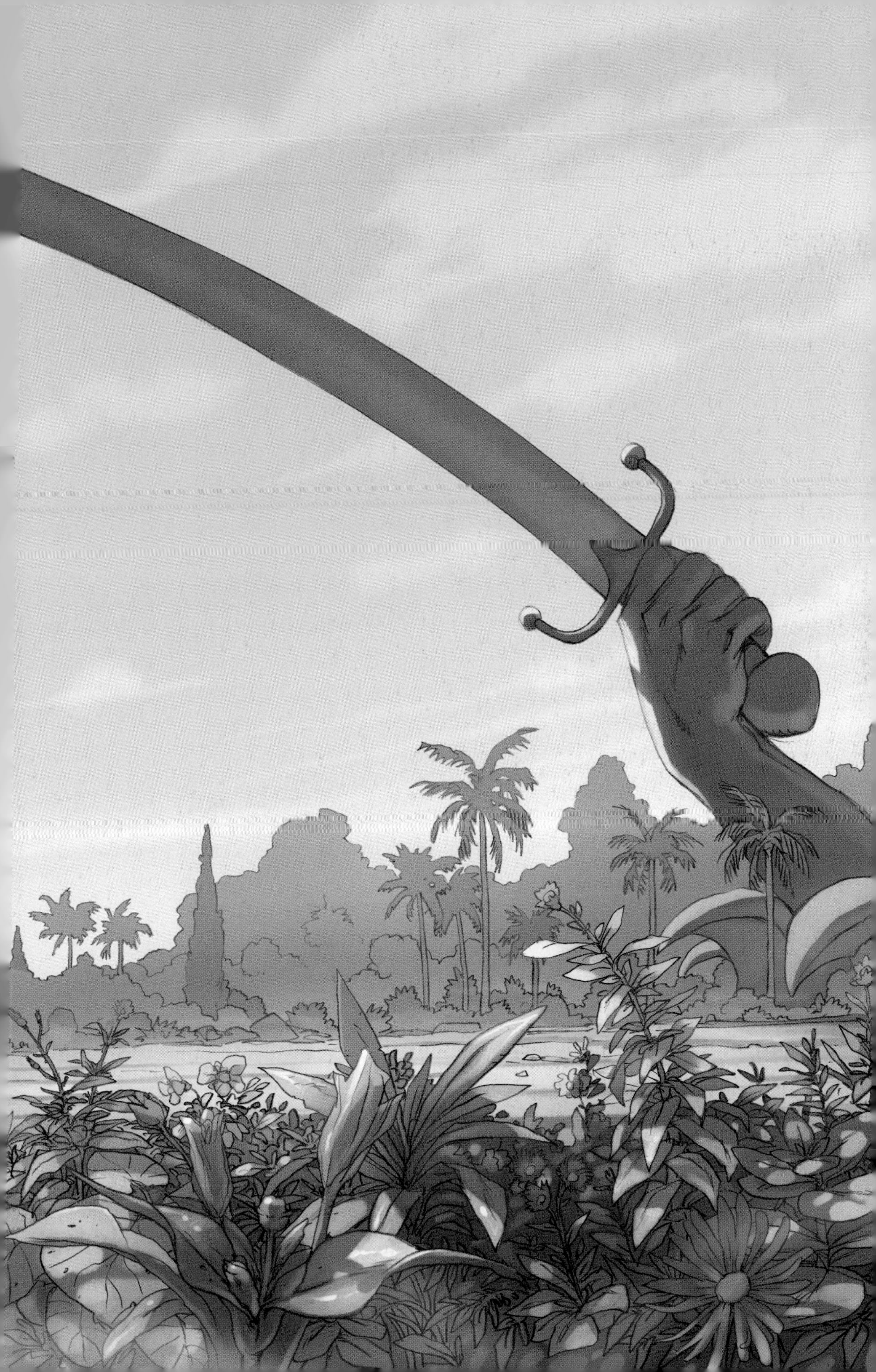

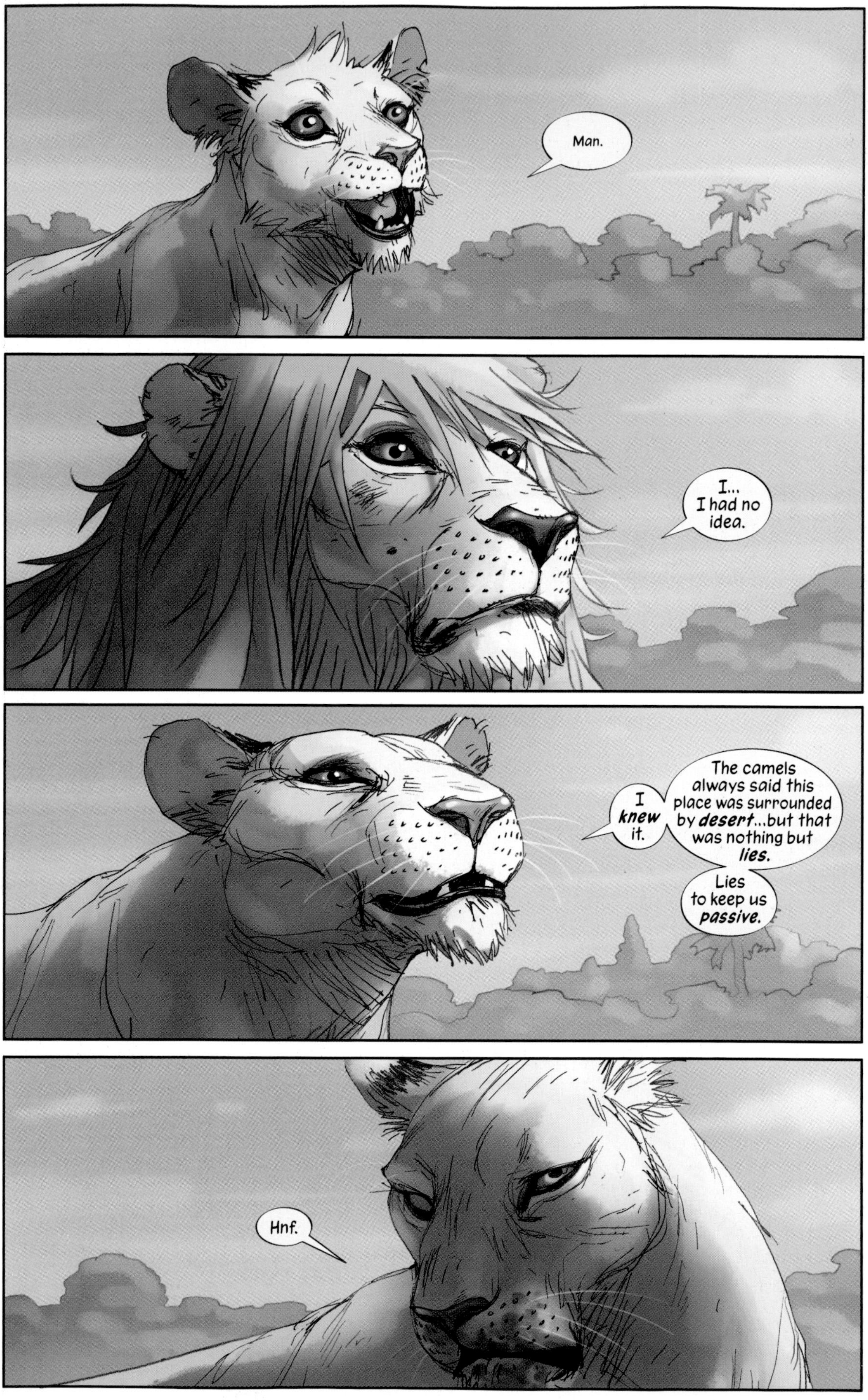
Man.
I... I had no idea.
I knew it.
The camels always said this place was surrounded by desert...but that was nothing but lies.
Lies to keep us passive.
Hnf.

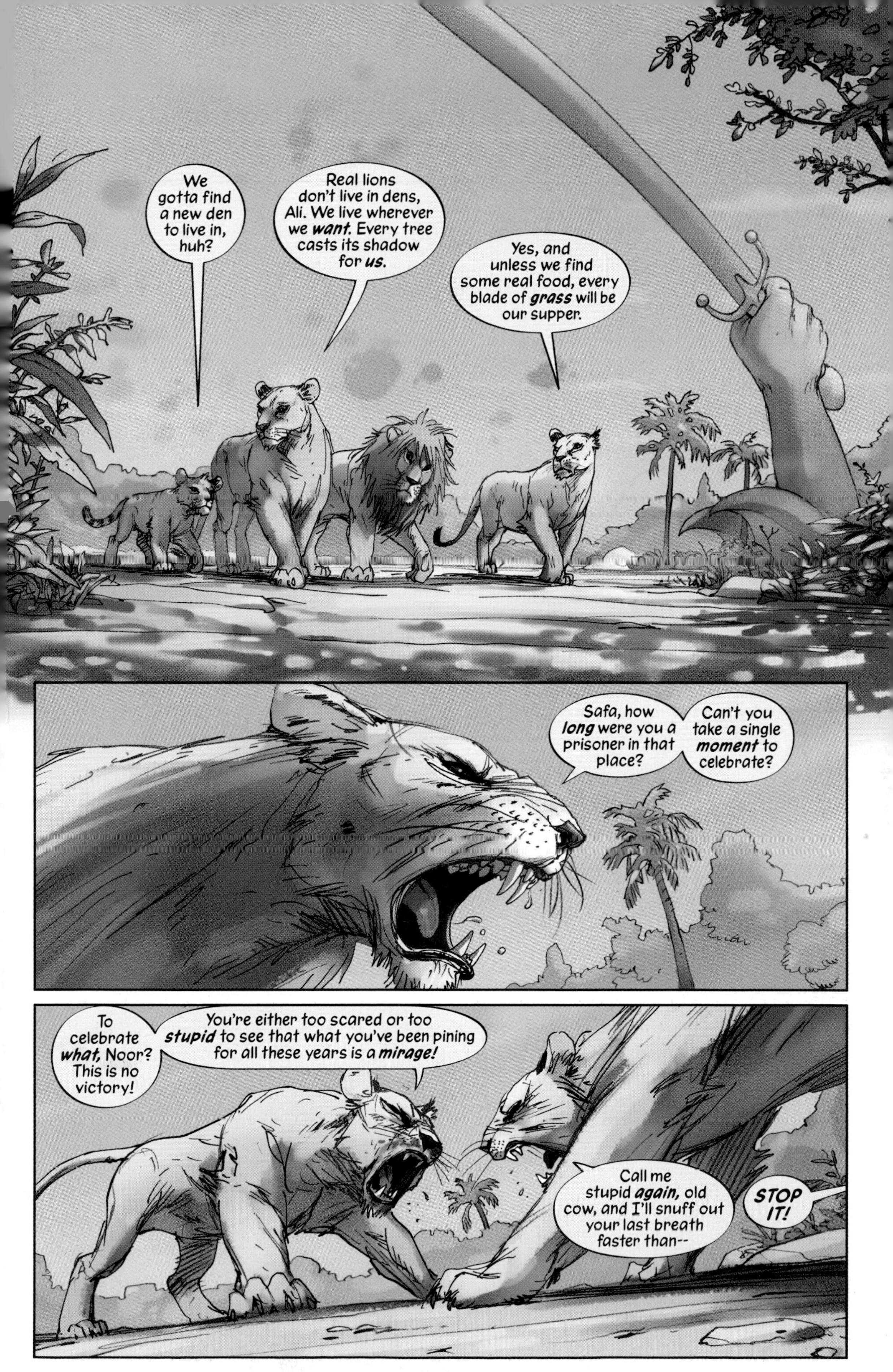
We gotta find a new den to live in, huh?
Real lions don't live in dens, Ali. We live wherever we *want*. Every tree casts its shadow for *us*.
Yes, and unless we find some real food, every blade of *grass* will be our supper.
Safa, how *long* were you a prisoner in that place?
Can't you take a single *moment* to celebrate?
To celebrate *what,* Noor? This is no victory!
You're either too scared or too *stupid* to see that what you've been pining for all these years is a *mirage!*
Call me stupid *again,* old cow, and I'll snuff out your last breath faster than--
STOP IT!

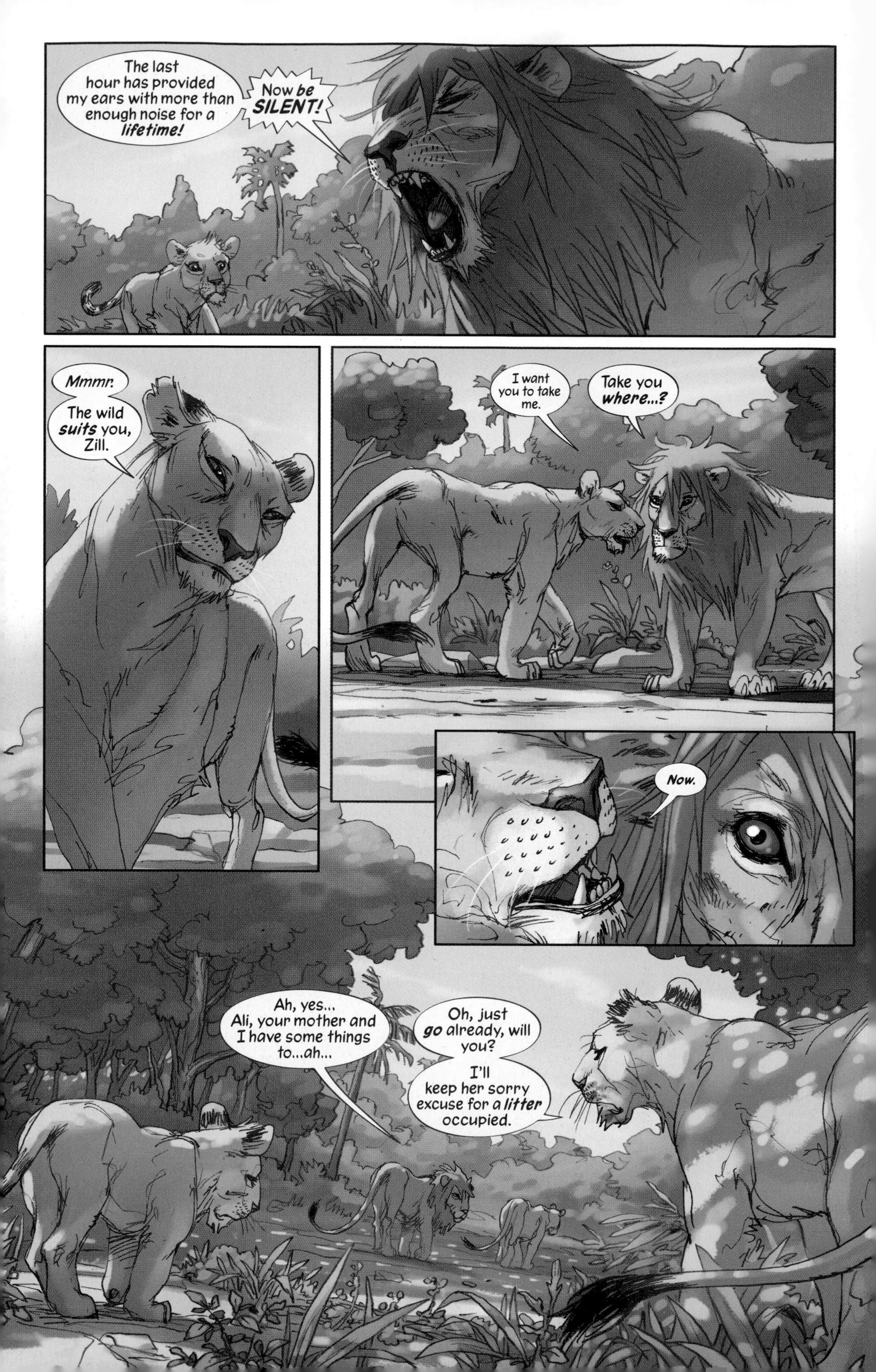
The last hour has provided my ears with more than enough noise for a *lifetime!*
Now *be SILENT!*
Mmmr.
The wild *suits* you, Zill.
I want you to take me.
Take you *where...?*
Now.
Ah, yes... Ali, your mother and I have some things to...ah...
Oh, just *go* already, will you?
I'll keep her sorry excuse for a *litter* occupied.

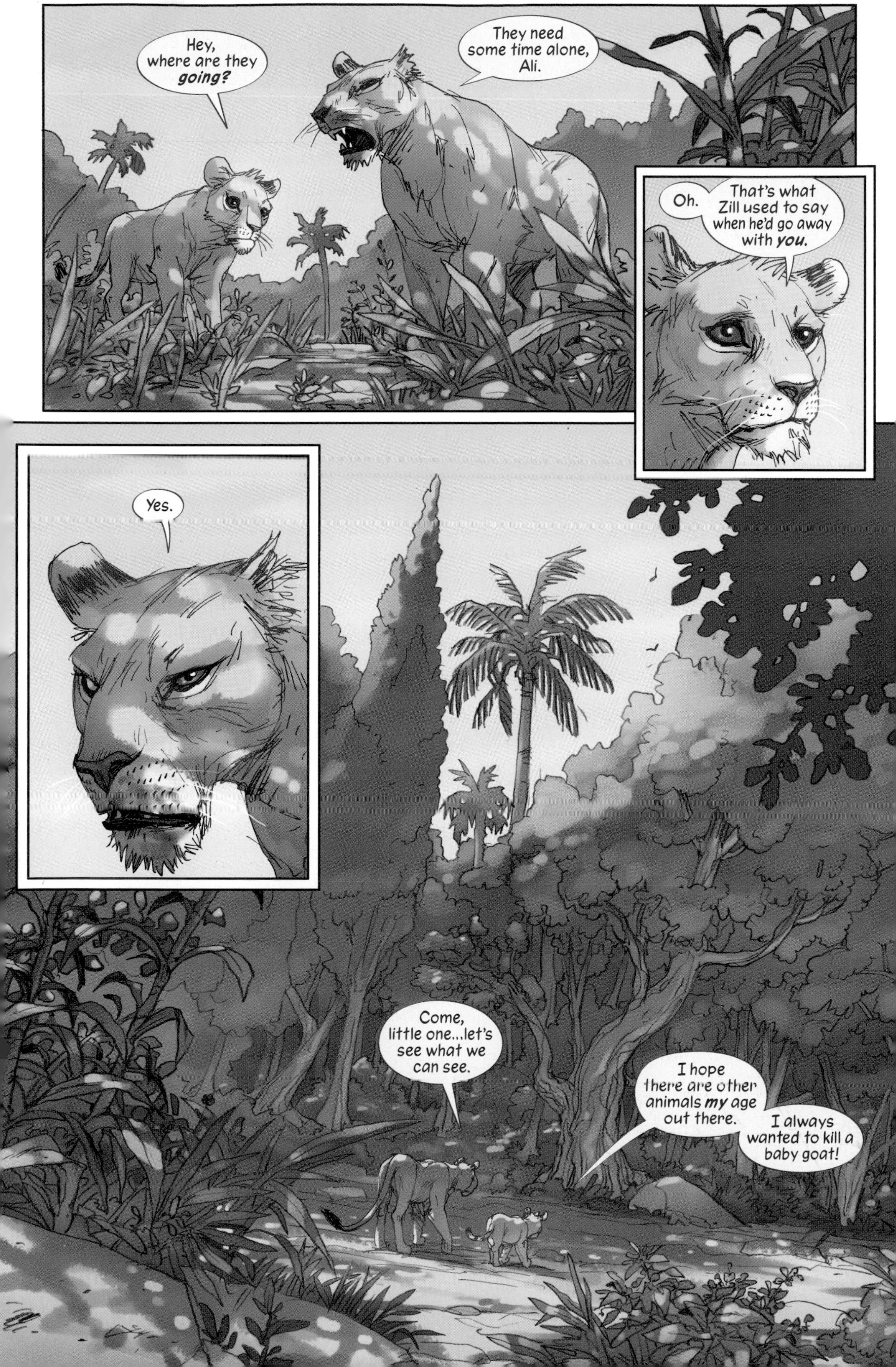
Hey, where are they *going?*
They need some time alone, Ali.
Oh.
That's what Zill used to say when he'd go away with *you.*
Yes.
Come, little one...let's see what we can see.
I hope there are other animals *my* age out there.
I always wanted to kill a baby goat!

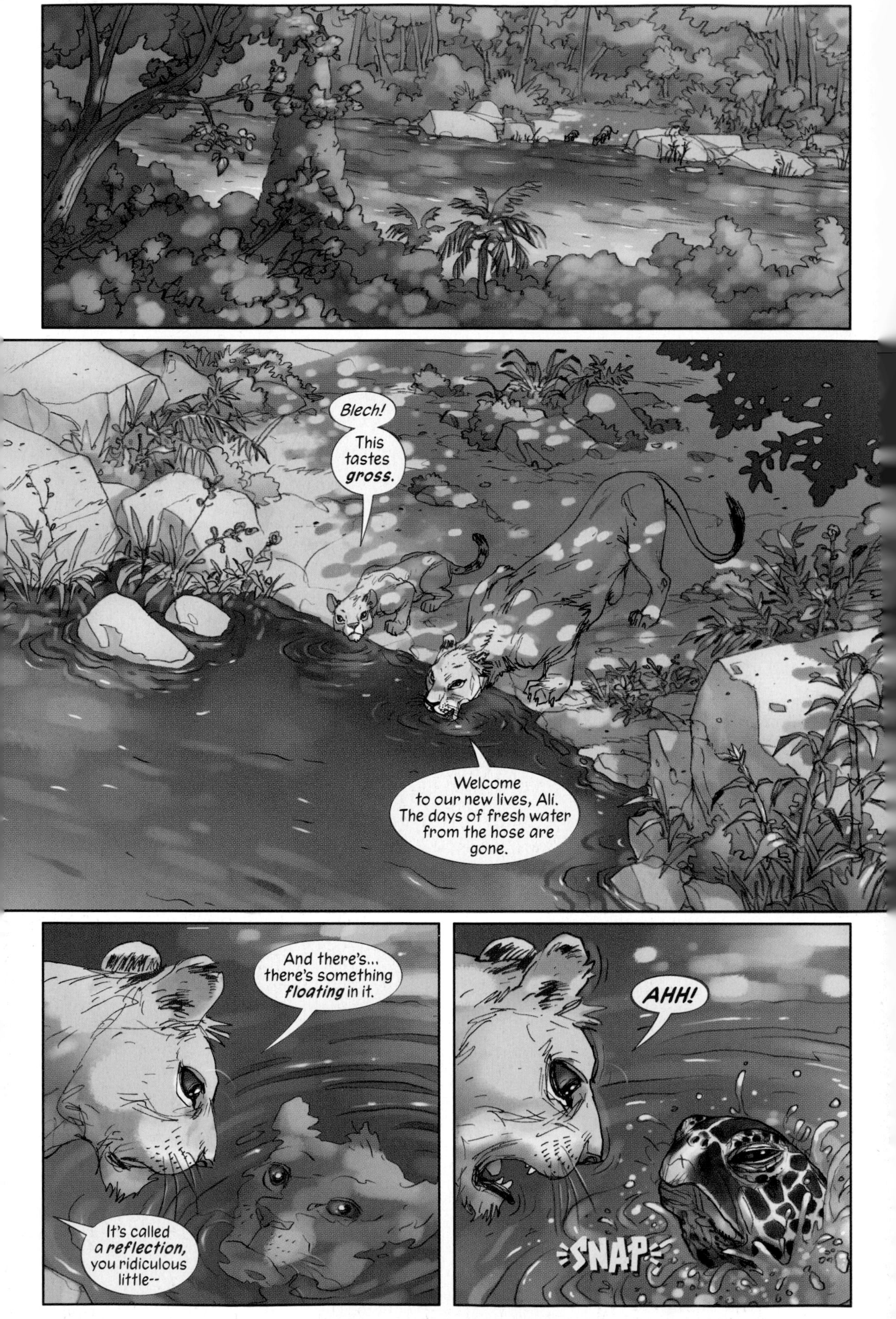
Blech!
This tastes *gross.*
Welcome to our new lives, Ali. The days of fresh water from the hose are gone.
And there's... there's something *floating* in it.
It's called a *reflection,* you ridiculous little--
AHH!
SNAP

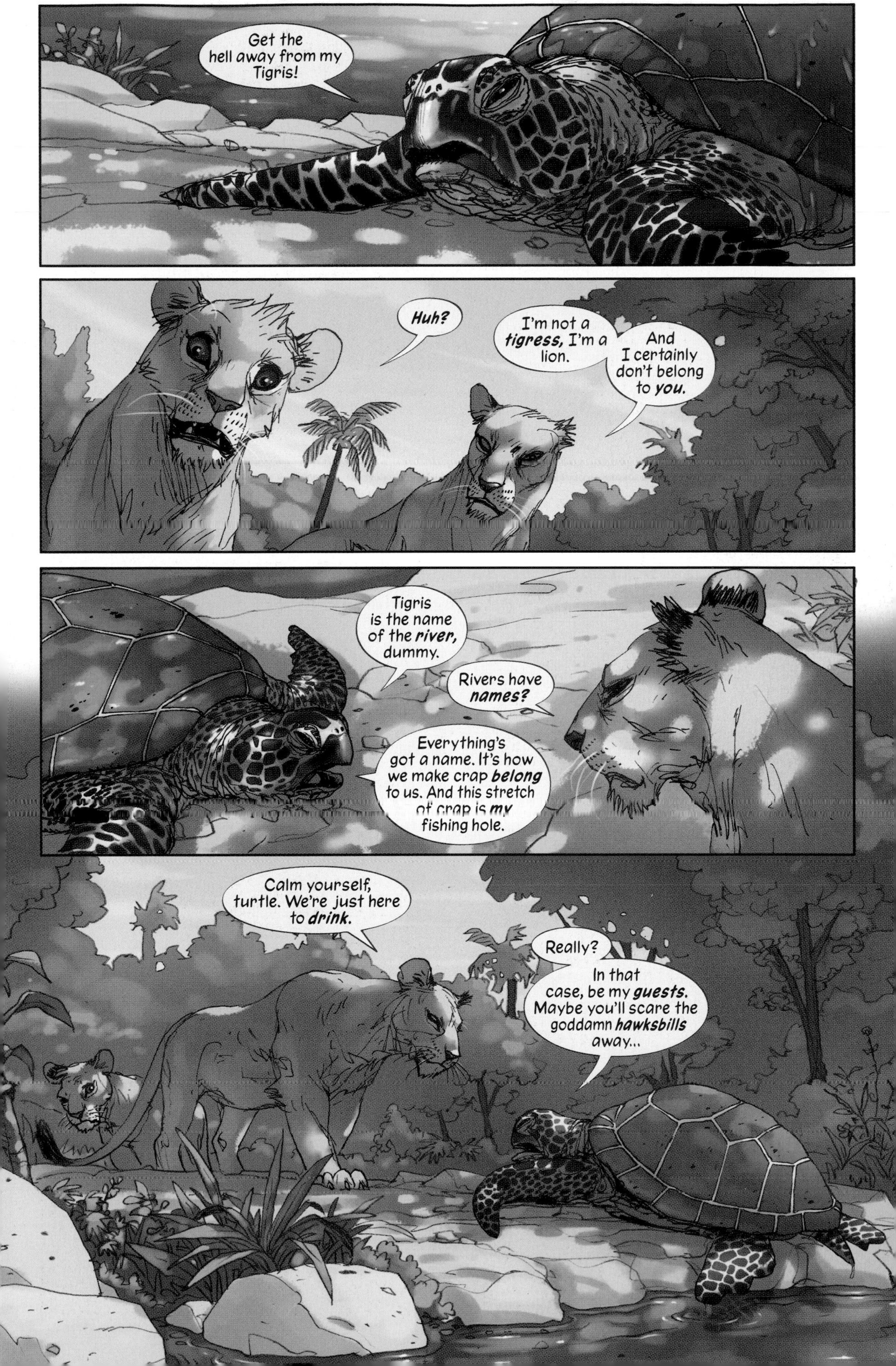
Get the hell away from my Tigris!
Huh?
I'm not a tigress, I'm a lion.
And I certainly don't belong to you.
Tigris is the name of the river, dummy.
Rivers have names?
Everything's got a name. It's how we make crap belong to us. And this stretch of crap is my fishing hole.
Calm yourself, turtle. We're just here to drink.
Really?
In that case, be my guests. Maybe you'll scare the goddamn hawksbills away...

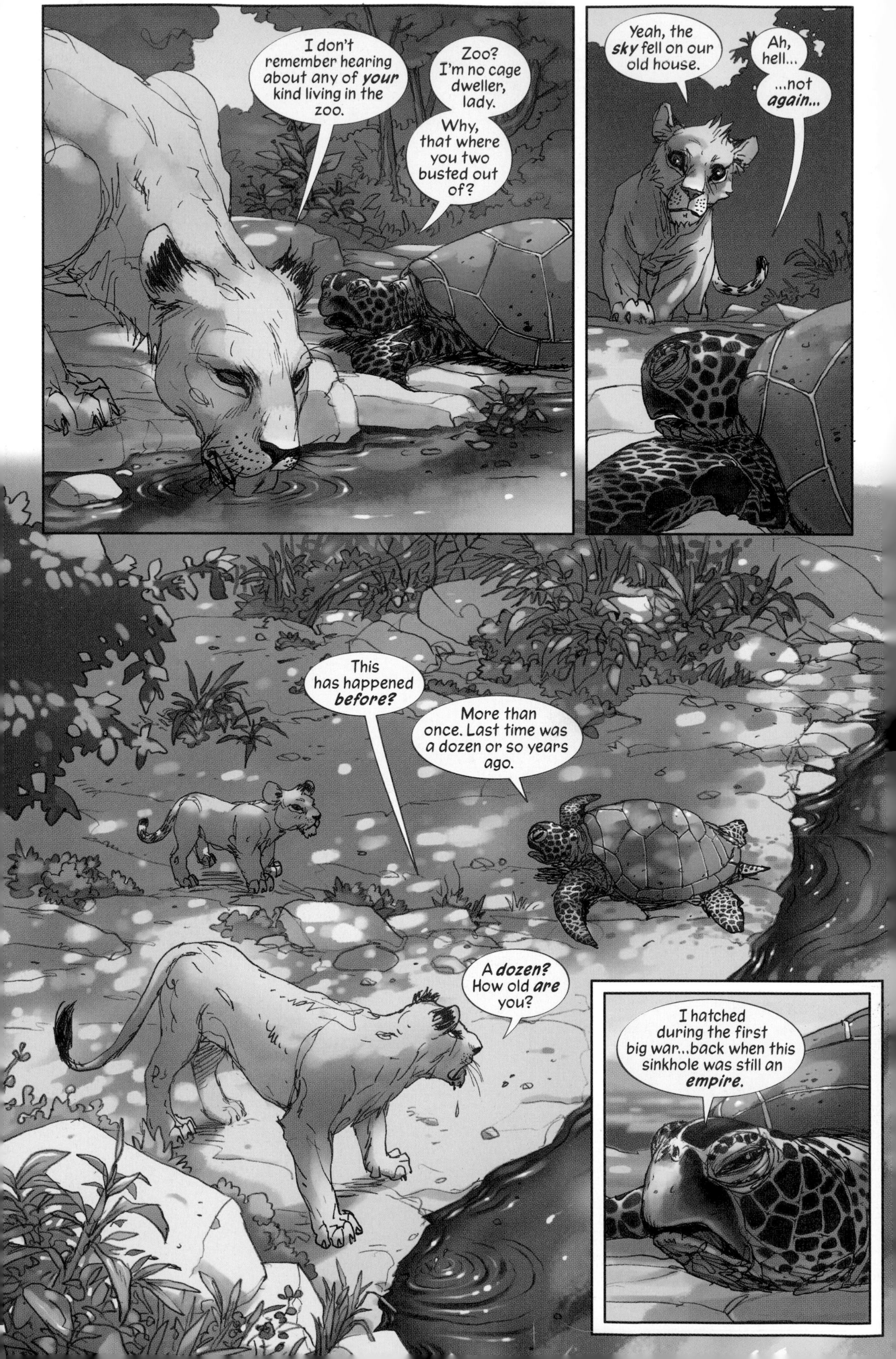
I don't remember hearing about any of *your* kind living in the zoo.
Zoo? I'm no cage dweller, lady.
Why, that where you two busted out of?
Yeah, the *sky* fell on our old house.
Ah, hell...
...not *again*...
This has happened *before?*
More than once. Last time was a dozen or so years ago.
A *dozen?* How old *are* you?
I hatched during the first big war...back when this sinkhole was still an *empire*.

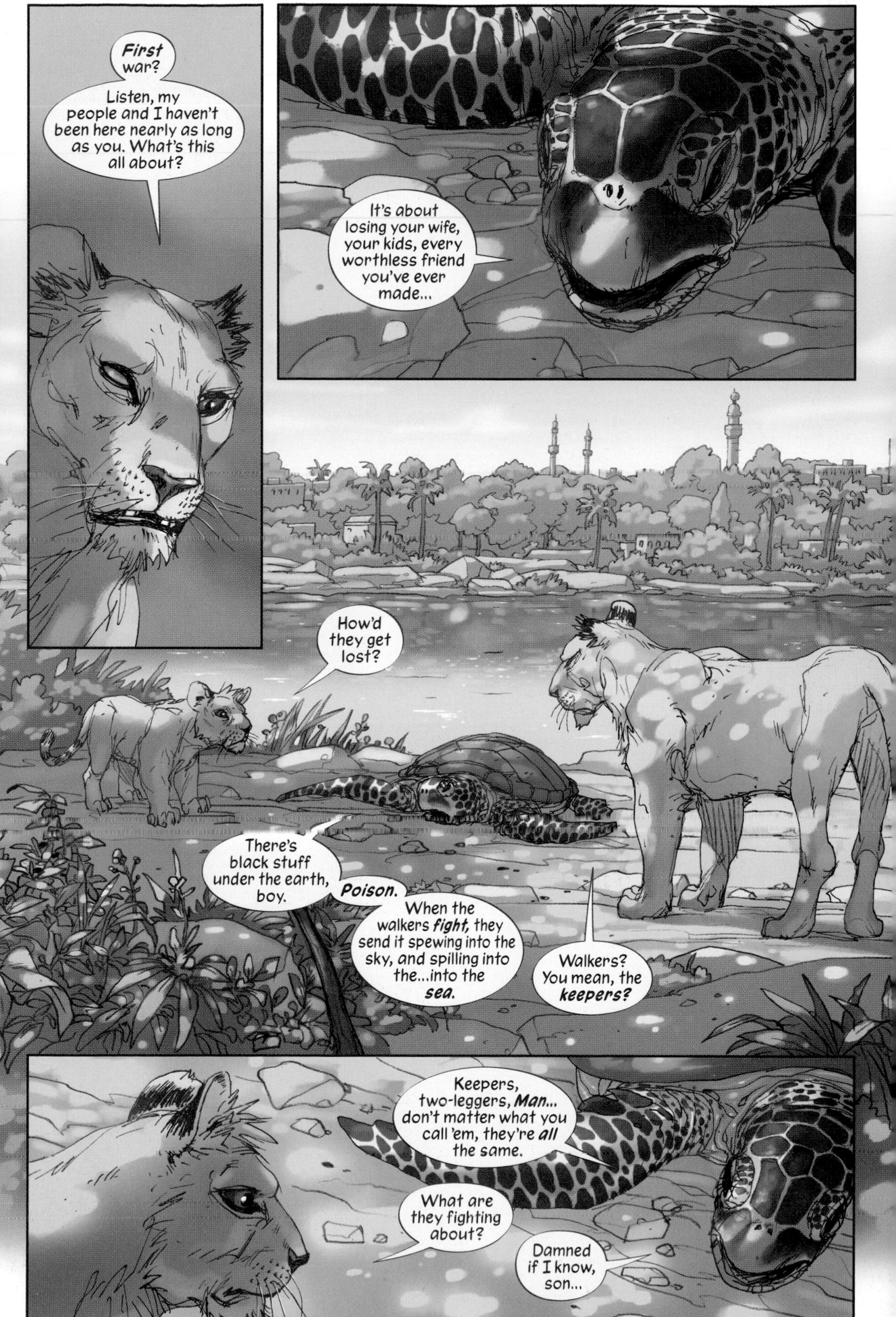
First war?
Listen, my people and I haven't been here nearly as long as you. What's this all about?
It's about losing your wife, your kids, every worthless friend you've ever made...
How'd they get lost?
There's black stuff under the earth, boy.
Poison.
When the walkers fight, they send it spewing into the sky, and spilling into the...into the sea.
Walkers? You mean, the keepers?
Keepers, two-leggers, Man... don't matter what you call 'em, they're all the same.
What are they fighting about?
Damned if I know, son...

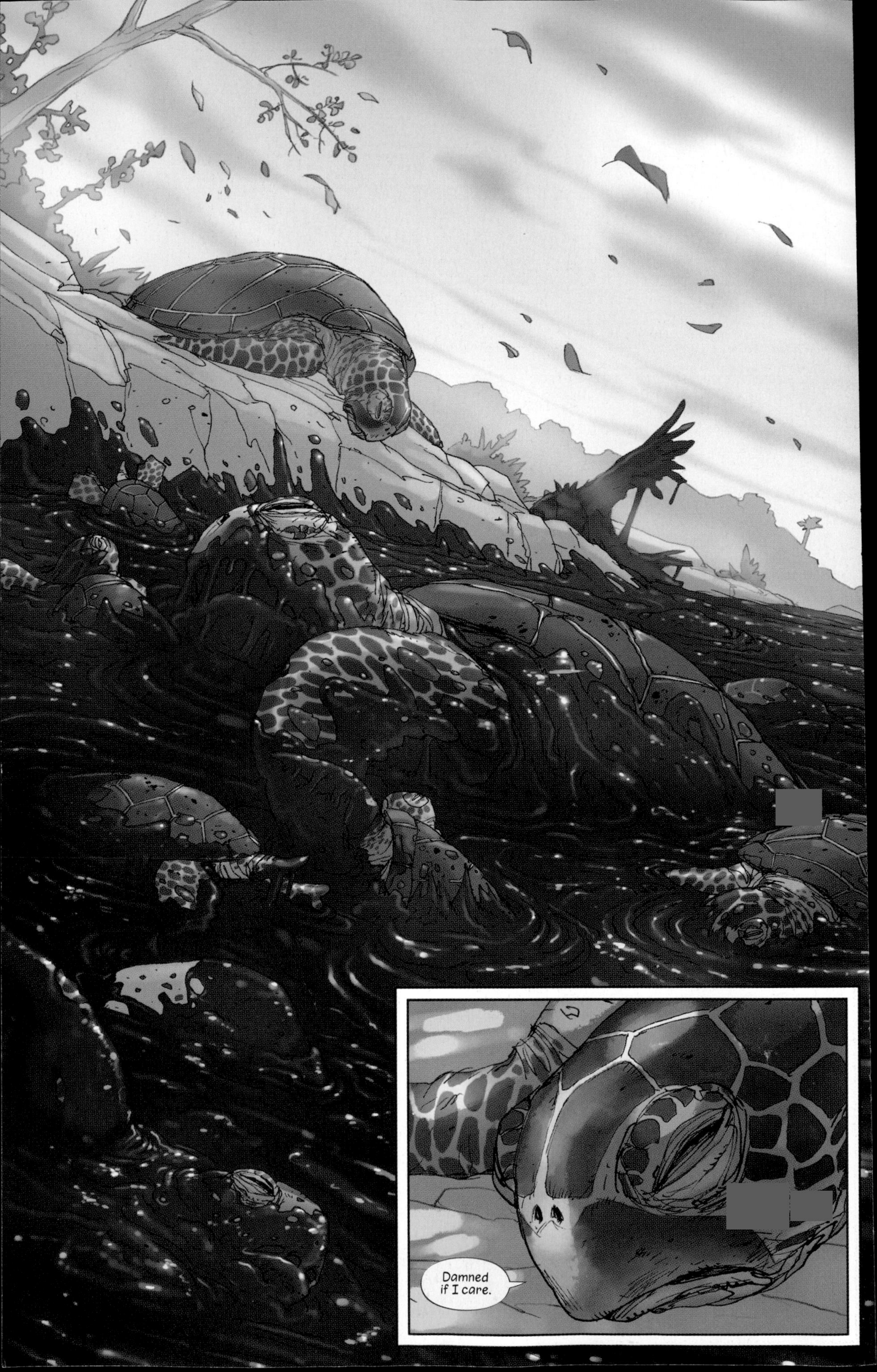
Damned if I care.

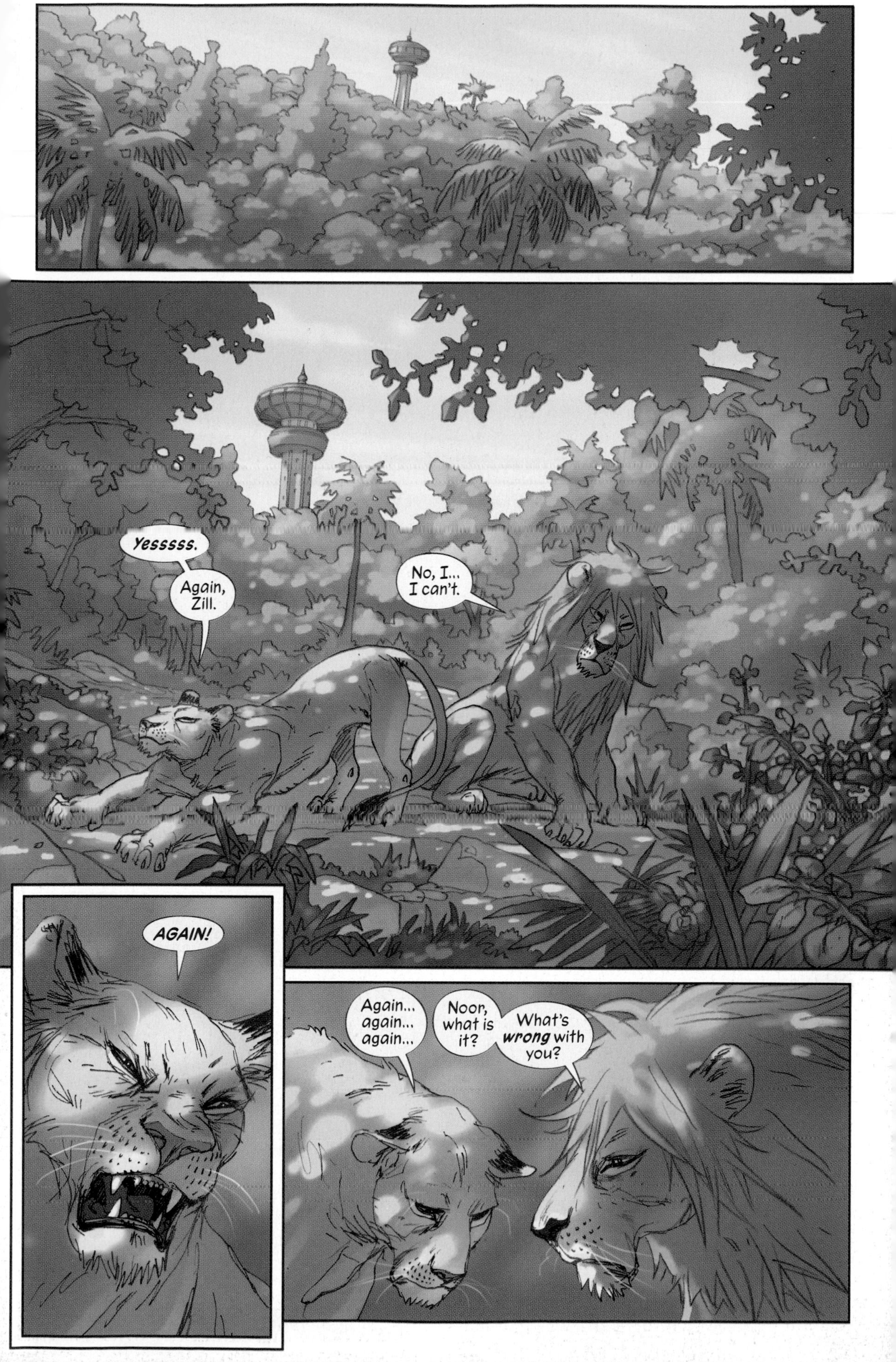
Yesssss.
Again, Zill.
No, I... I can't.
AGAIN!
Again... again... again...
Noor, what is it?
What's wrong with you?

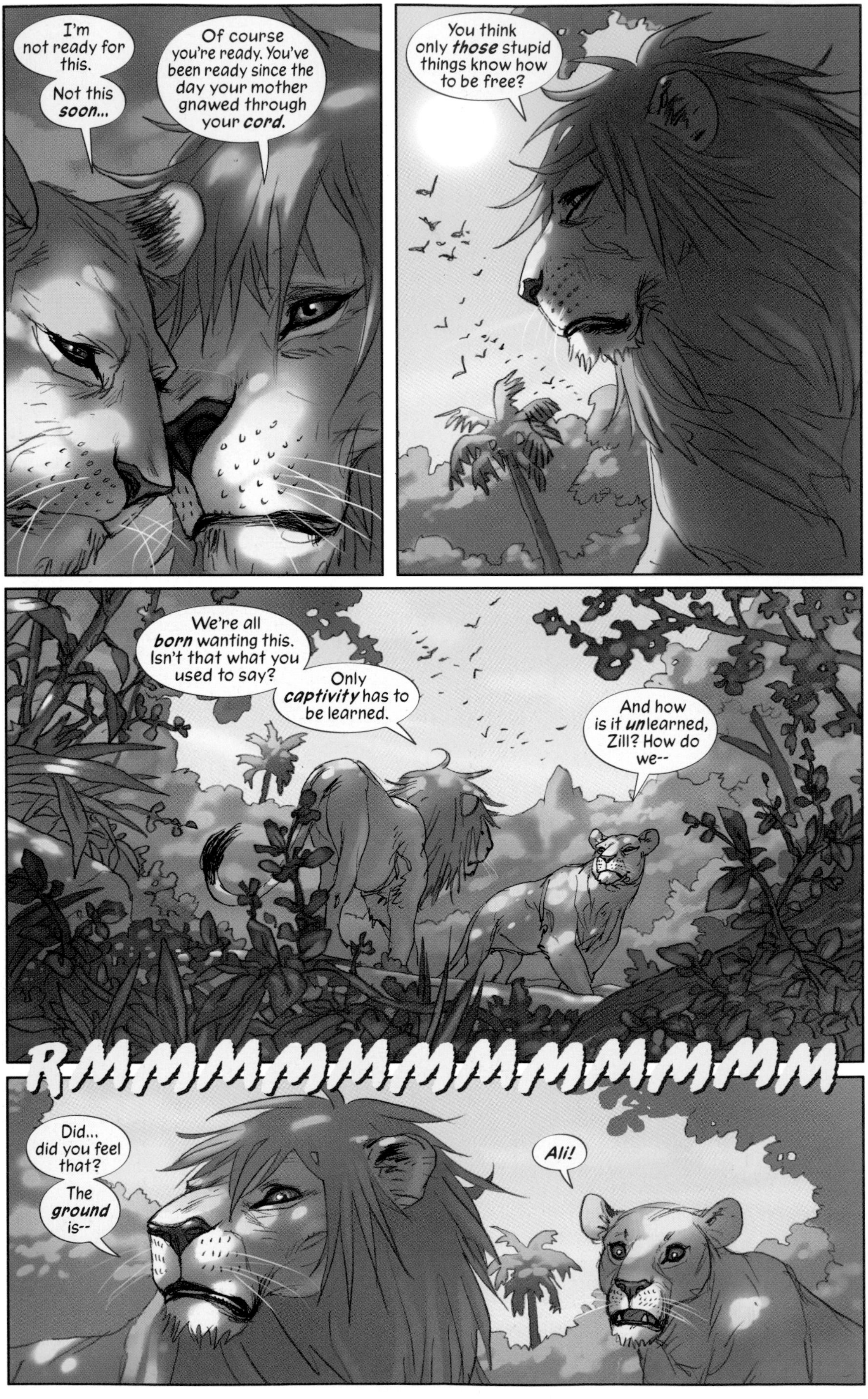
I'm not ready for this.
Not this soon...
Of course you're ready. You've been ready since the day your mother gnawed through your cord.
You think only those stupid things know how to be free?
We're all born wanting this. Isn't that what you used to say?
Only captivity has to be learned.
And how is it unlearned, Zill? How do we--
RMMMMMMMMMMMMMMMMM
Did... did you feel that?
The ground is--
Ali!

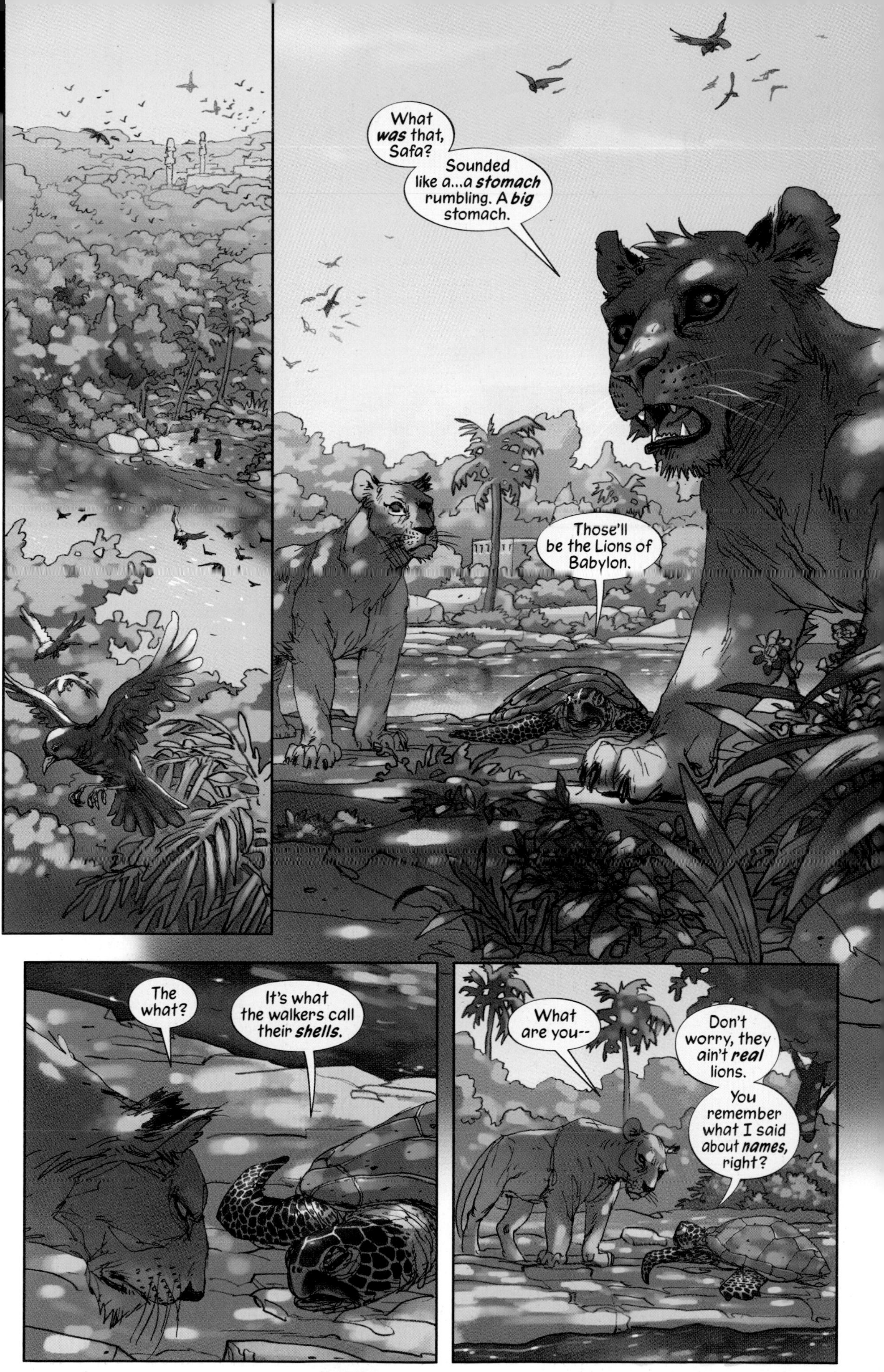
What *was* that, Safa?
Sounded like a...a *stomach* rumbling. A *big* stomach.
Those'll be the Lions of Babylon.
The what?
It's what the walkers call their *shells*.
What are you--
Don't worry, they ain't *real* lions.
You remember what I said about *names*, right?

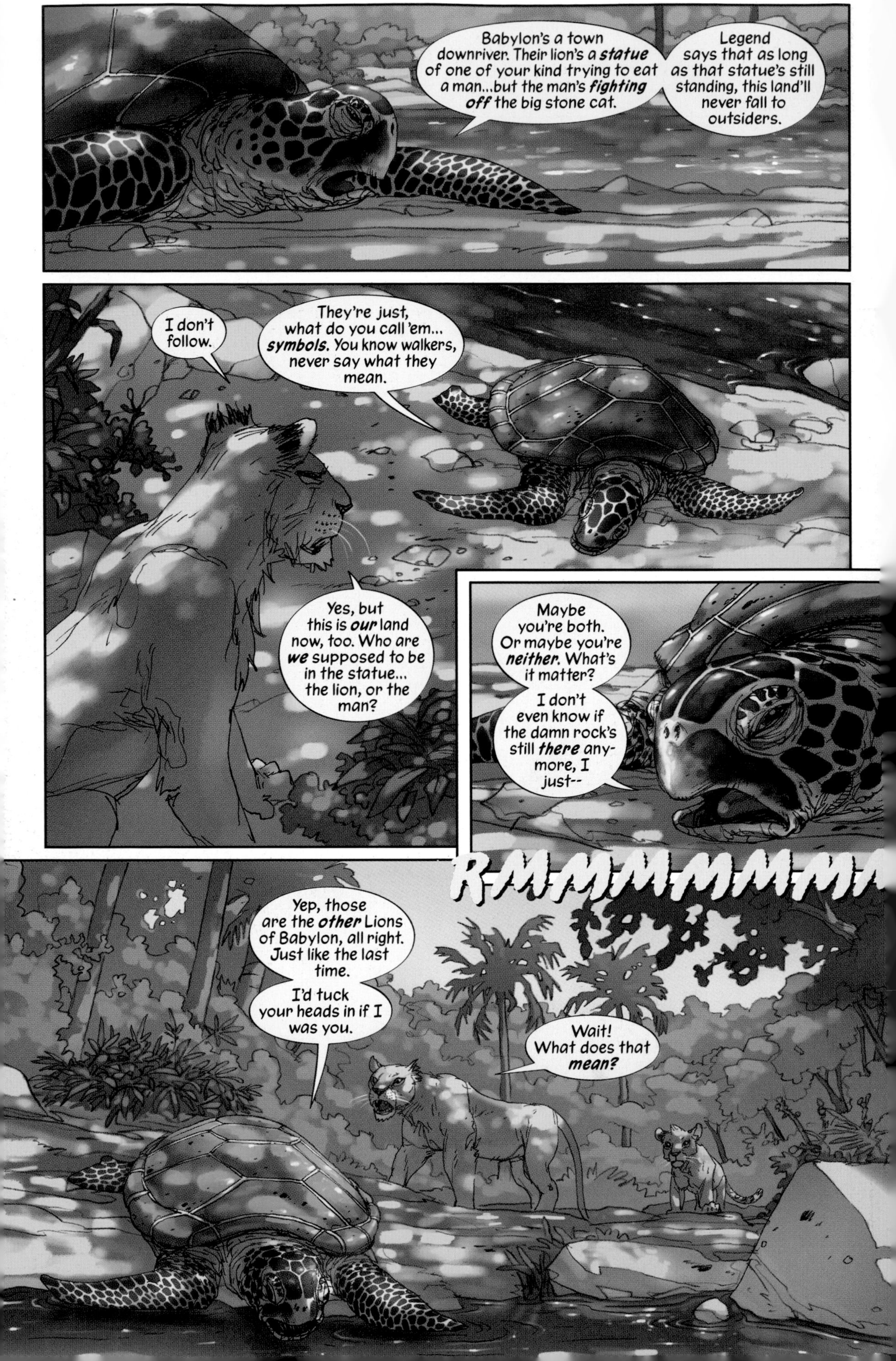
Babylon's a town downriver. Their lion's a *statue* of one of your kind trying to eat a man...but the man's *fighting off* the big stone cat.
Legend says that as long as that statue's still standing, this land'll never fall to outsiders.
I don't follow.
They're just, what do you call 'em... *symbols.* You know walkers, never say what they mean.
Yes, but this is *our* land now, too. Who are *we* supposed to be in the statue... the lion, or the man?
Maybe you're both. Or maybe you're *neither.* What's it matter?
I don't even know if the damn rock's still *there* anymore, I just--
RMMMMMMMM
Yep, those are the *other* Lions of Babylon, all right. Just like the last time.
I'd tuck your heads in if I was you.
Wait! What does that *mean?*

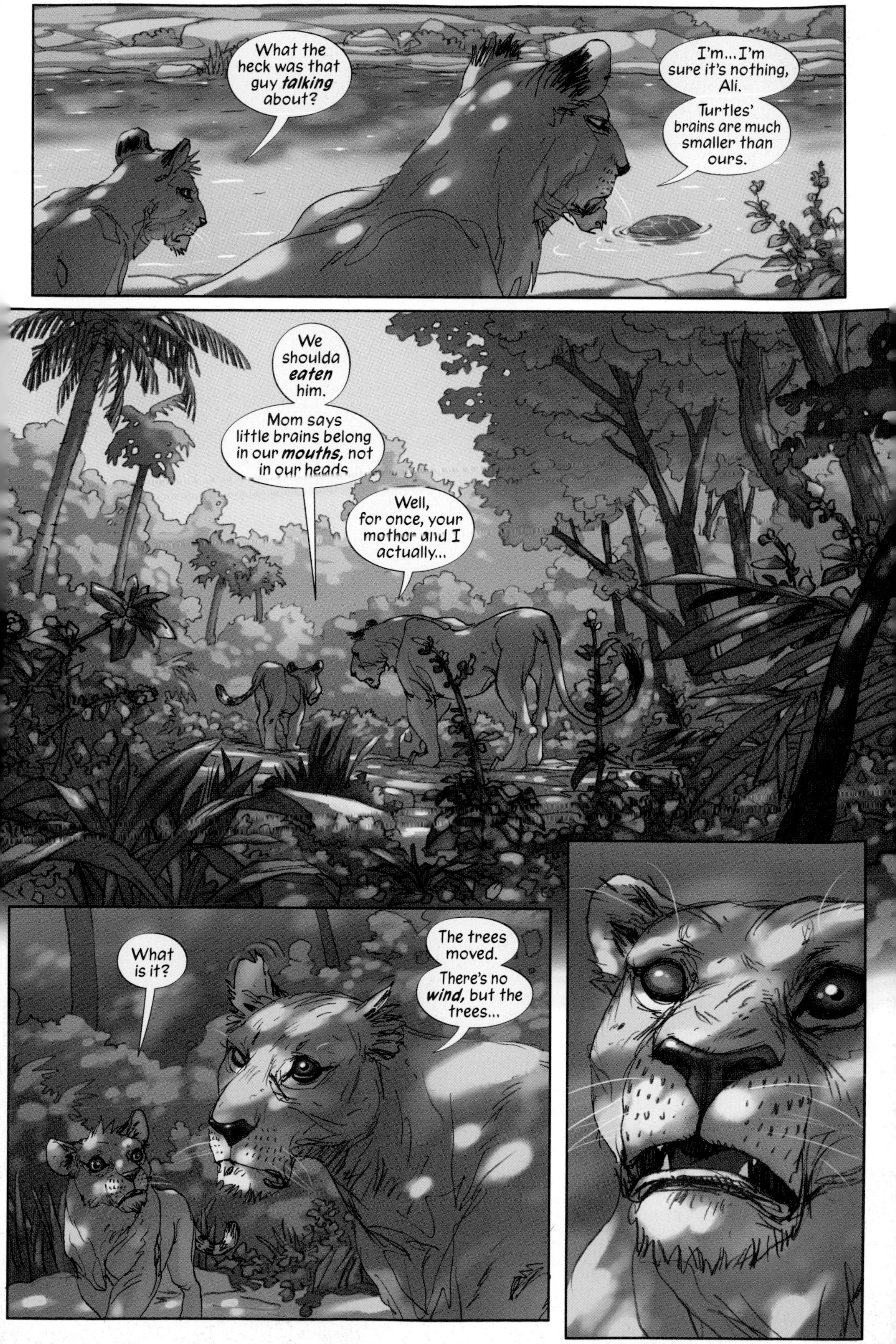

What the heck was that guy *talking* about?
I'm... I'm sure it's nothing, Ali.
Turtles' brains are much smaller than ours.
We shoulda *eaten* him.
Mom says little brains belong in our *mouths,* not in our heads.
Well, for once, your mother and I actually...
What is it?
The trees moved.
There's no *wind,* but the trees...

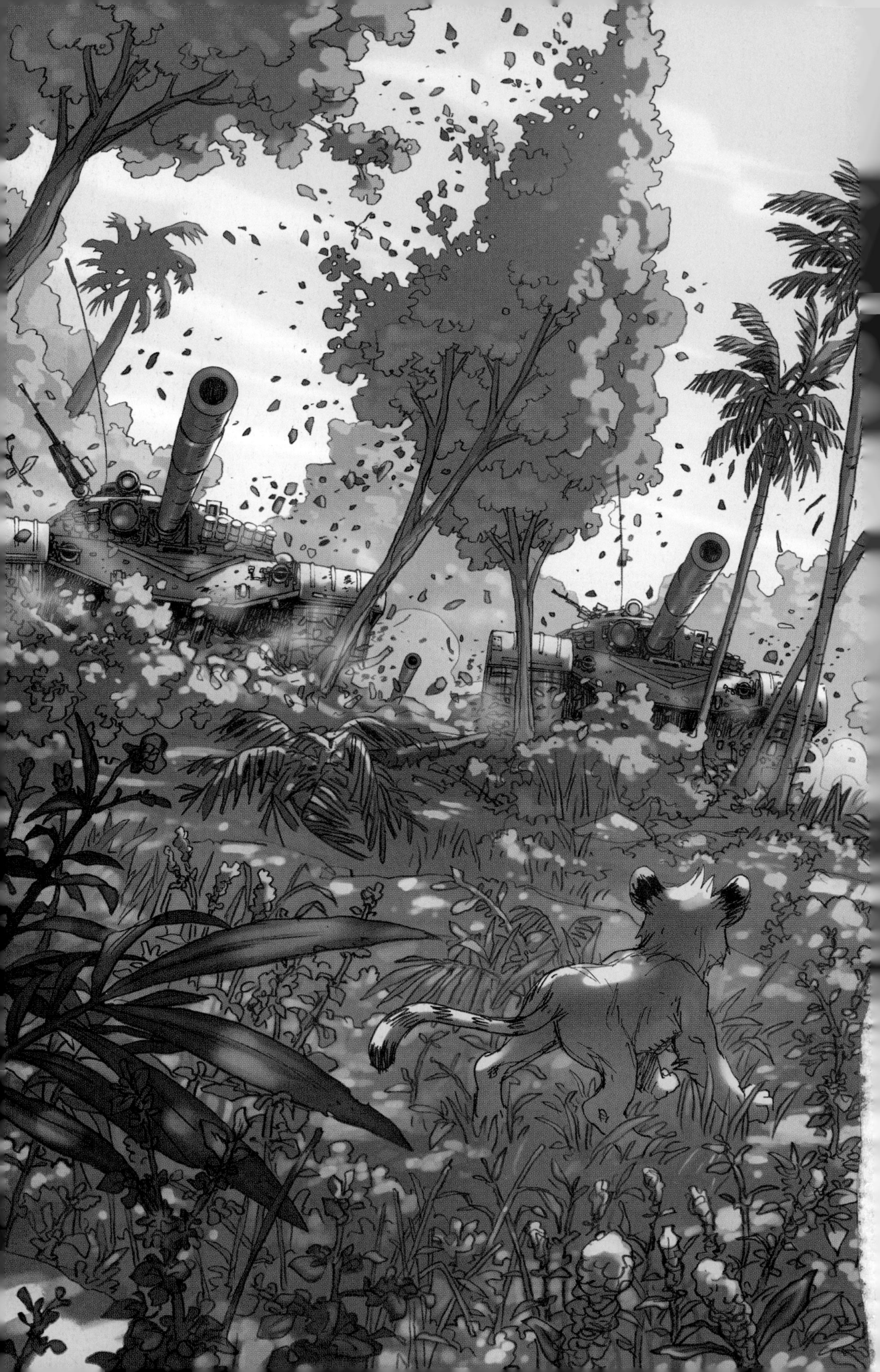

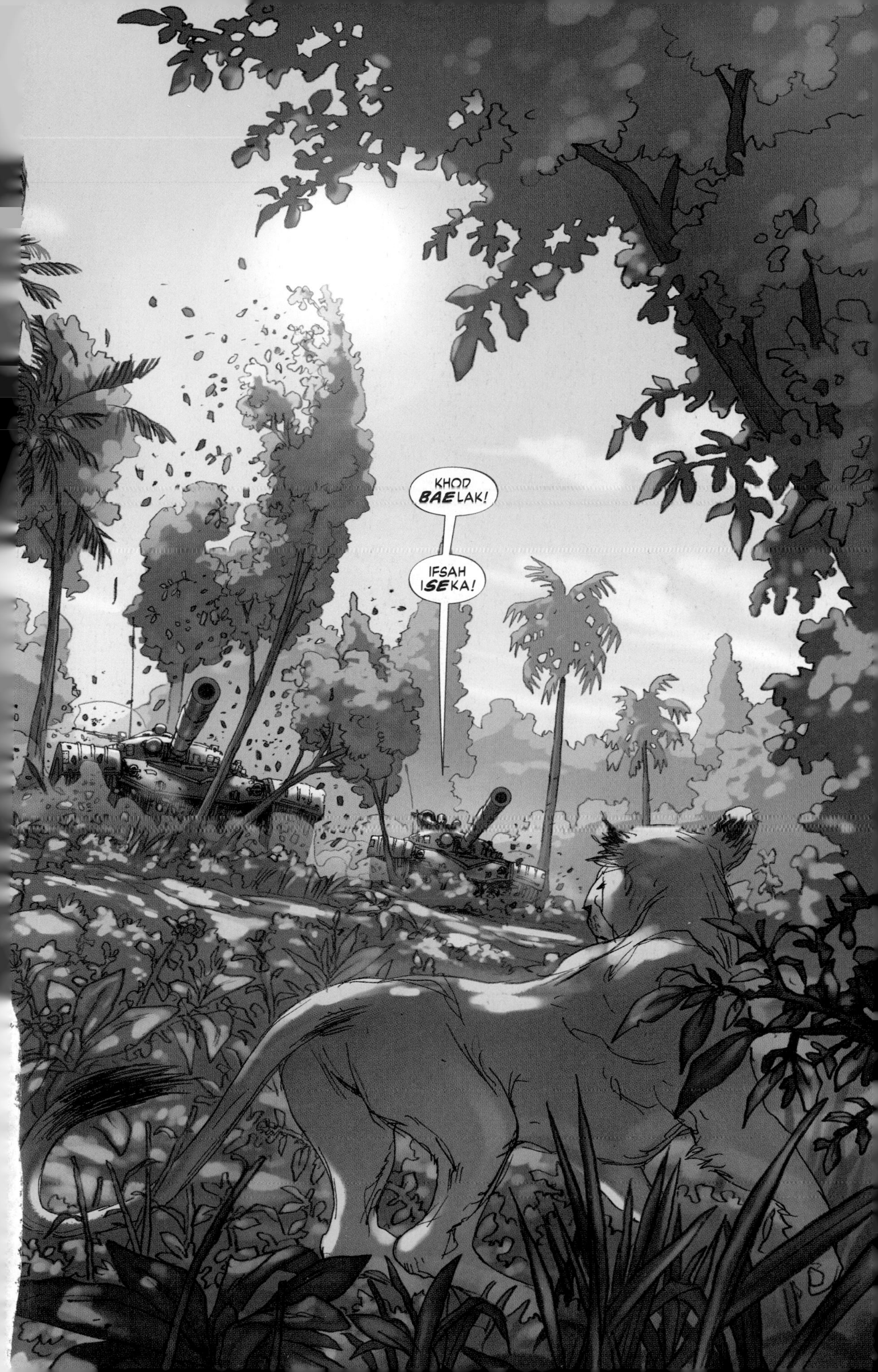
KHOD BAE LAK!
IFSAH ISE KA!

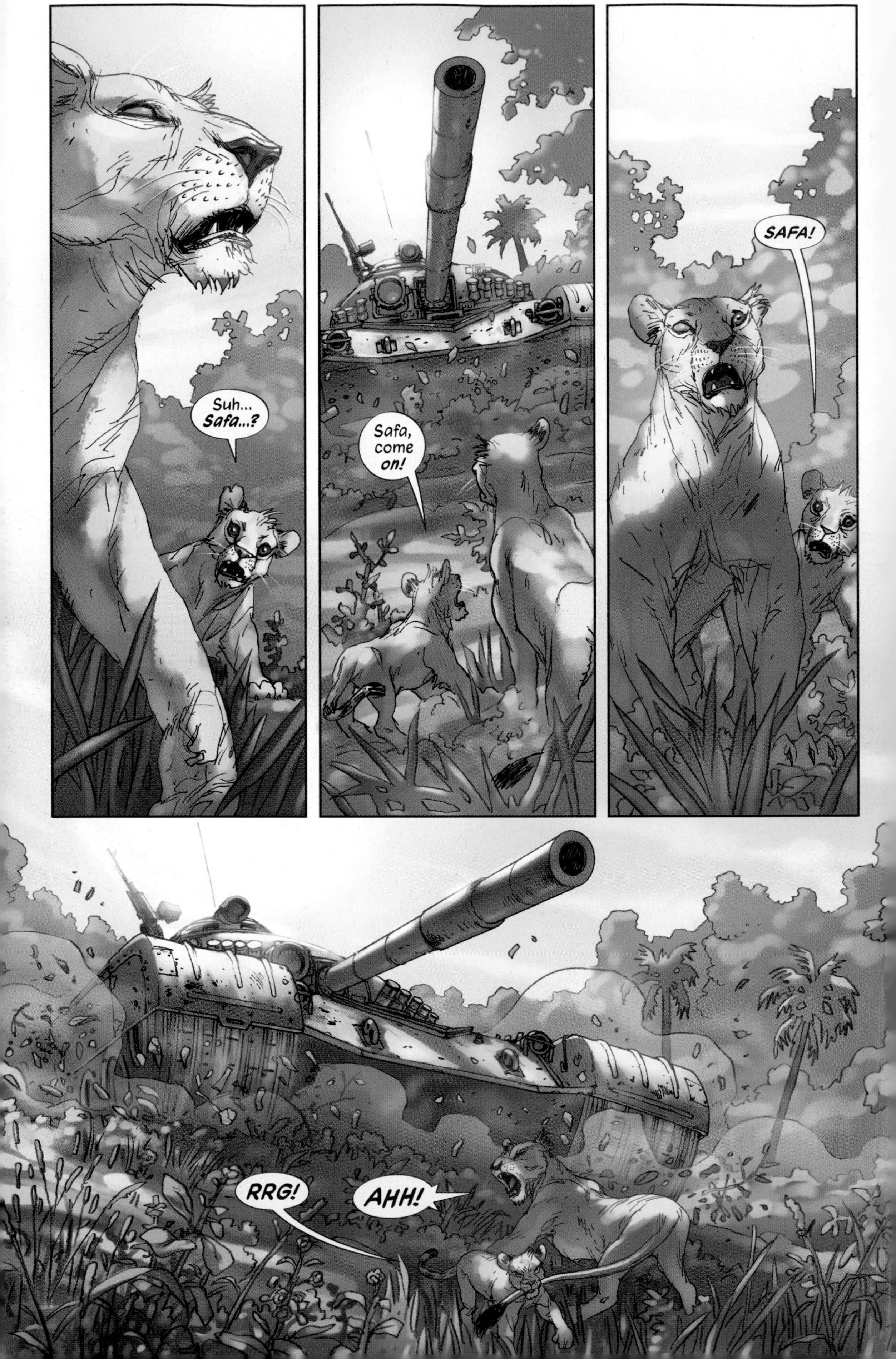
Suh...
Safa...?
Safa, come on!
SAFA!
RRG!
AHH!

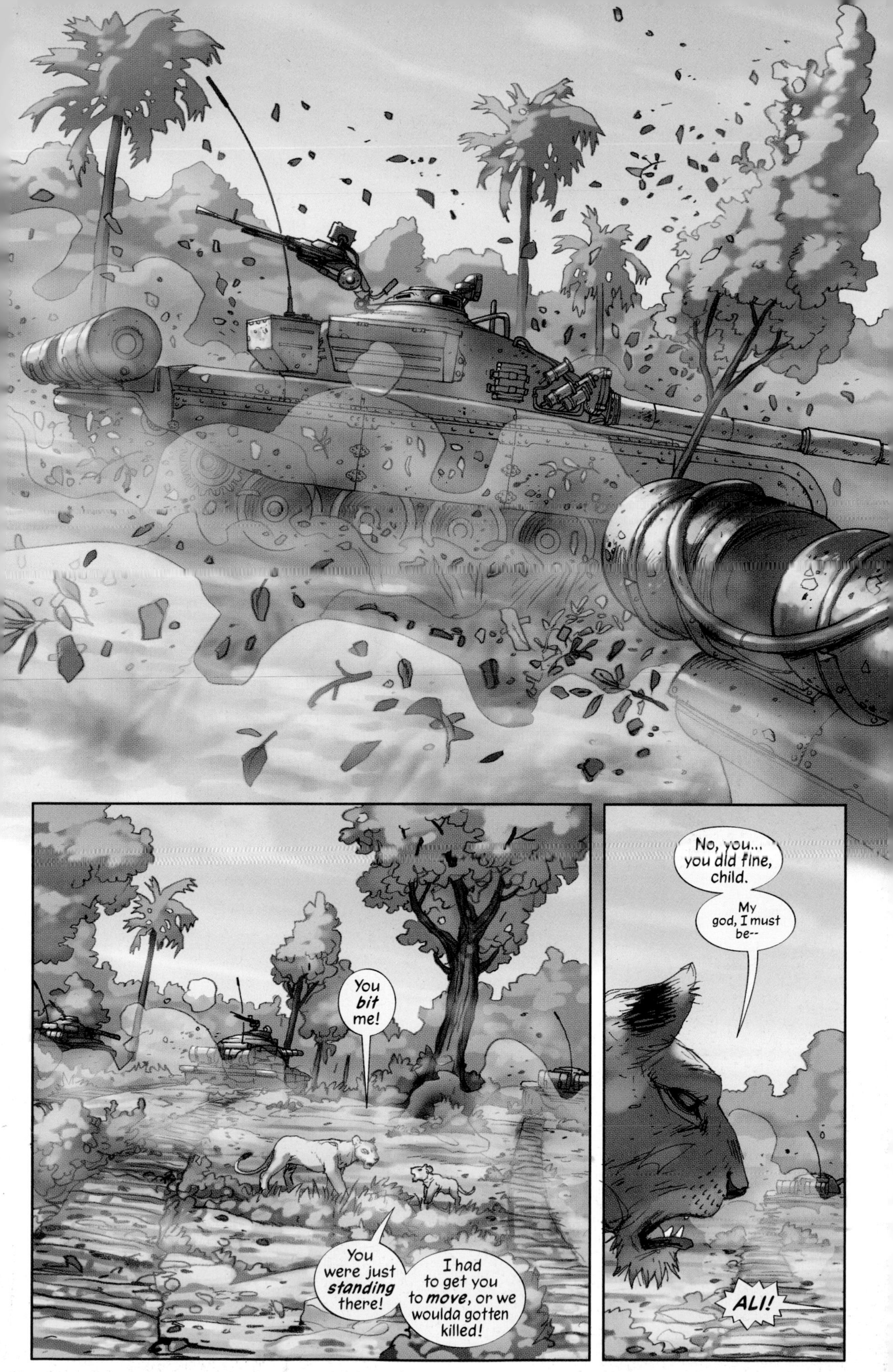

You *bit* me!
You were just *standing* there!
I had to get you to *move*, or we woulda gotten killed!
No, you... you did fine, child.
My god, I must be--
ALI!

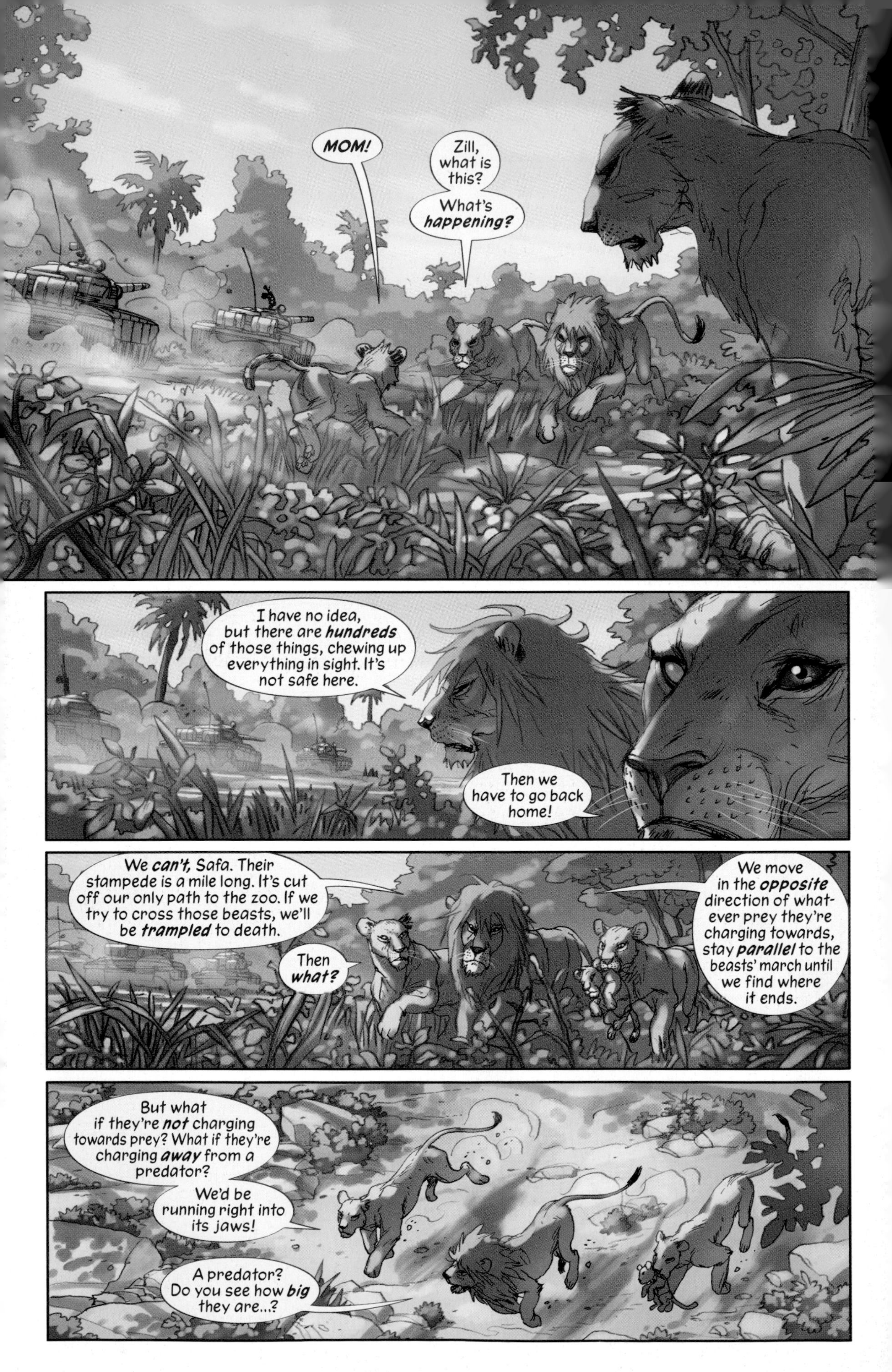
MOM!
Zill, what is this?
What's happening?
I have no idea, but there are hundreds of those things, chewing up everything in sight. It's not safe here.
Then we have to go back home!
We can't, Safa. Their stampede is a mile long. It's cut off our only path to the zoo. If we try to cross those beasts, we'll be trampled to death.
Then what?
We move in the opposite direction of whatever prey they're charging towards, stay parallel to the beasts' march until we find where it ends.
But what if they're not charging towards prey? What if they're charging away from a predator?
We'd be running right into its jaws!
A predator? Do you see how big they are...?

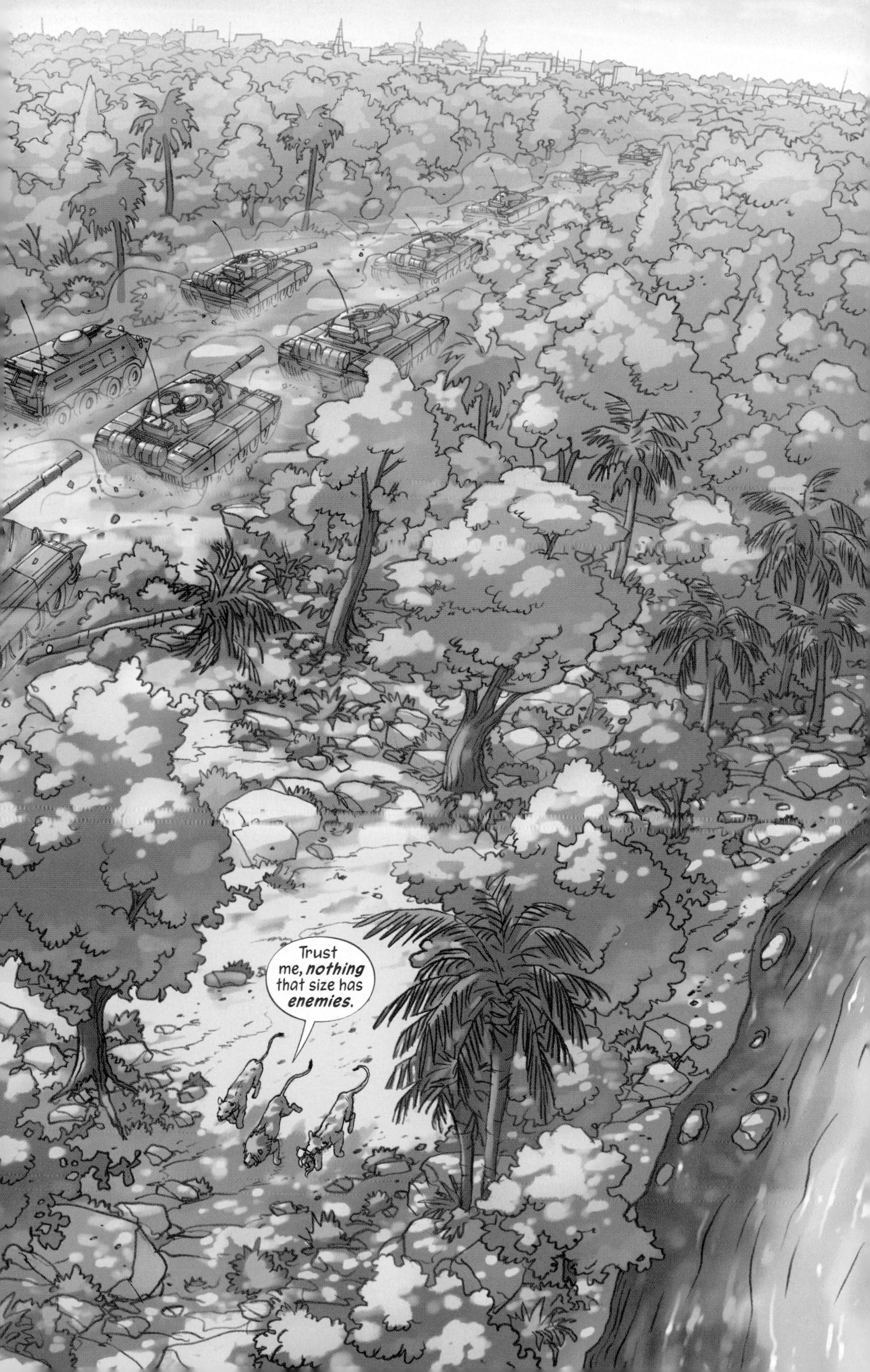
Trust me, **nothing** that size has **enemies**.

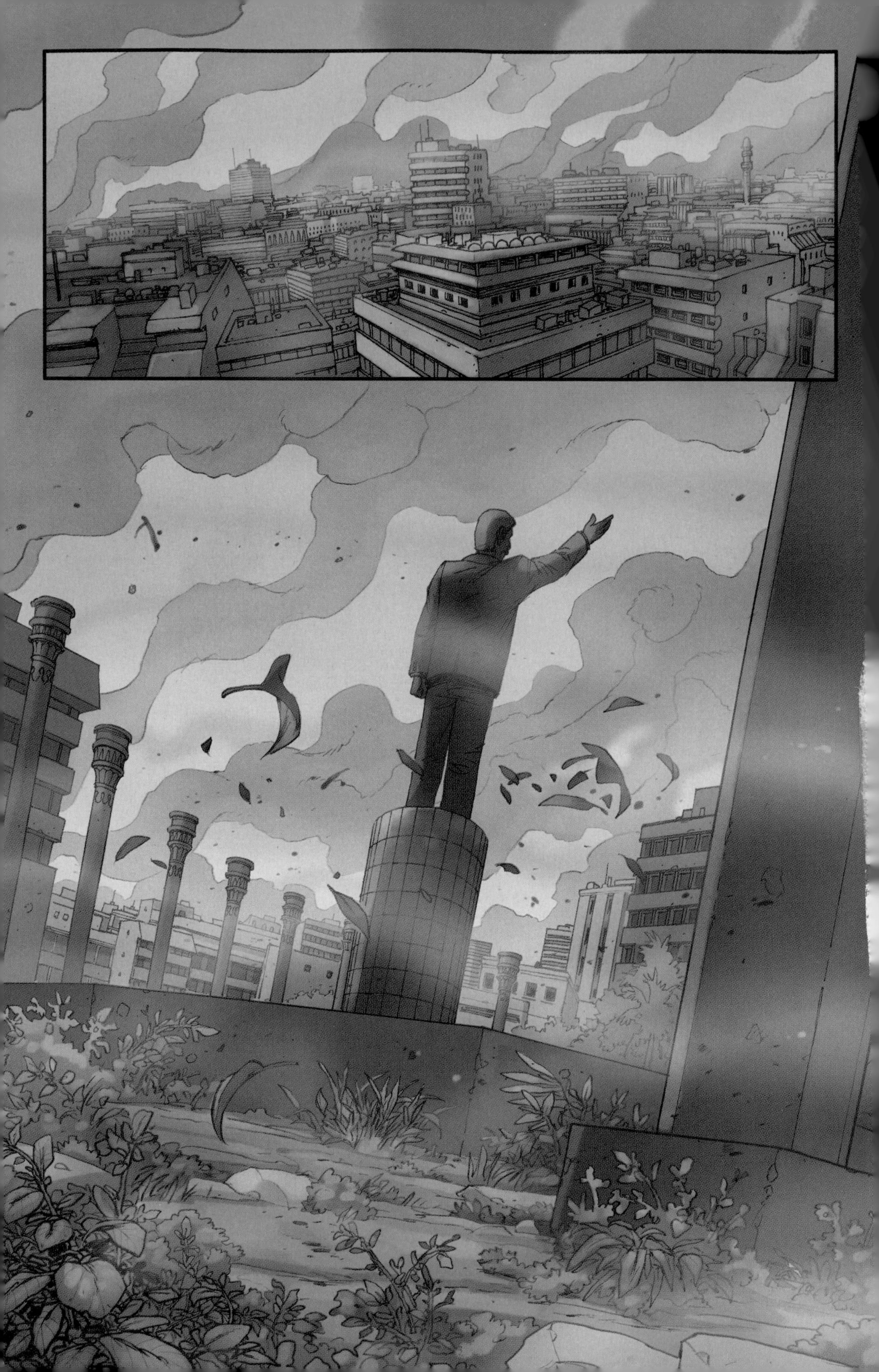

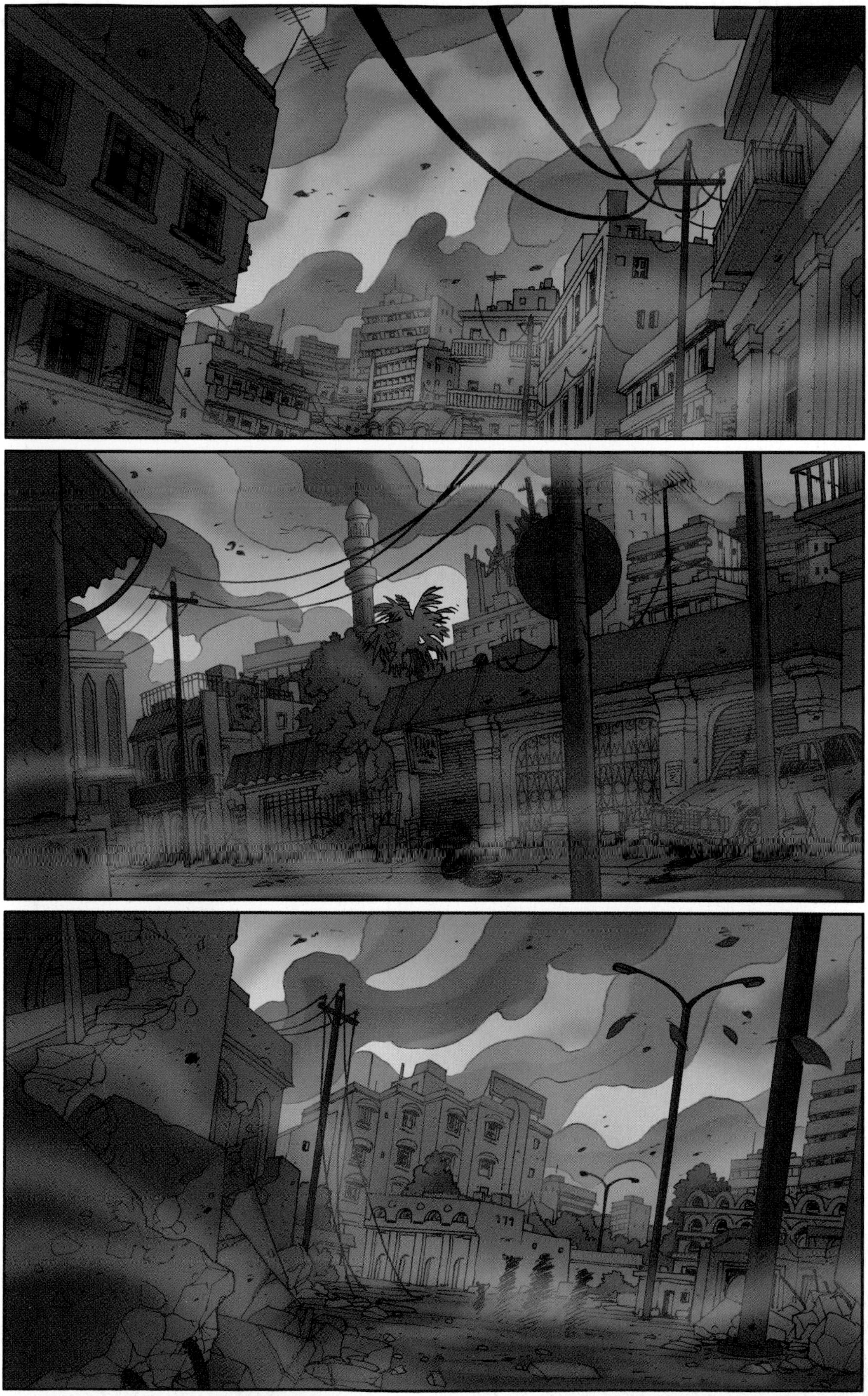

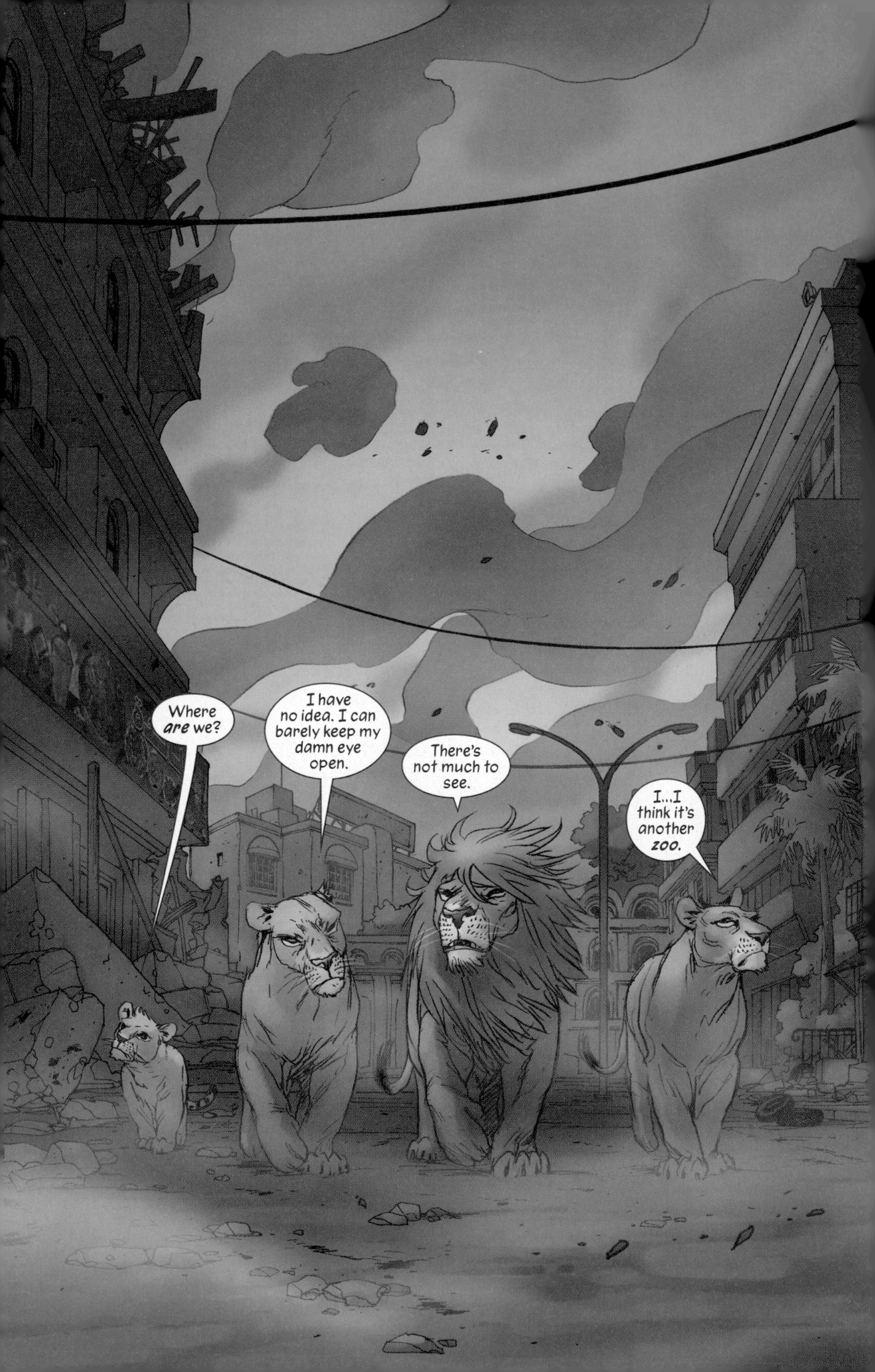
Where *are* we?
I have no idea. I can barely keep my damn eye open.
There's not much to see.
I...I think it's another *zoo*.

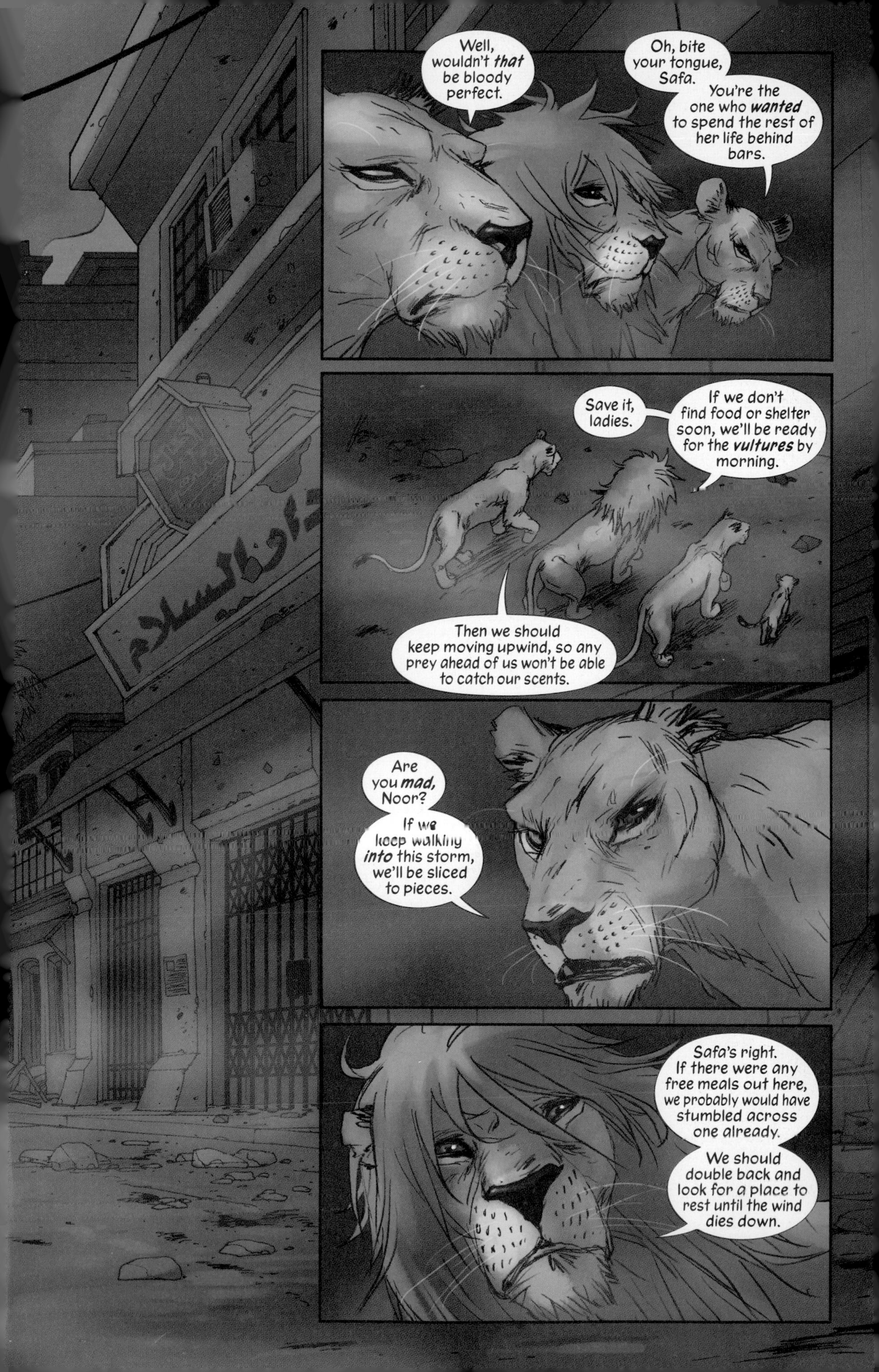
Well, wouldn't *that* be bloody perfect.
Oh, bite your tongue, Safa.
You're the one who *wanted* to spend the rest of her life behind bars.
Save it, ladies.
If we don't find food or shelter soon, we'll be ready for the *vultures* by morning.
Then we should keep moving upwind, so any prey ahead of us won't be able to catch our scents.
Are you *mad*, Noor?
If we keep walking *into* this storm, we'll be sliced to pieces.
Safa's right. If there were any free meals out here, we probably would have stumbled across one already.
We should double back and look for a place to rest until the wind dies down.

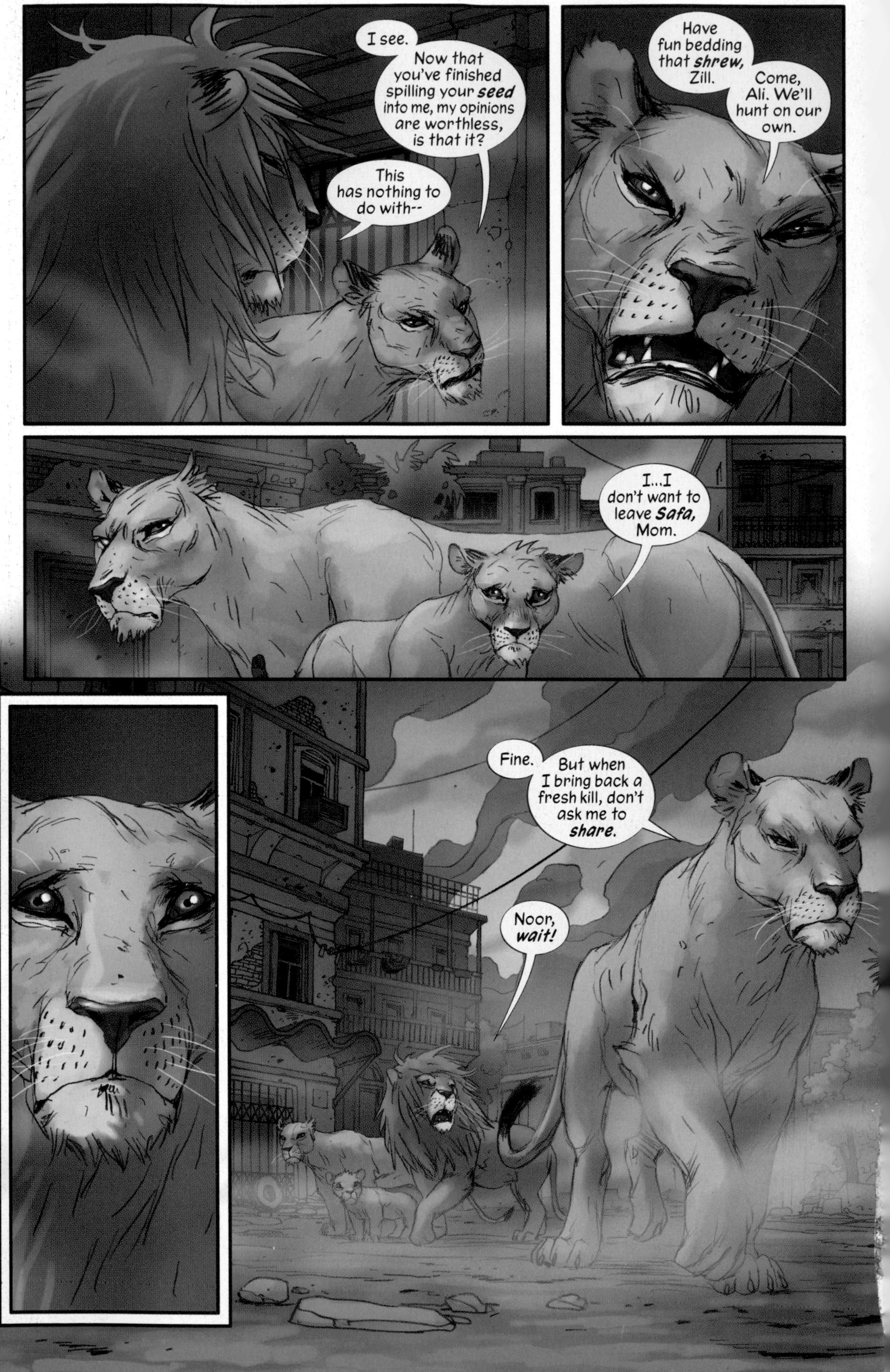
I see.
Now that you've finished spilling your seed into me, my opinions are worthless, is that it?
This has nothing to do with--
Have fun bedding that shrew, Zill.
Come, Ali. We'll hunt on our own.
I...I don't want to leave Safa, Mom.
Fine.
But when I bring back a fresh kill, don't ask me to share.
Noor, wait!

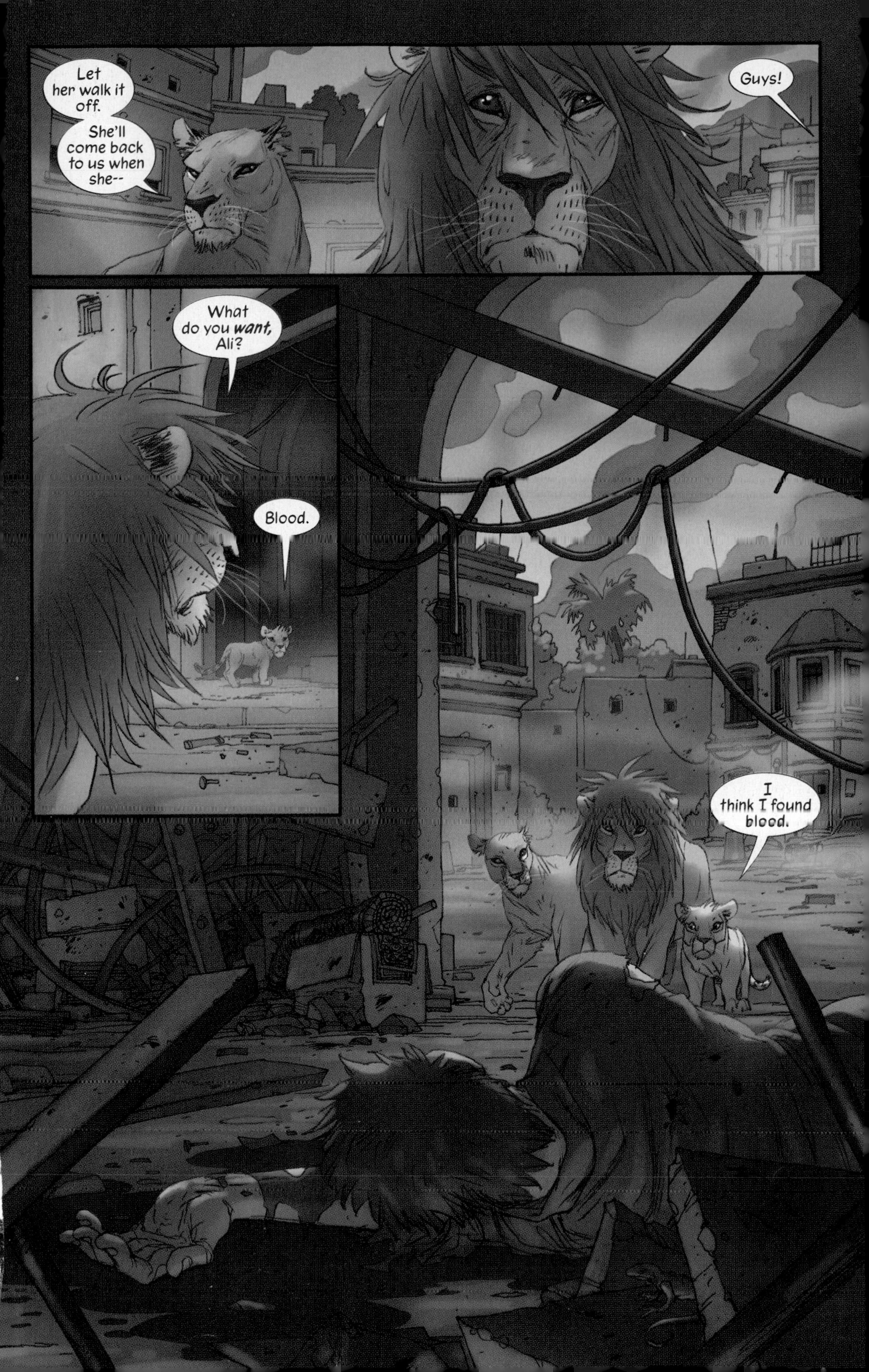
Let her walk it off.
She'll come back to us when she--
Guys!
What do you *want,* Ali?
Blood.
I think I found blood.

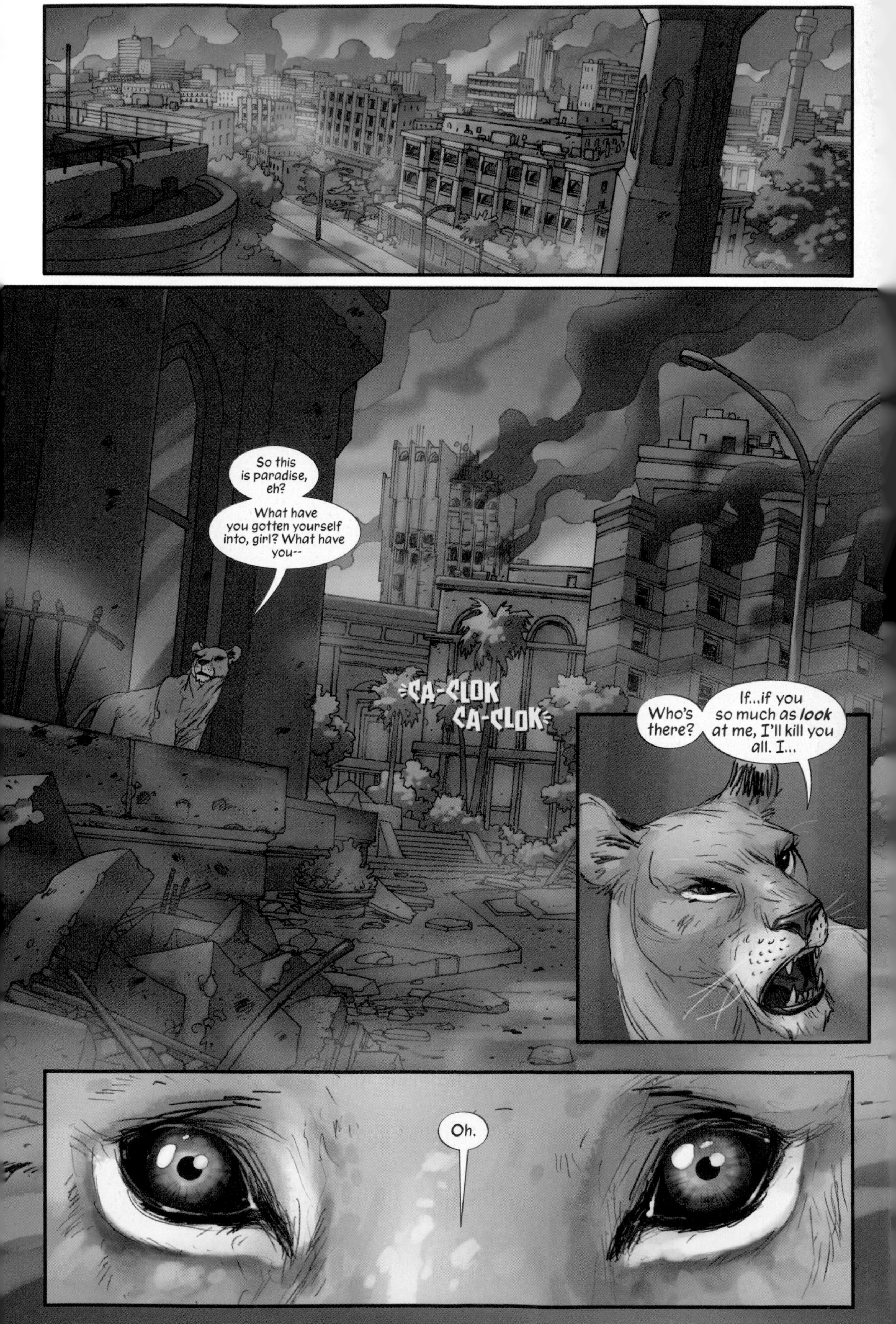

So this is paradise, eh?
What have you gotten yourself into, girl? What have you--
CA-CLOK
CA-CLOK
Who's there?
If...if you so much as *look* at me, I'll kill you all. I...
Oh.

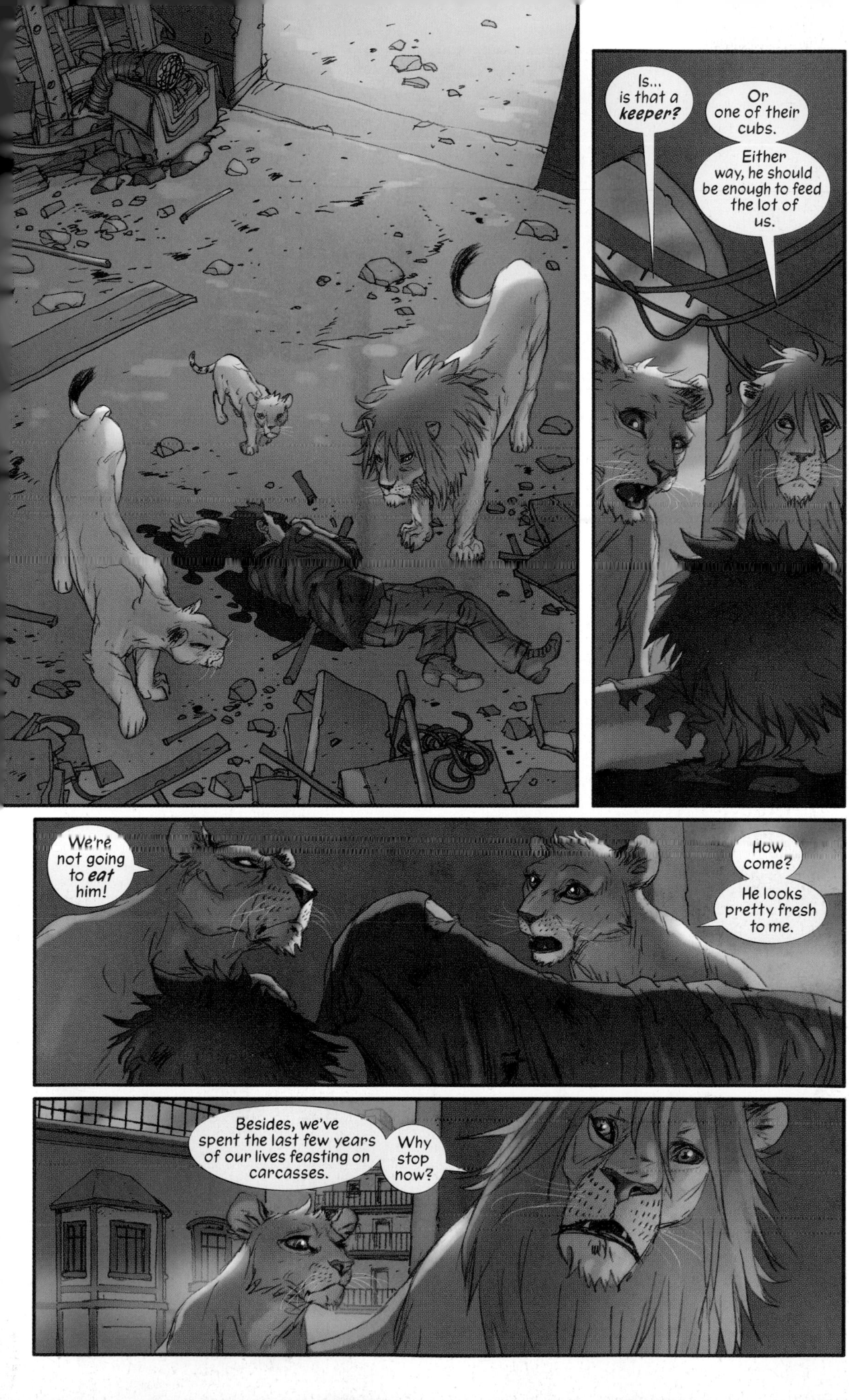
Is... is that a keeper?
Or one of their cubs.
Either way, he should be enough to feed the lot of us.
We're not going to eat him!
How come?
He looks pretty fresh to me.
Besides, we've spent the last few years of our lives feasting on carcasses.
Why stop now?

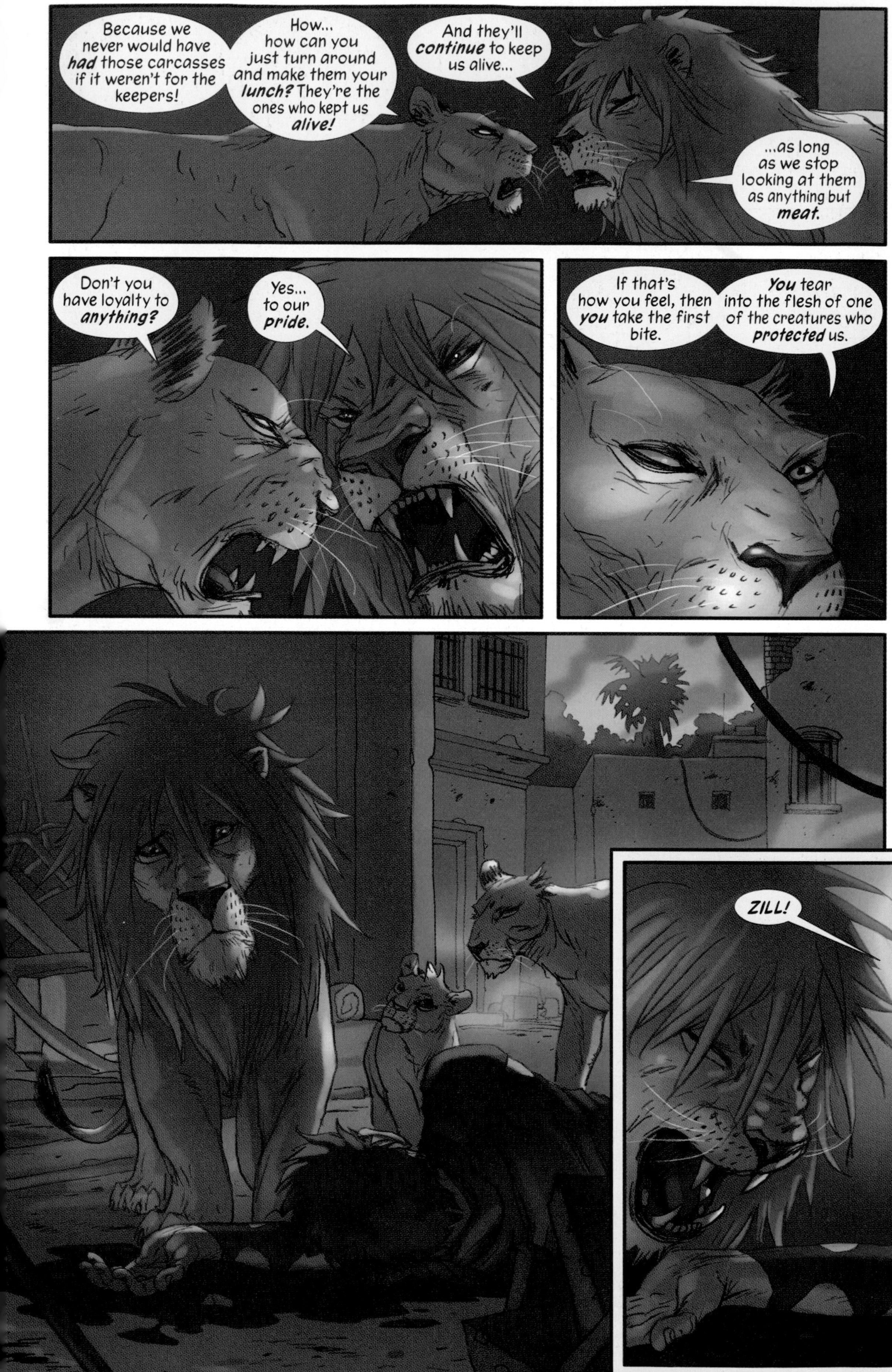

Because we never would have had those carcasses if it weren't for the keepers!
How... how can you just turn around and make them your lunch? They're the ones who kept us alive!
And they'll continue to keep us alive...
...as long as we stop looking at them as anything but meat.
Don't you have loyalty to anything?
Yes... to our pride.
If that's how you feel, then you take the first bite.
You tear into the flesh of one of the creatures who protected us.
ZILL!

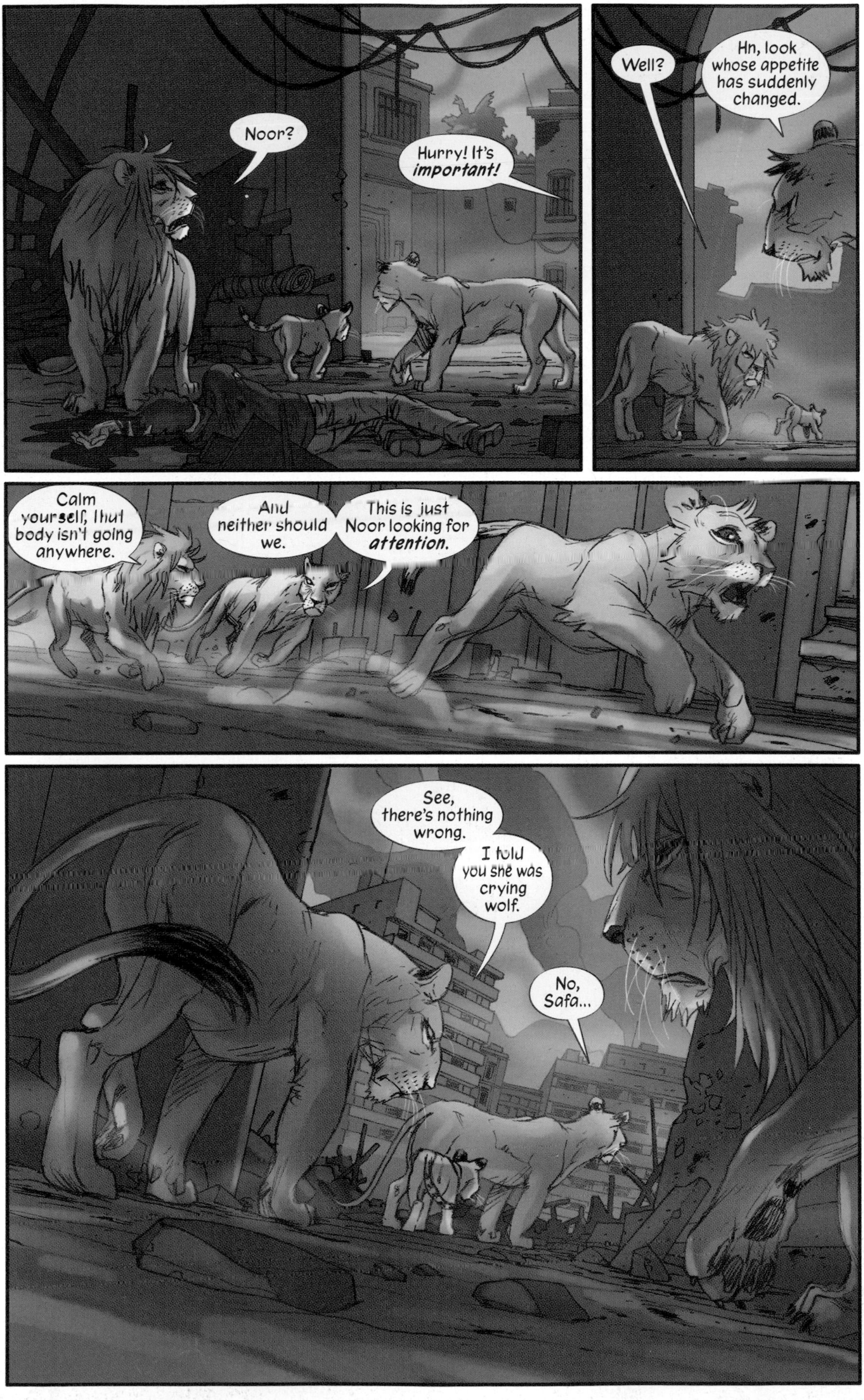
Noor?
Hurry! It's *important!*
Well?
Hn, look whose appetite has suddenly changed.
Calm yourself, that body isn't going anywhere.
And neither should we.
This is just Noor looking for *attention.*
See, there's nothing wrong.
I told you she was crying wolf.
No, Safa...

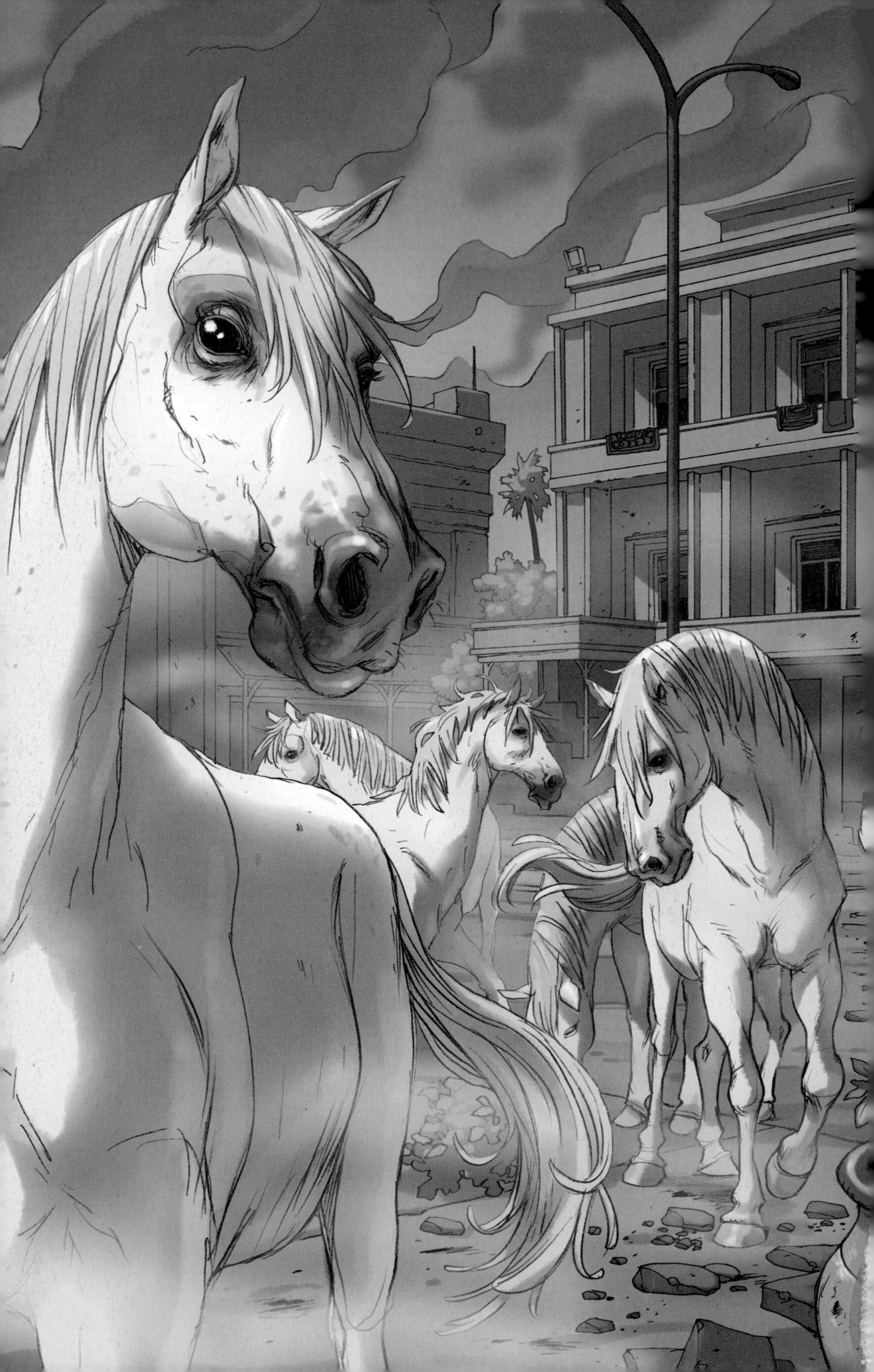

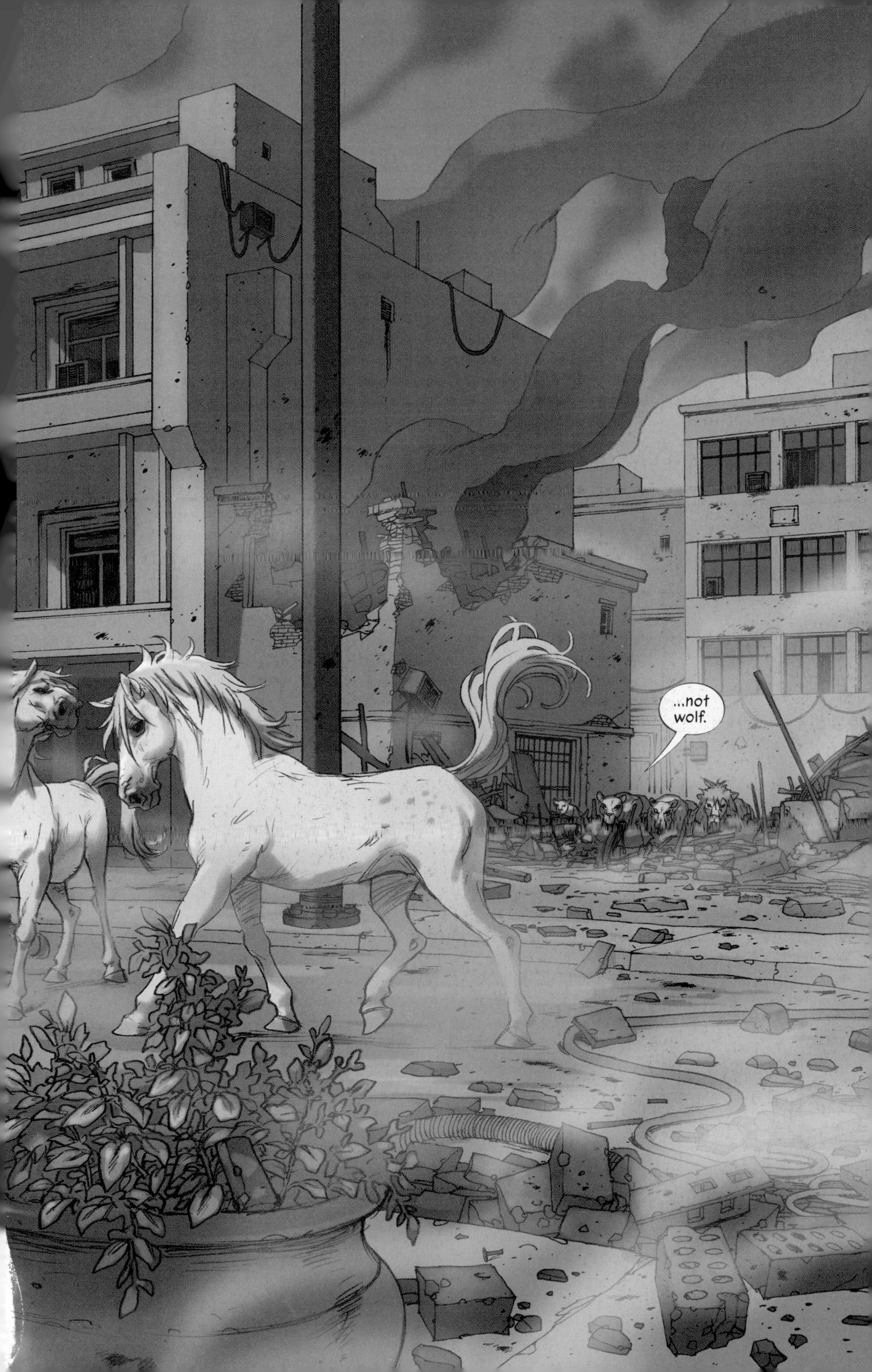
...not wolf.

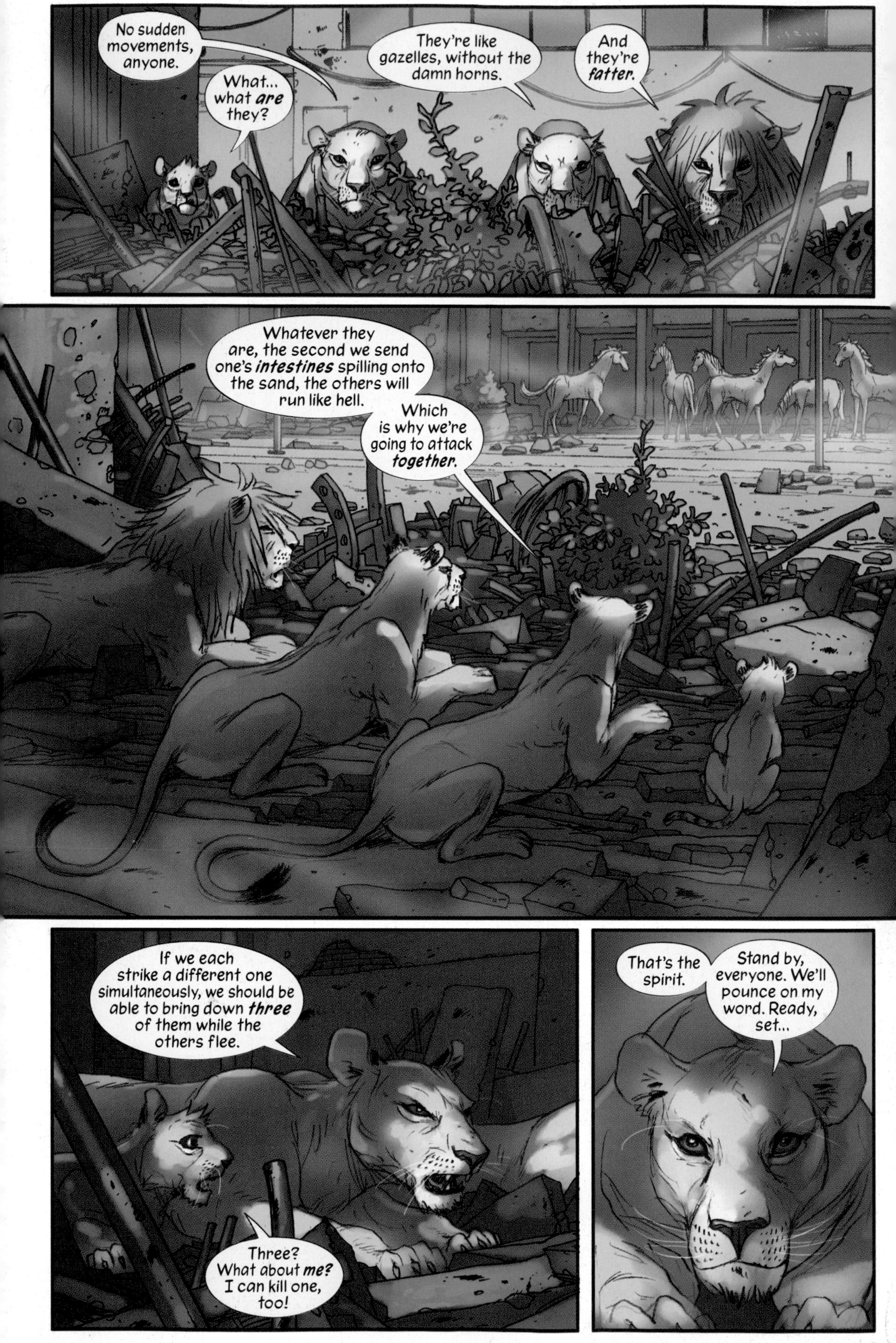
No sudden movements, anyone.
What... what *are* they?
They're like gazelles, without the damn horns.
And they're *fatter*.
Whatever they are, the second we send one's *intestines* spilling onto the sand, the others will run like hell.
Which is why we're going to attack *together*.
If we each strike a different one simultaneously, we should be able to bring down *three* of them while the others flee.
Three? What about *me?* I can kill one, too!
That's the spirit.
Stand by, everyone. We'll pounce on my word. Ready, set...

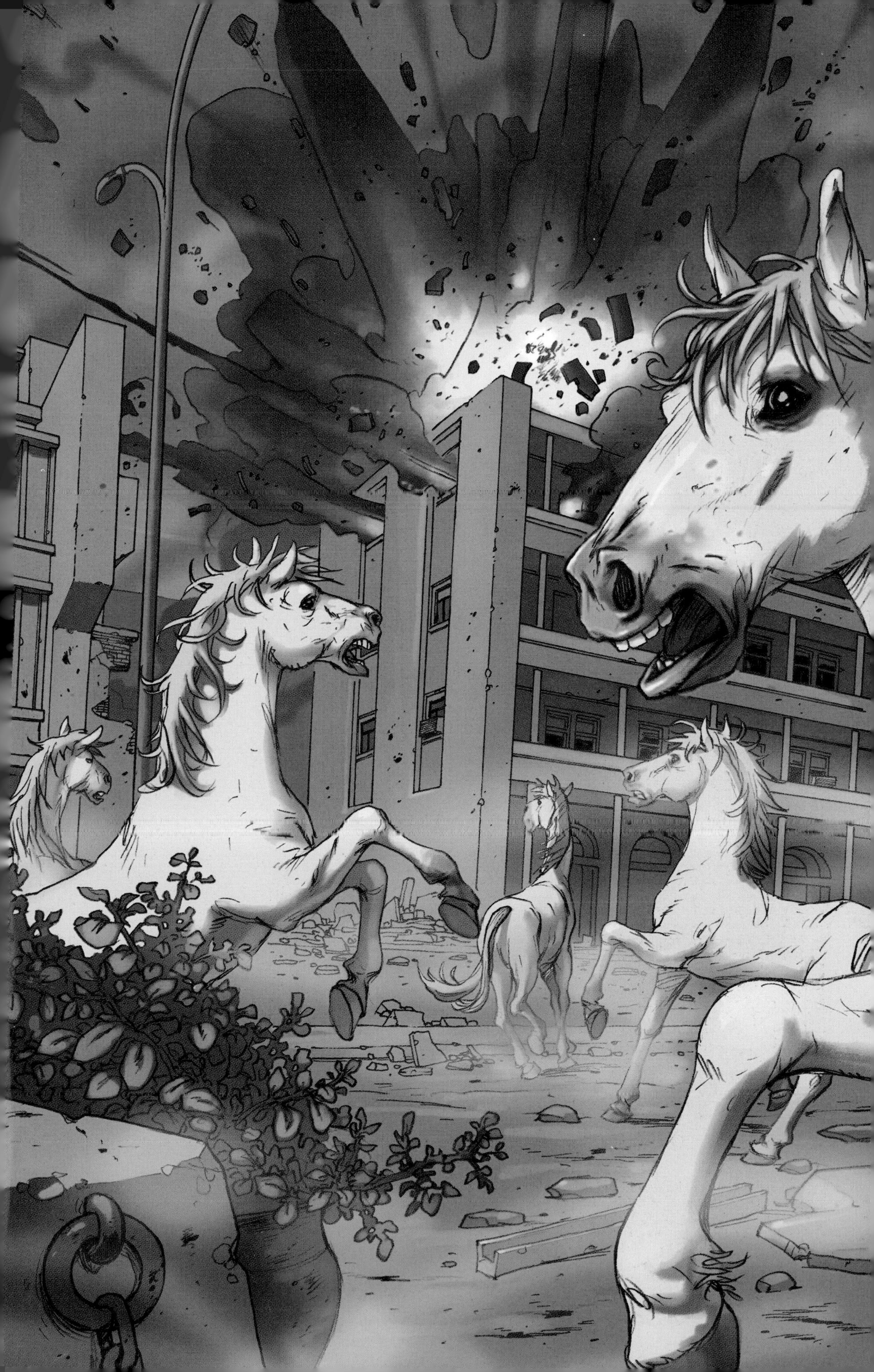

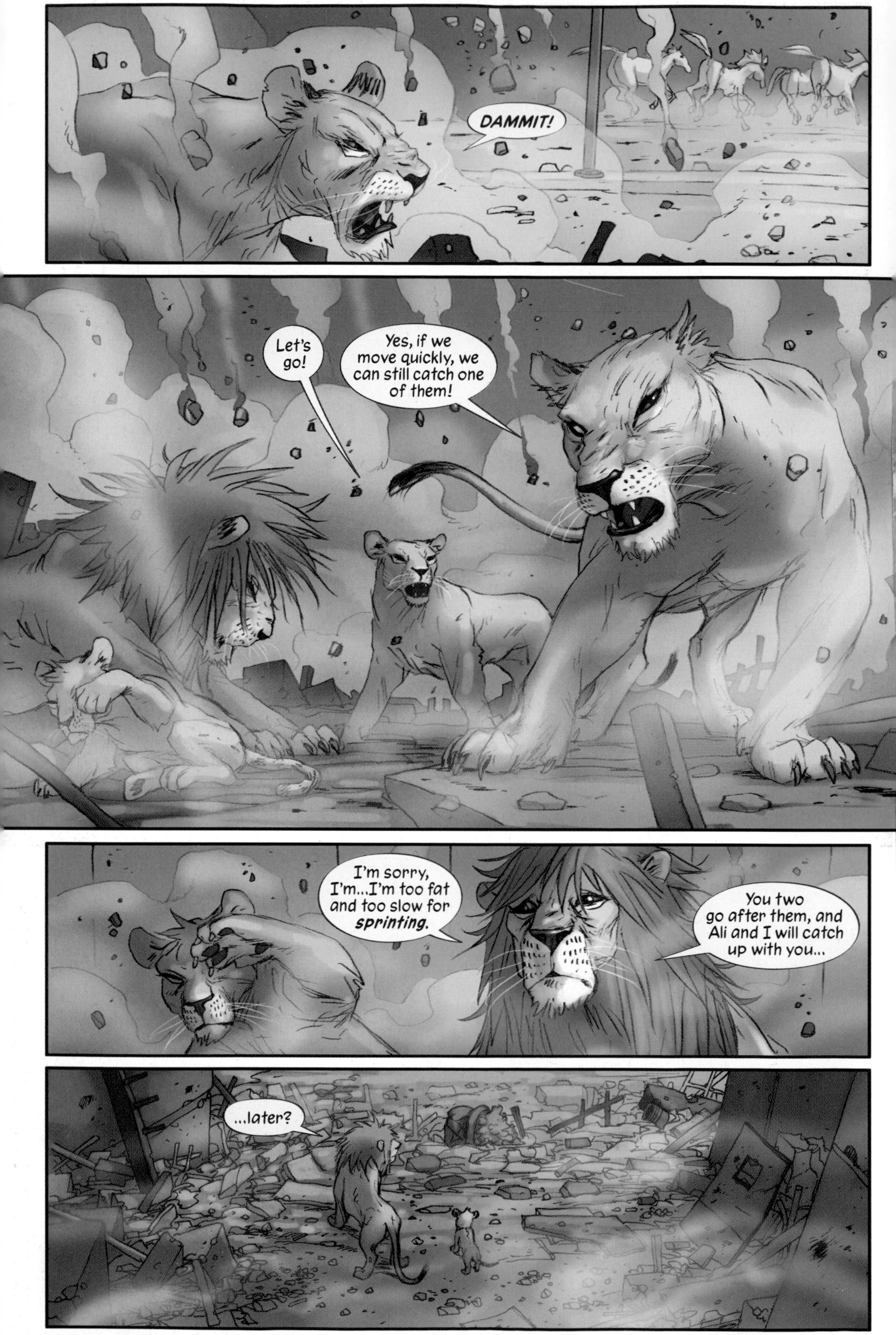
DAMMIT!
Let's go!
Yes, if we move quickly, we can still catch one of them!
I'm sorry, I'm...I'm too fat and too slow for *sprinting*.
You two go after them, and Ali and I will catch up with you...
...later?

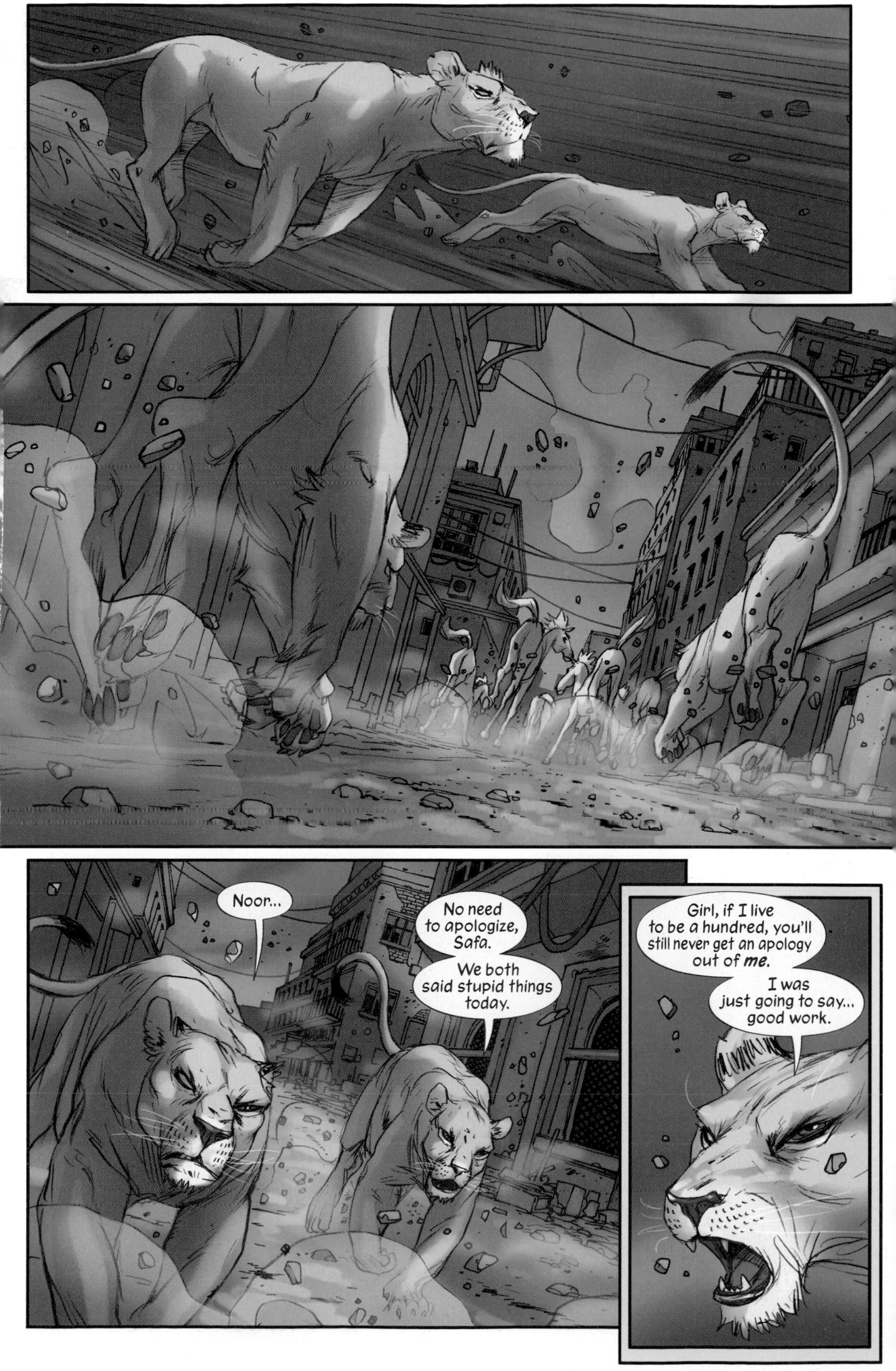
Noor...
No need to apologize, Safa.
We both said stupid things today.
Girl, if I live to be a hundred, you'll still never get an apology out of **me**.
I was just going to say... good work.

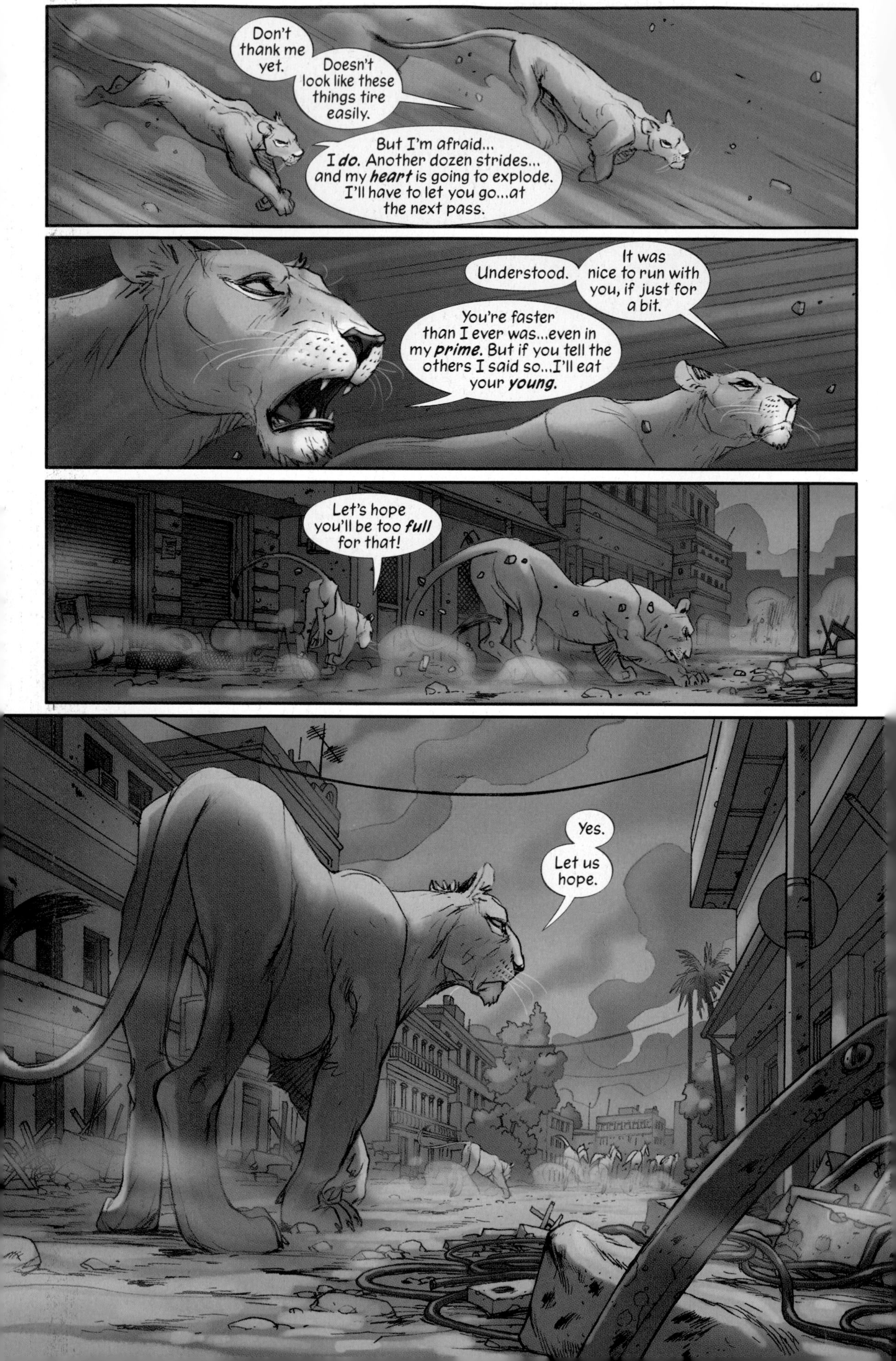
Don't thank me yet.
Doesn't look like these things tire easily.
But I'm afraid... I *do.* Another dozen strides... and my *heart* is going to explode. I'll have to let you go...at the next pass.
Understood.
It was nice to run with you, if just for a bit.
You're faster than I ever was...even in my *prime.* But if you tell the others I said so...I'll eat your *young.*
Let's hope you'll be too *full* for that!
Yes.
Let us hope.

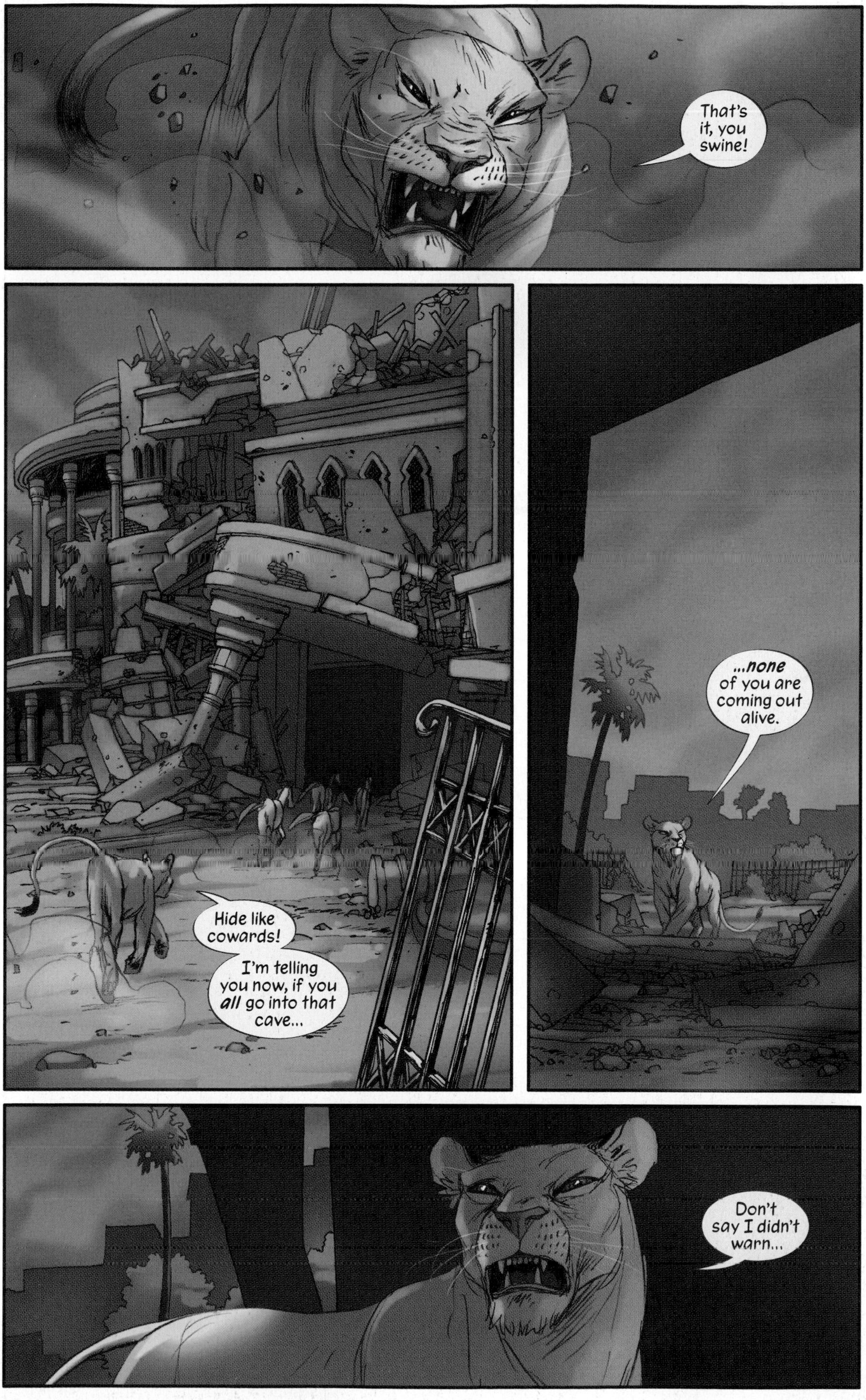

That's it, you swine!
Hide like cowards!
I'm telling you now, if you *all* go into that cave...
...*none* of you are coming out alive.
Don't say I didn't warn...

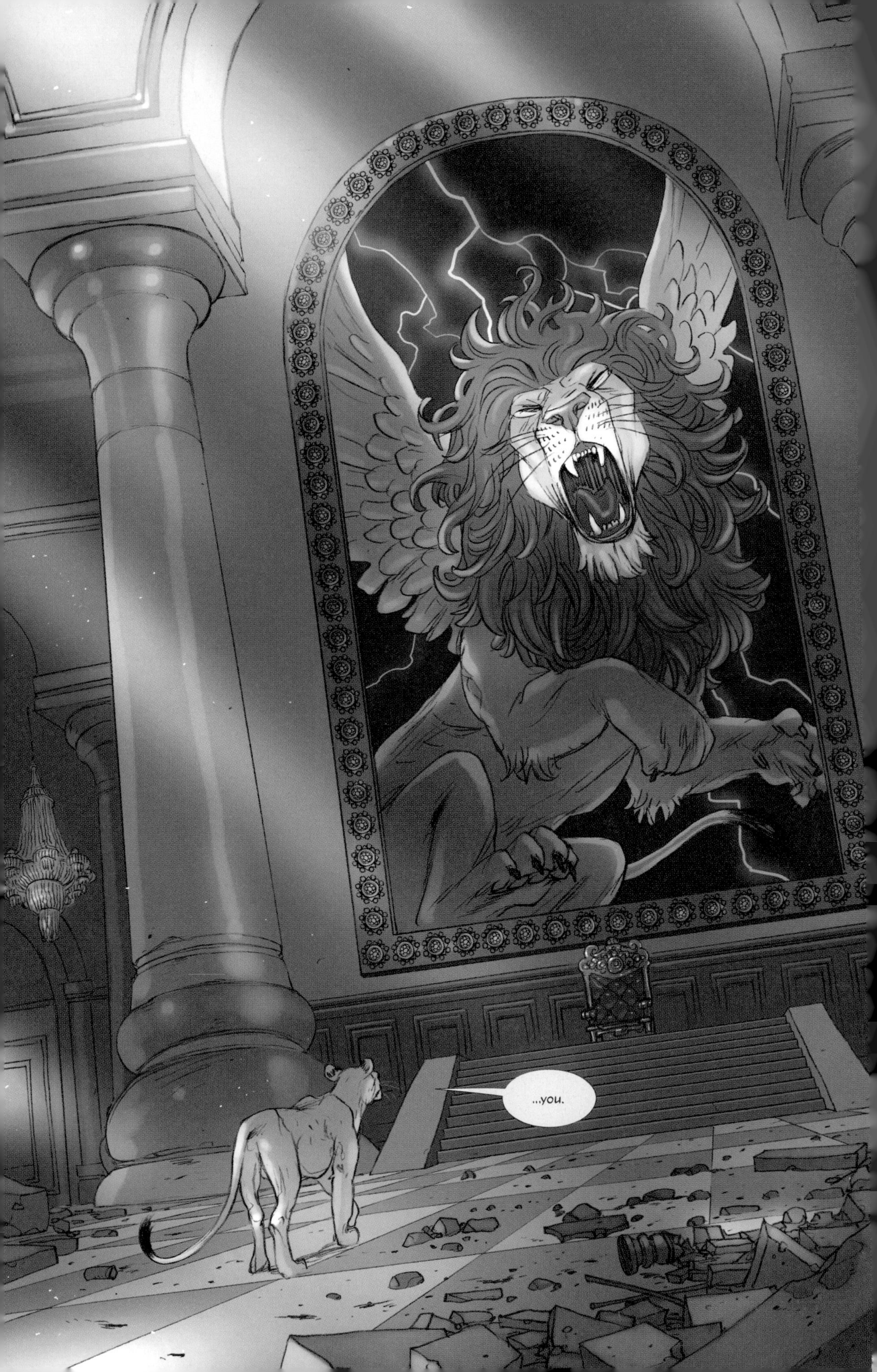
...you.

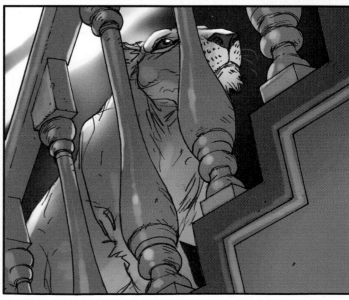

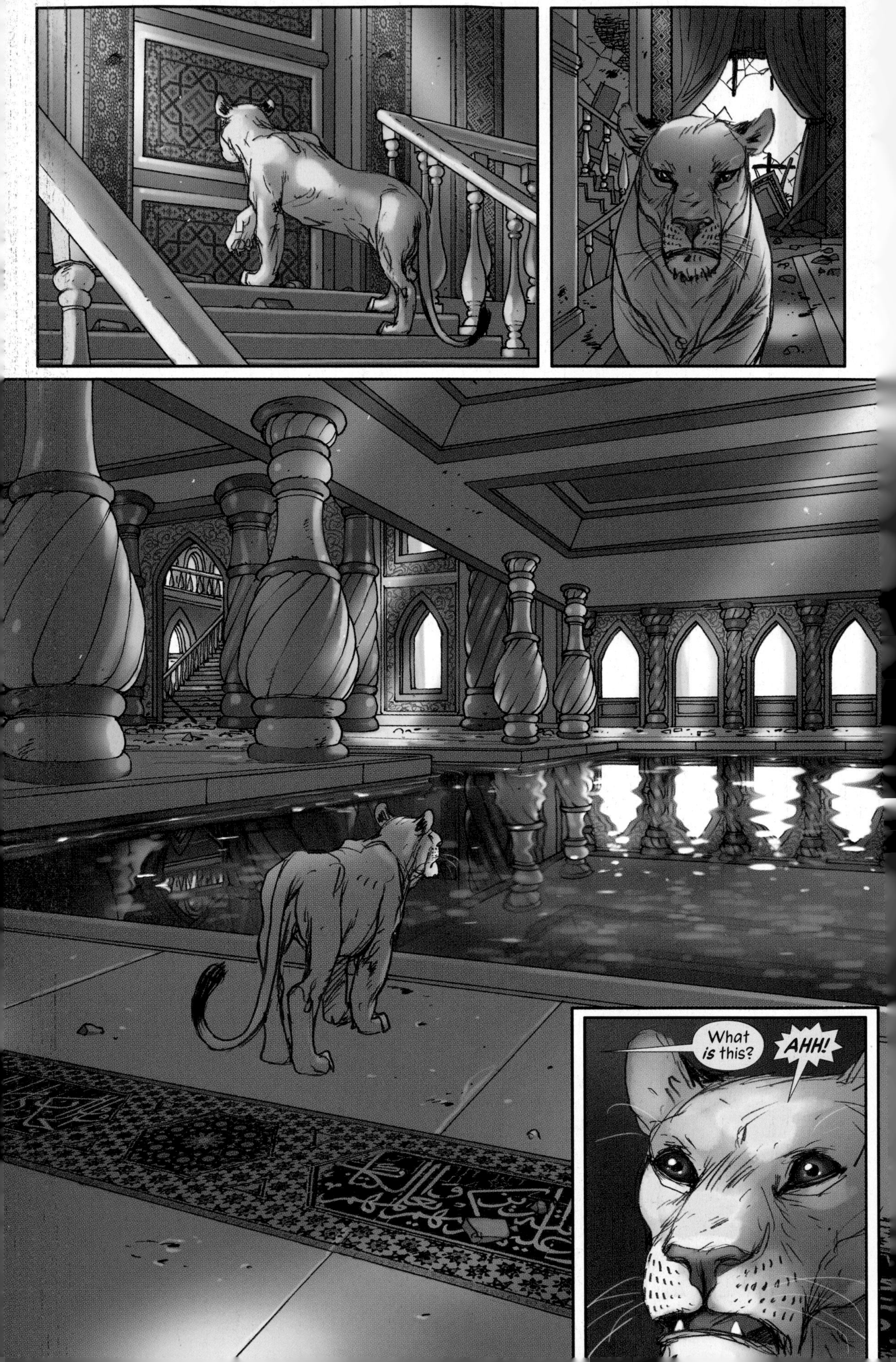
What is this?
AHH!

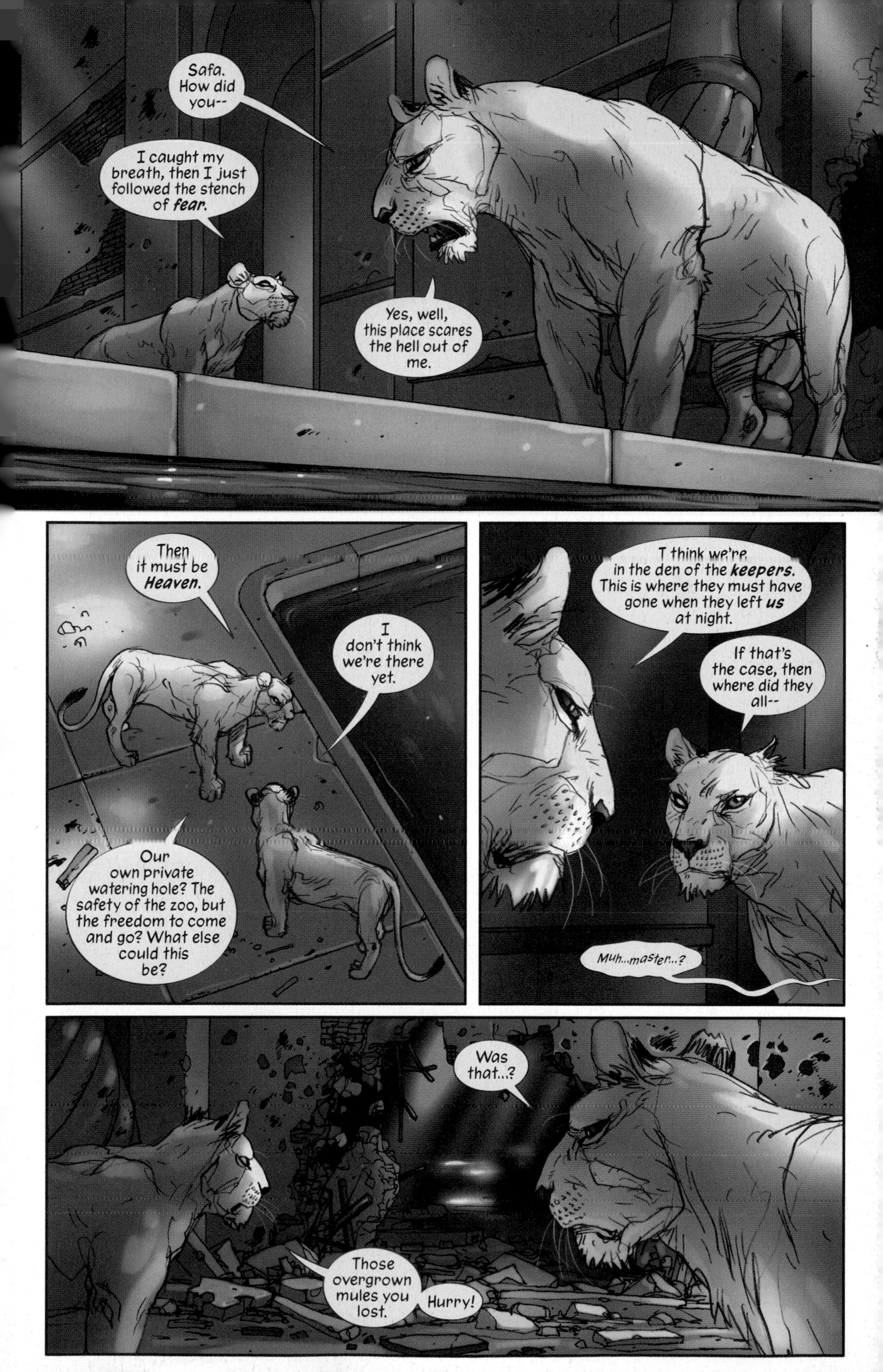
Safa. How did you--
I caught my breath, then I just followed the stench of *fear*.
Yes, well, this place scares the hell out of me.
Then it must be *Heaven*.
I don't think we're there yet.
Our own private watering hole? The safety of the zoo, but the freedom to come and go? What else could this be?
I think we're in the den of the *keepers*. This is where they must have gone when they left *us* at night.
If that's the case, then where did they all--
Muh...master...?
Was that...?
Those overgrown mules you lost.
Hurry!

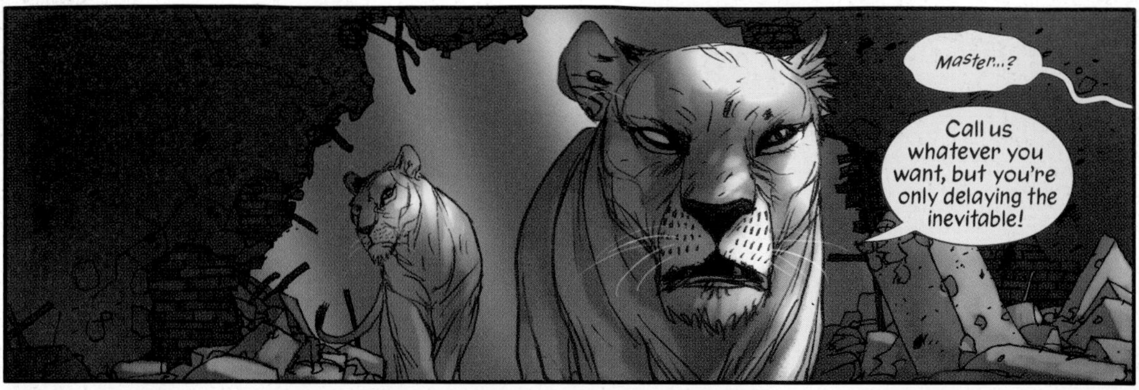
Master...?
Call us whatever you want, but you're only delaying the inevitable!

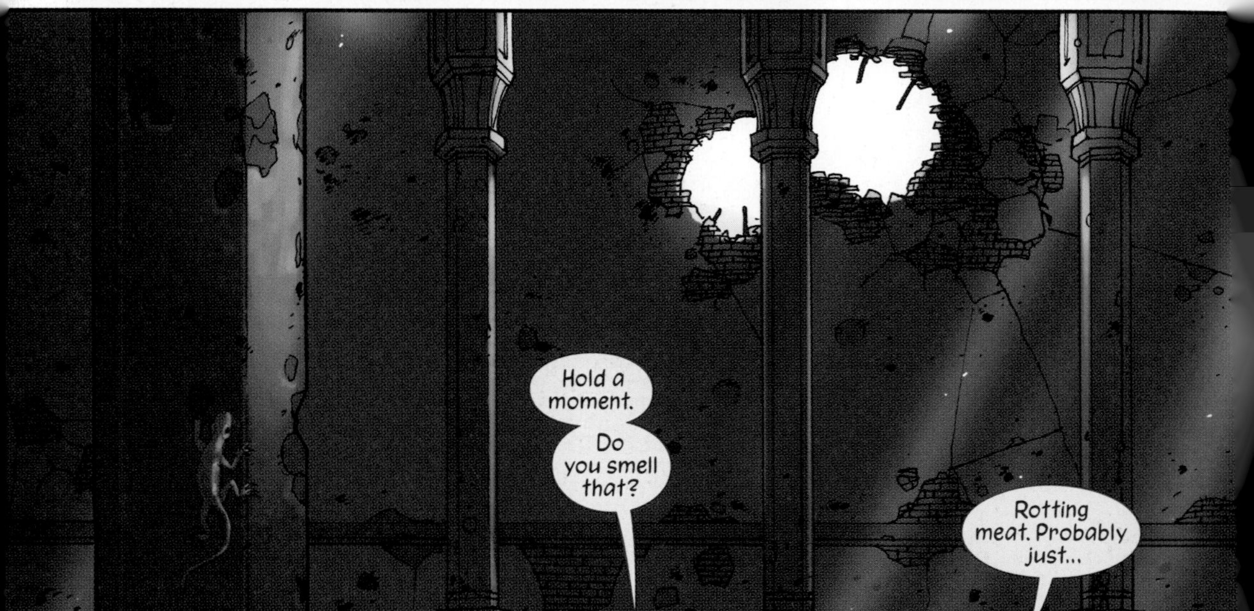
Hold a moment.
Do you smell that?
Rotting meat. Probably just...

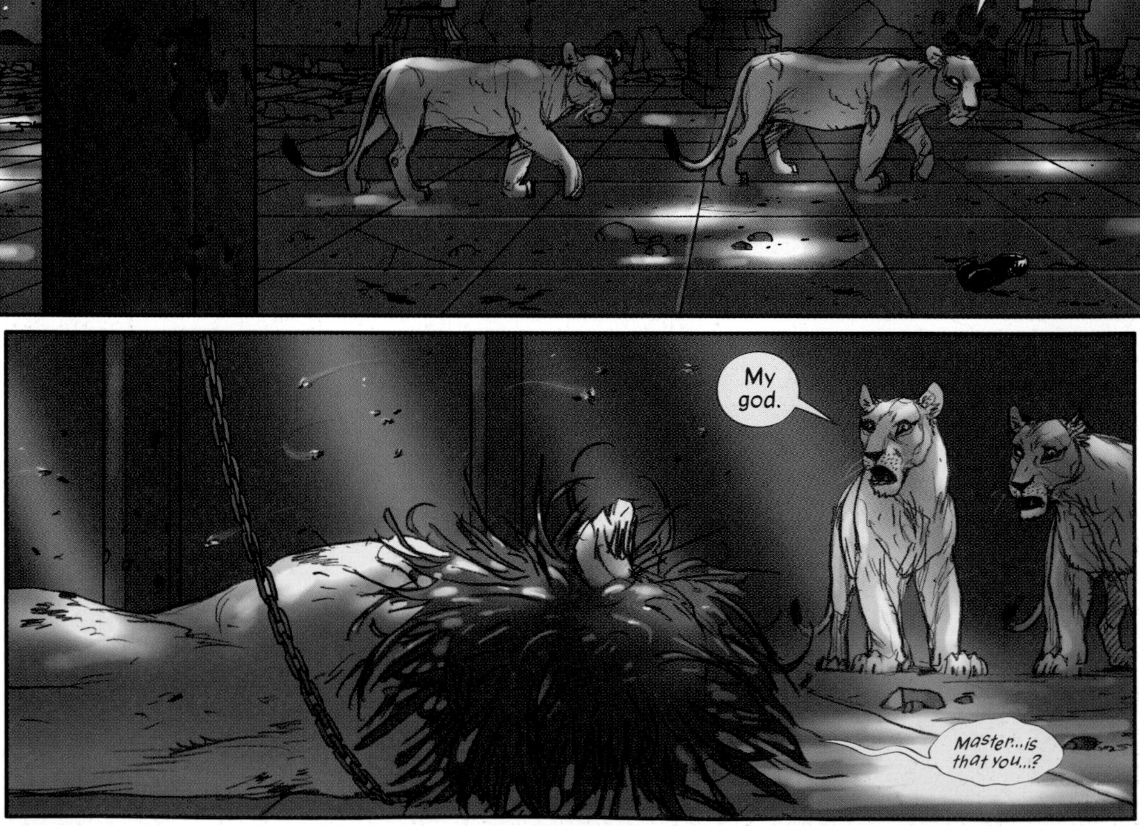
My god.
Master...is that you...?

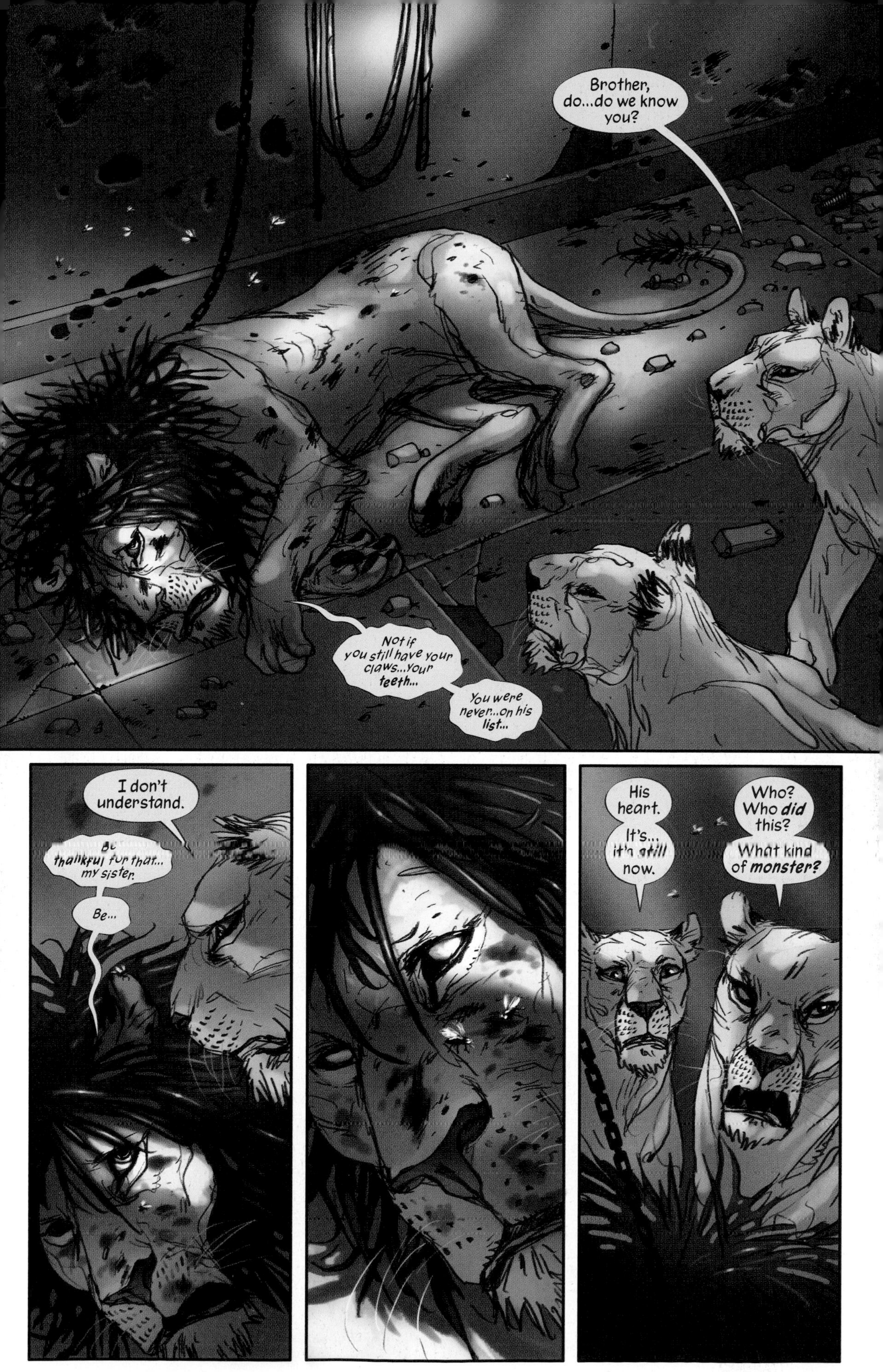
Brother, do...do we know you?
Not if you still have your claws...your **teeth**...
You were never...on his list...
I don't understand.
Be thankful for that... my sister.
Be...
His heart.
It's... it's still now.
Who? Who **did** this?
What kind of **monster?**

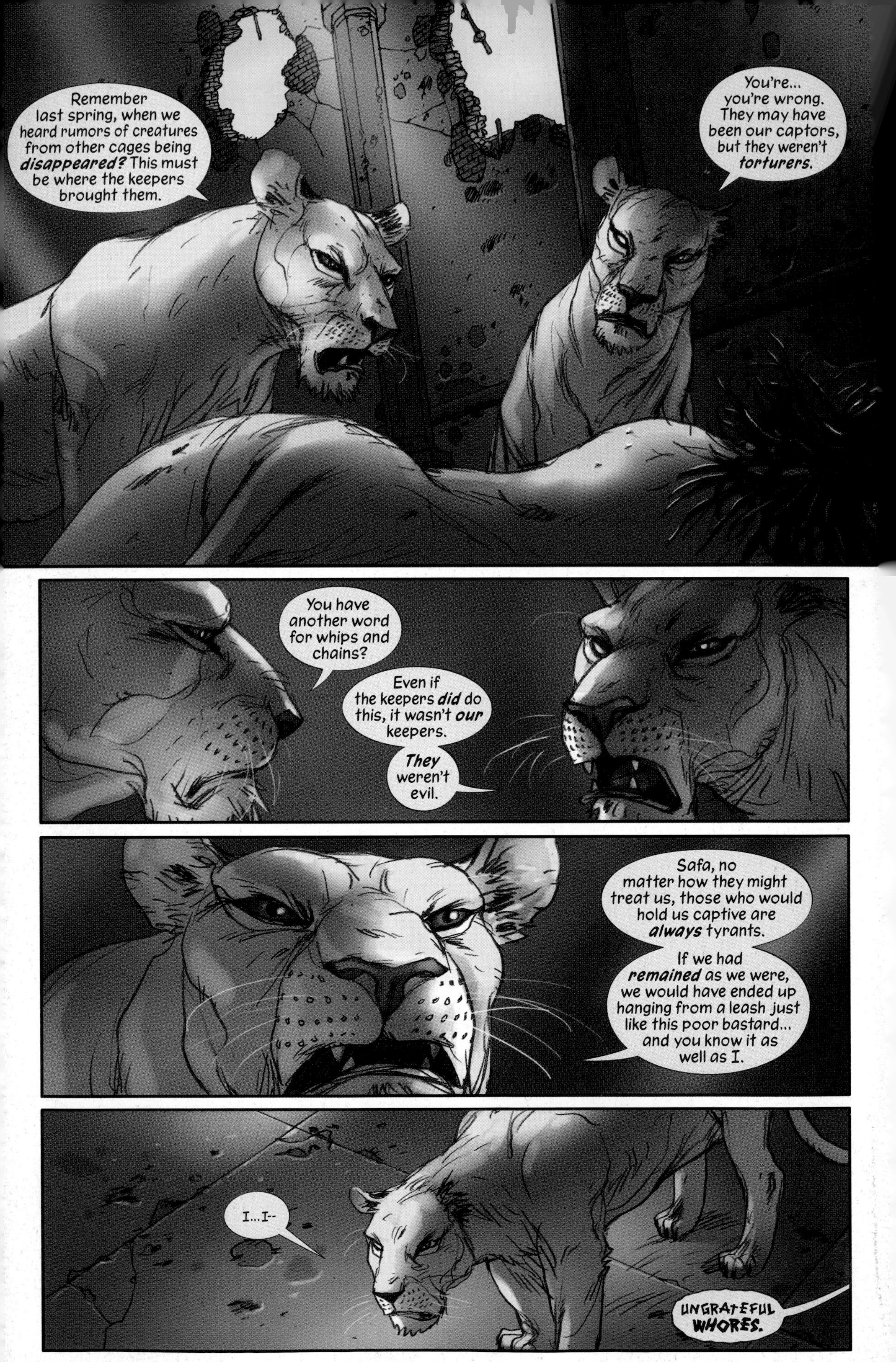
Remember last spring, when we heard rumors of creatures from other cages being *disappeared?* This must be where the keepers brought them.
You're... you're wrong. They may have been our captors, but they weren't *torturers.*
You have another word for whips and chains?
Even if the keepers *did* do this, it wasn't *our* keepers.
They weren't evil.
Safa, no matter how they might treat us, those who would hold us captive are *always* tyrants.
If we had *remained* as we were, we would have ended up hanging from a leash just like this poor bastard... and you know it as well as I.
I... I--
UNGRATEFUL WHORES.

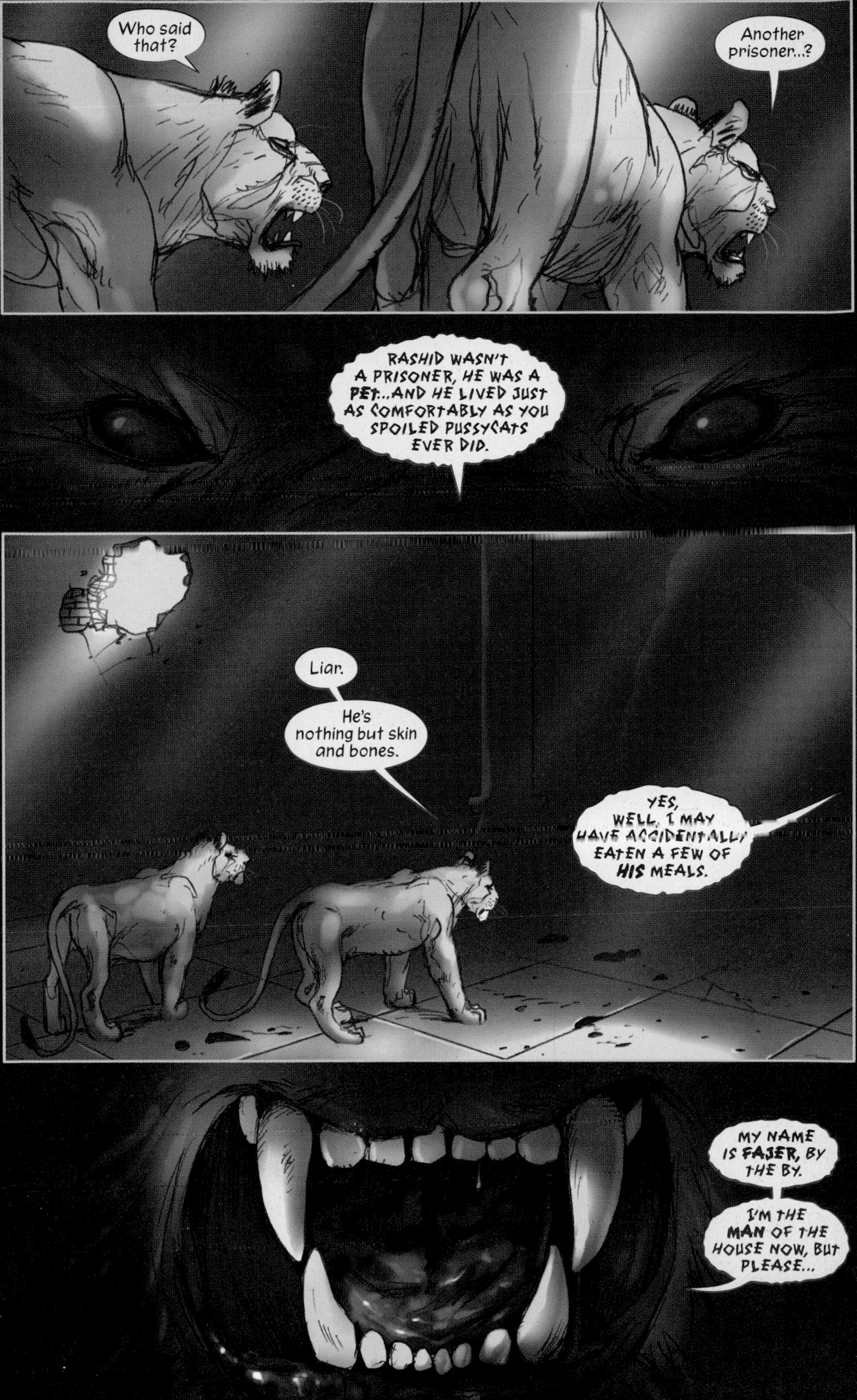
Who said that?
Another prisoner...?
RASHID WASN'T A PRISONER, HE WAS A PET...AND HE LIVED JUST AS COMFORTABLY AS YOU SPOILED PUSSYCATS EVER DID.
Liar.
He's nothing but skin and bones.
YES, WELL, I MAY HAVE ACCIDENTALLY EATEN A FEW OF HIS MEALS.
MY NAME IS FAJER, BY THE BY.
I'M THE MAN OF THE HOUSE NOW, BUT PLEASE...

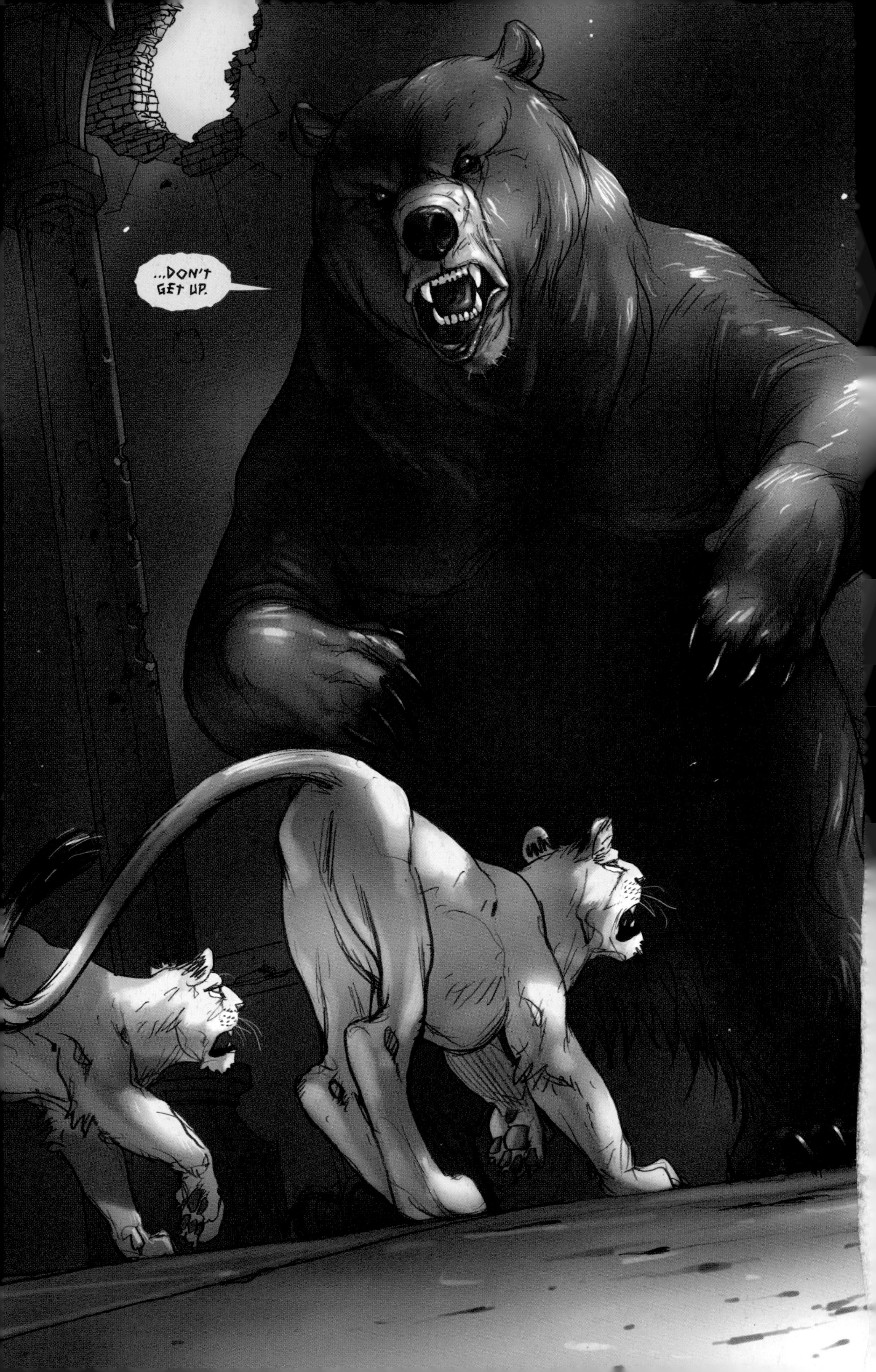
...DON'T GET UP.

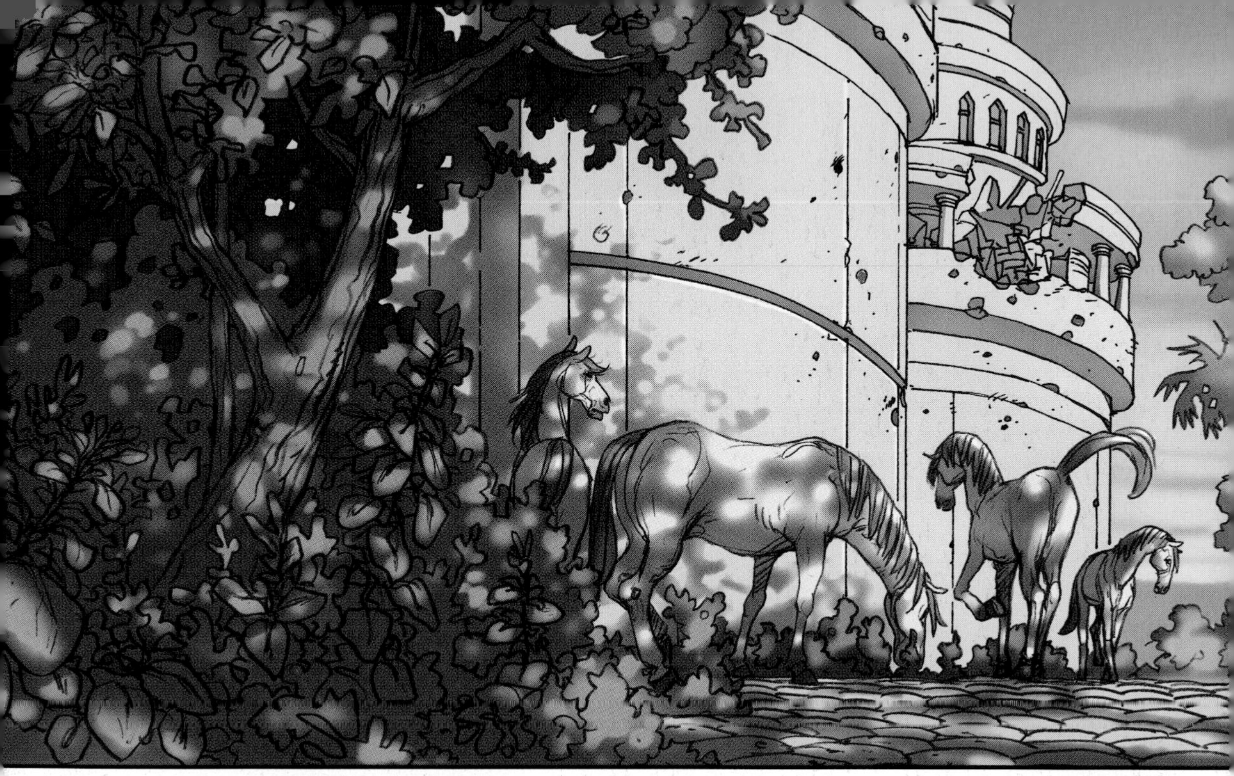

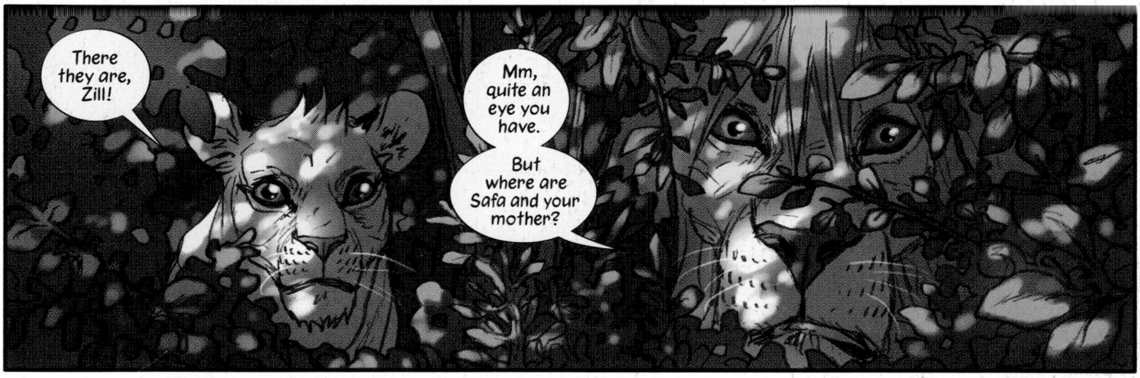
There they are, Zill!
Mm, quite an eye you have.
But where are Safa and your mother?

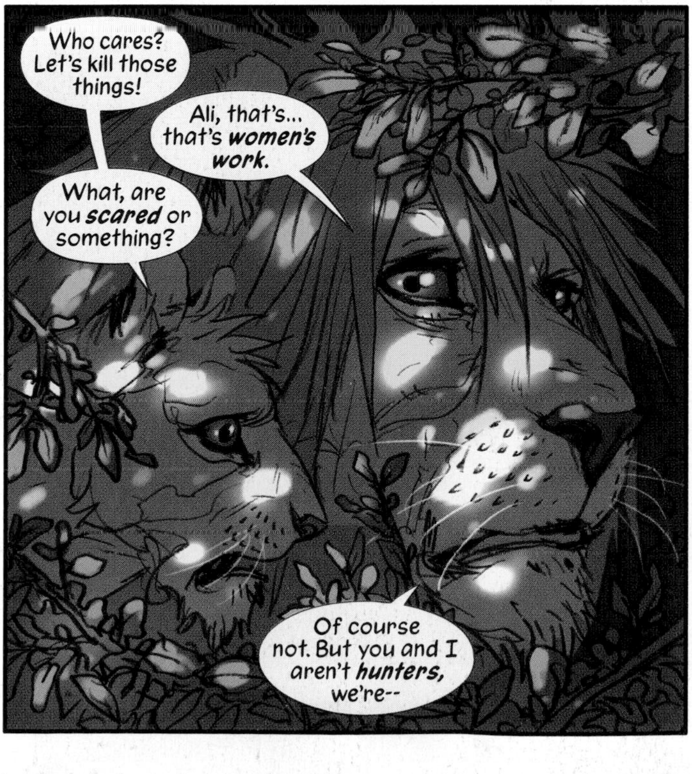
Who cares? Let's kill those things!
Ali, that's... that's *women's work.*
What, are you *scared* or something?
Of course not. But you and I aren't *hunters,* we're--

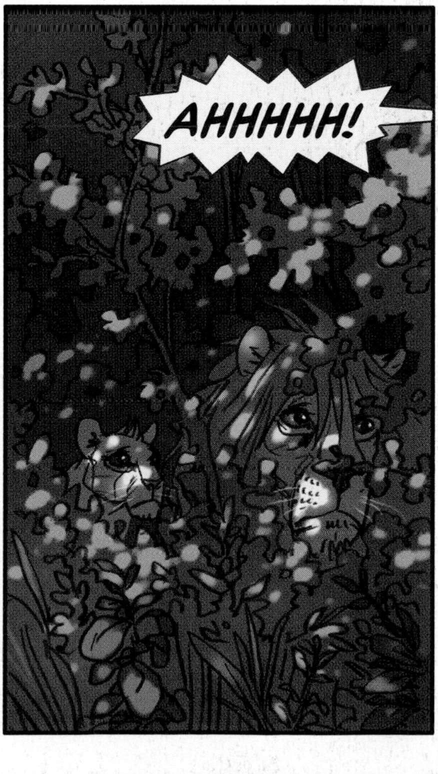
AHHHHH!

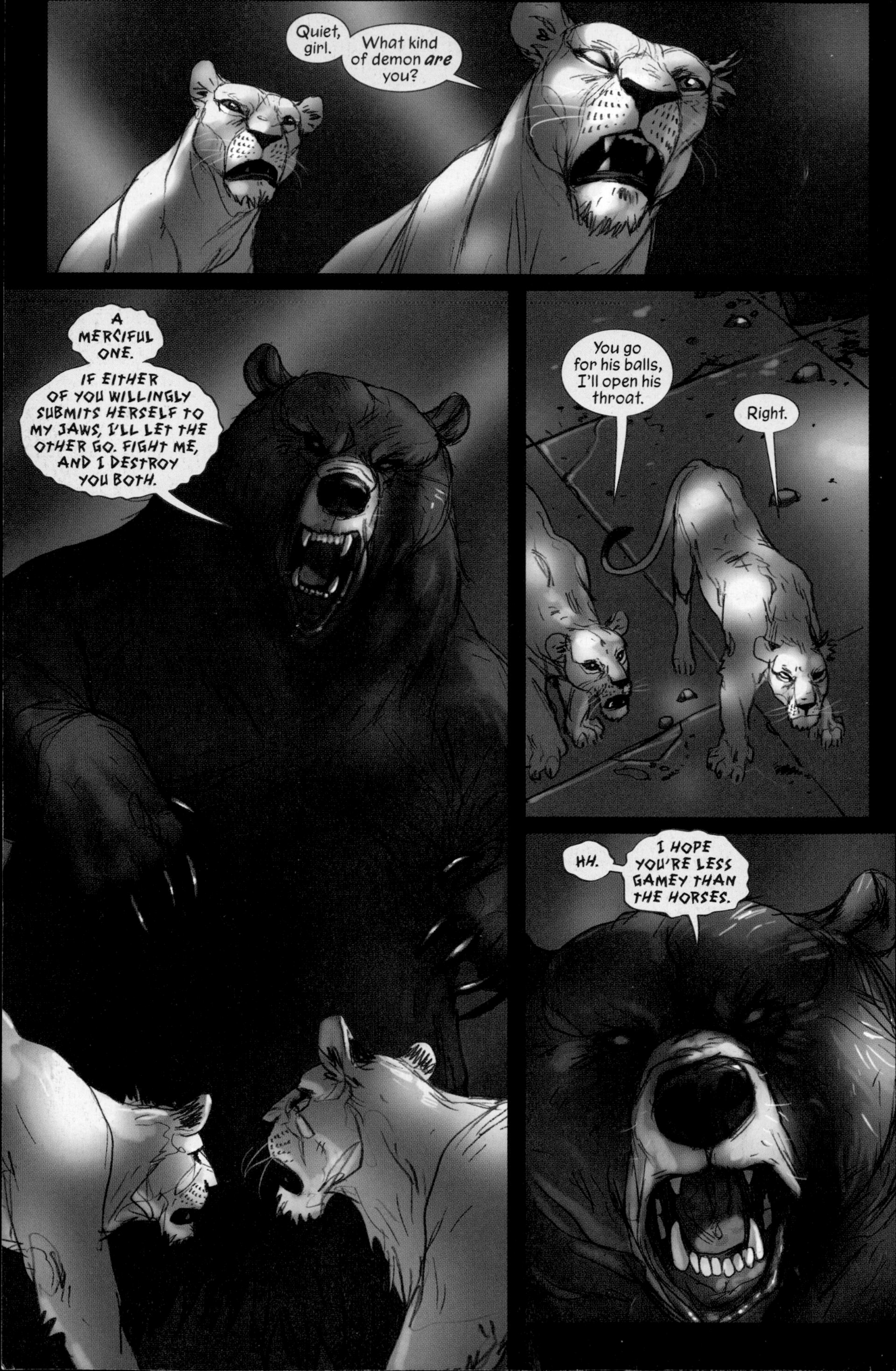
Quiet, girl.
What kind of demon *are* you?
A MERCIFUL ONE.
IF EITHER OF YOU WILLINGLY SUBMITS HERSELF TO MY JAWS, I'LL LET THE OTHER GO. FIGHT ME, AND I DESTROY YOU BOTH.
You go for his balls, I'll open his throat.
Right.
HH.
I HOPE YOU'RE LESS GAMEY THAN THE HORSES.

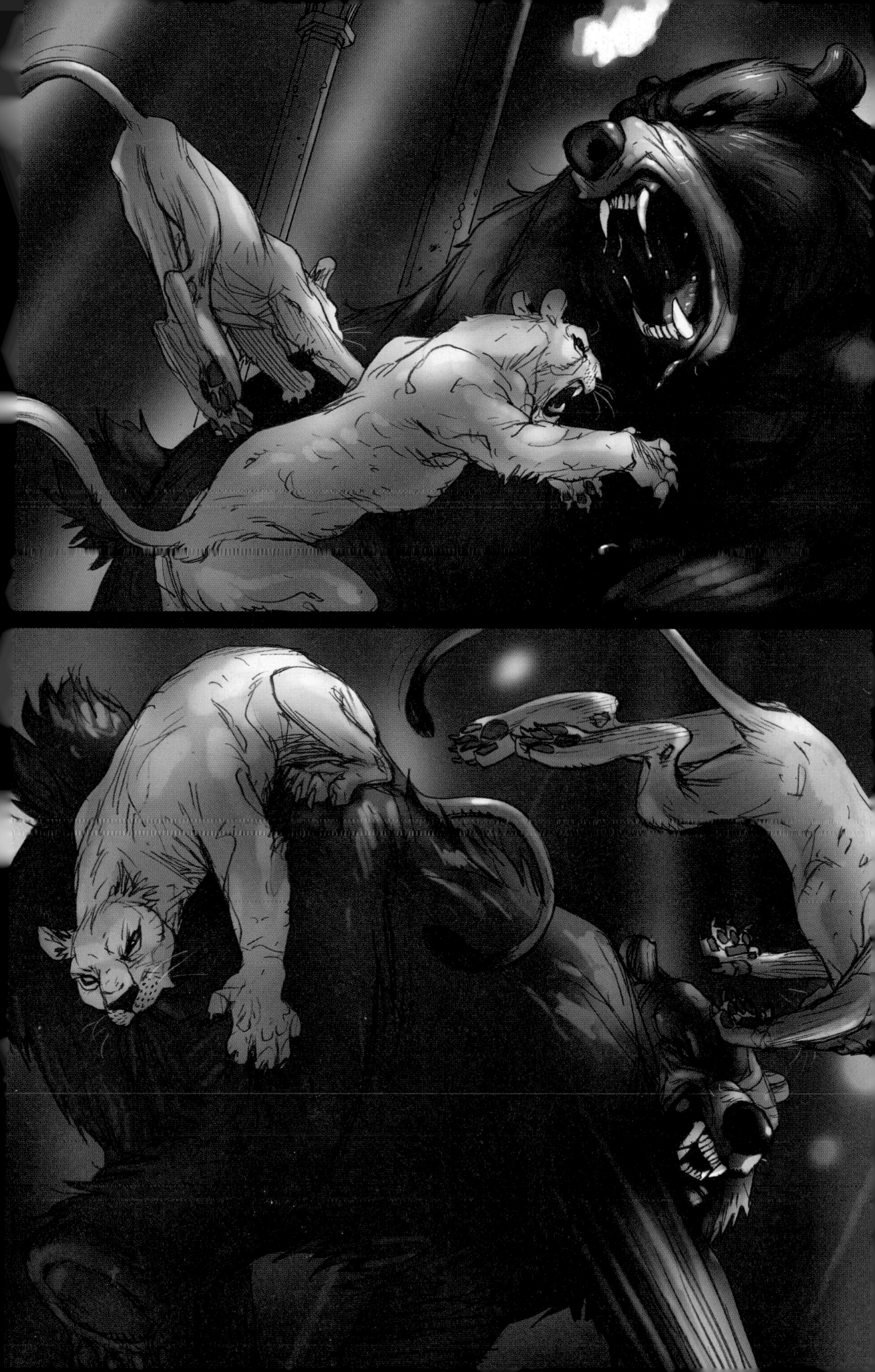

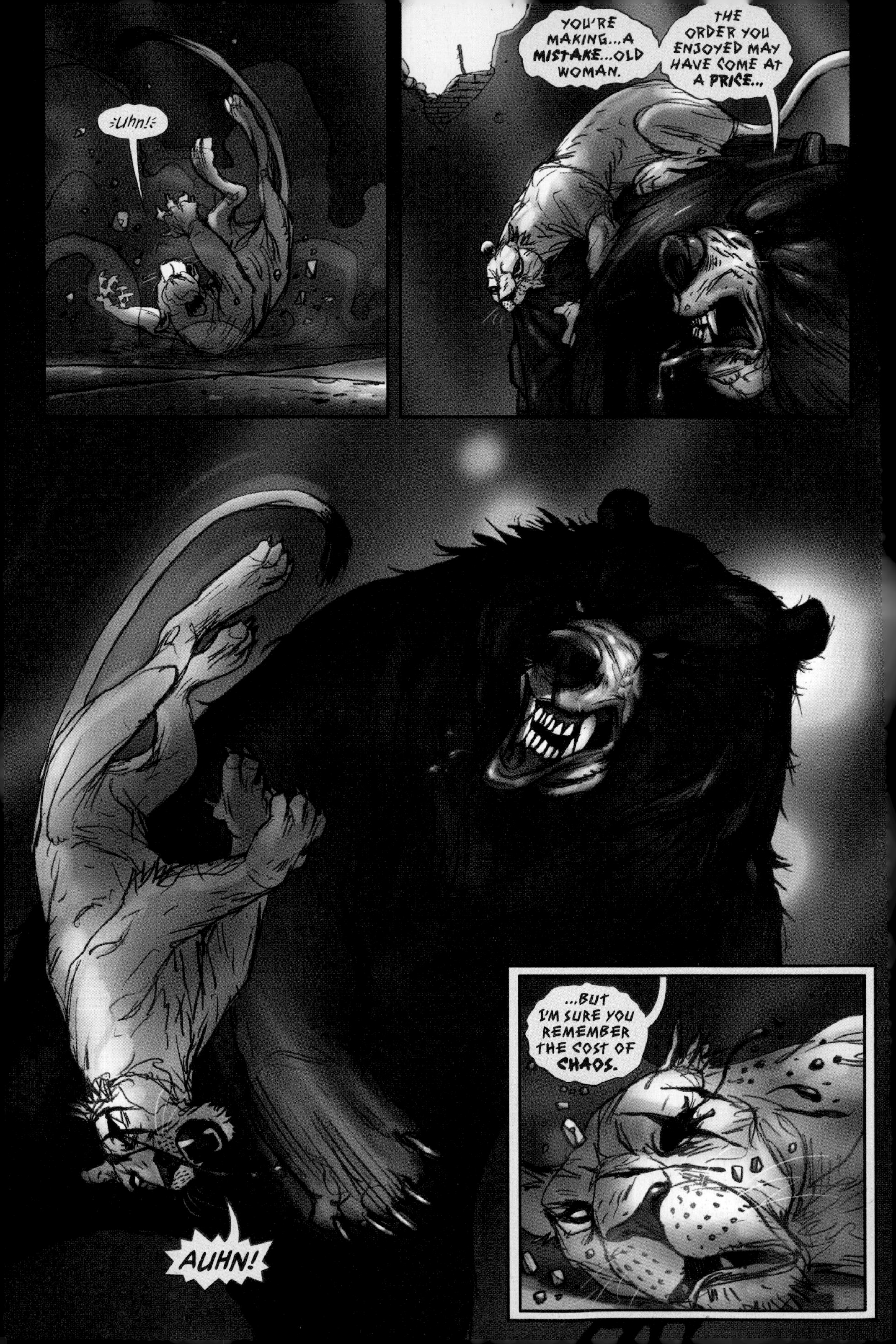
Uhn!
YOU'RE MAKING...A MISTAKE...OLD WOMAN.
THE ORDER YOU ENJOYED MAY HAVE COME AT A PRICE...
AUHN!
...BUT I'M SURE YOU REMEMBER THE COST OF CHAOS.

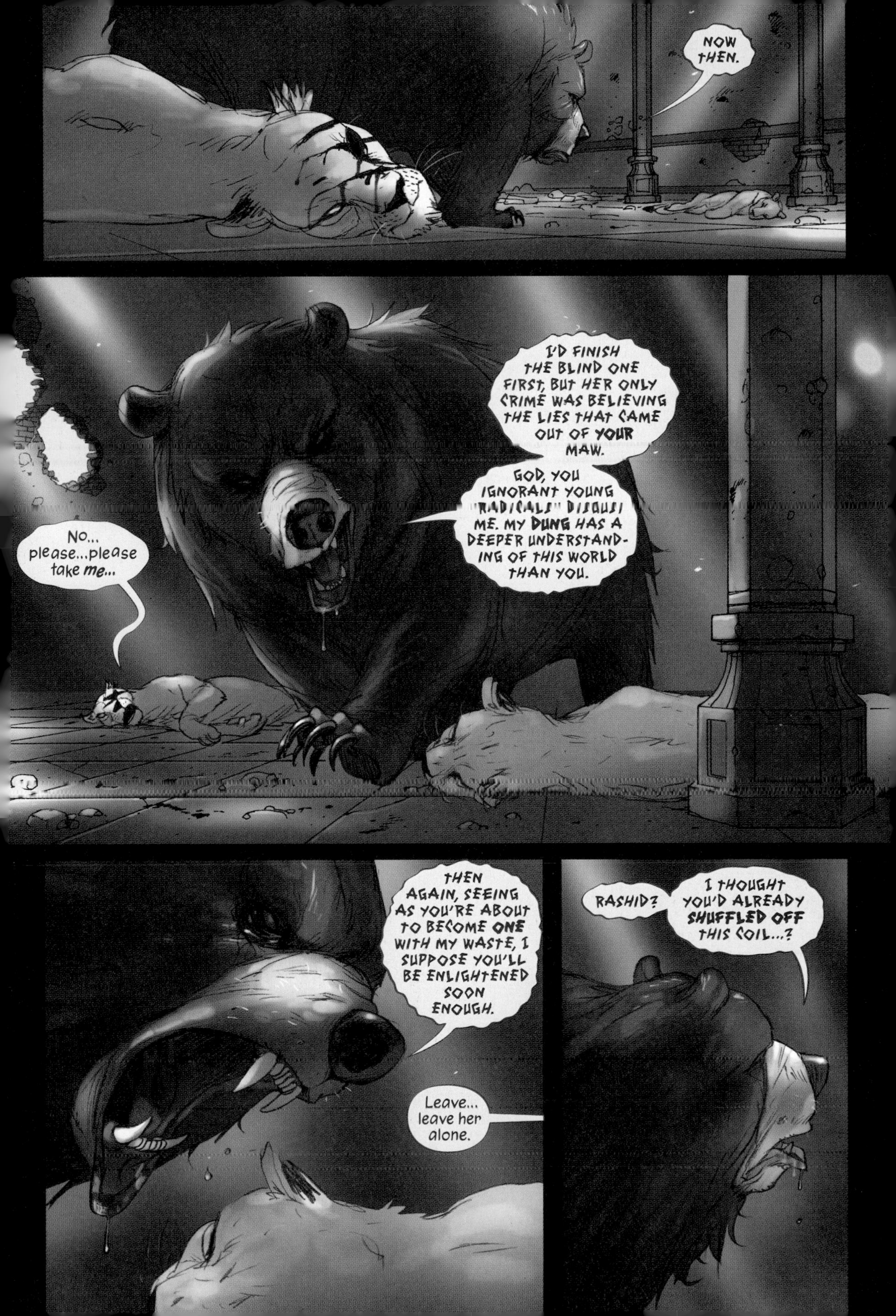
NOW THEN.
I'D FINISH THE BLIND ONE FIRST, BUT HER ONLY CRIME WAS BELIEVING THE LIES THAT CAME OUT OF YOUR MAW.
GOD, YOU IGNORANT YOUNG "RADICALS" DISGUST ME. MY DUNG HAS A DEEPER UNDERSTANDING OF THIS WORLD THAN YOU.
No... please...please take me...
THEN AGAIN, SEEING AS YOU'RE ABOUT TO BECOME ONE WITH MY WASTE, I SUPPOSE YOU'LL BE ENLIGHTENED SOON ENOUGH.
Leave... leave her alone.
RASHID?
I THOUGHT YOU'D ALREADY SHUFFLED OFF THIS COIL...?

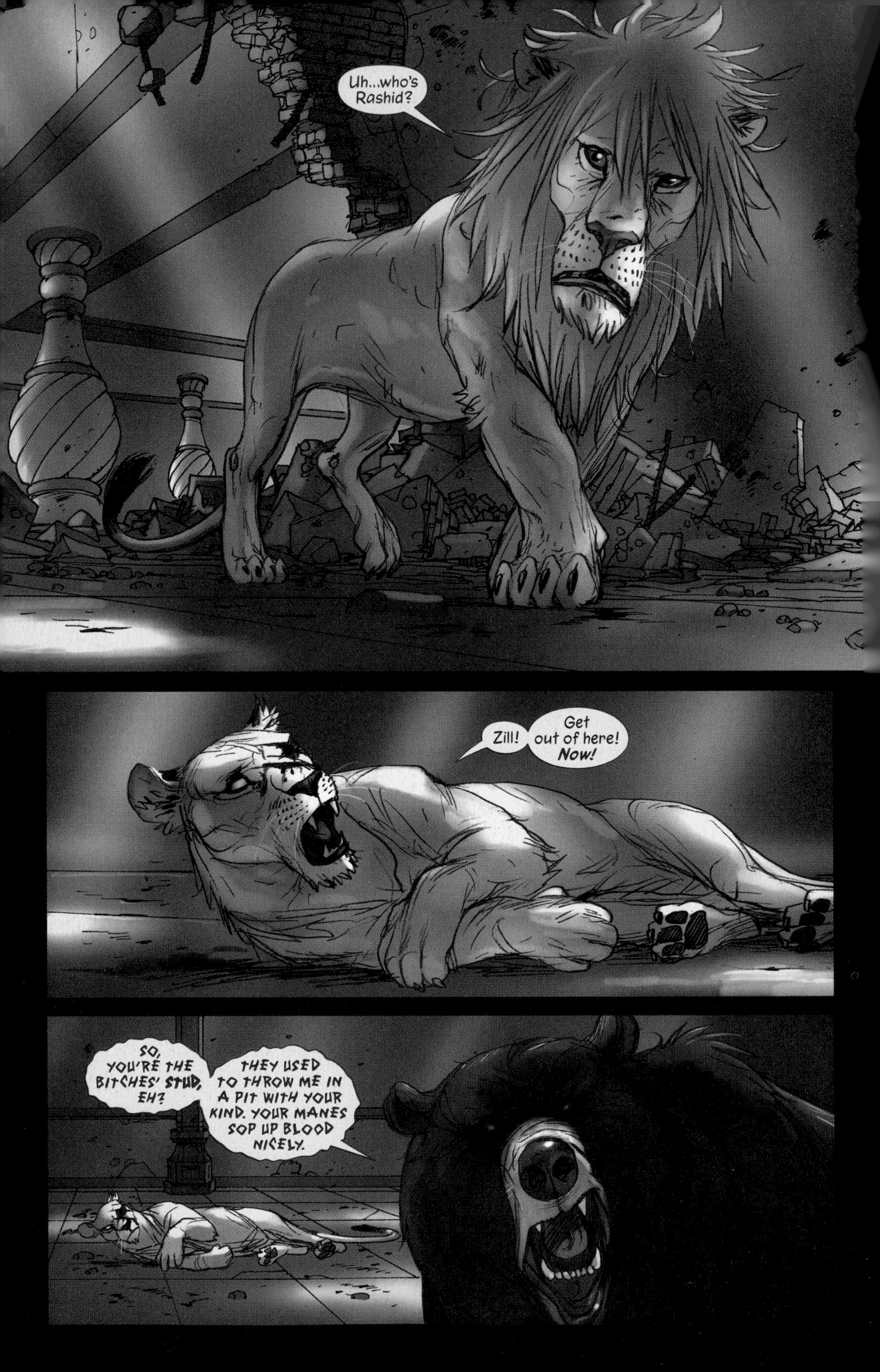
Uh...who's Rashid?
Zill!
Get out of here! Now!
SO, YOU'RE THE BITCHES' STUD, EH?
THEY USED TO THROW ME IN A PIT WITH YOUR KIND. YOUR MANES SOP UP BLOOD NICELY.

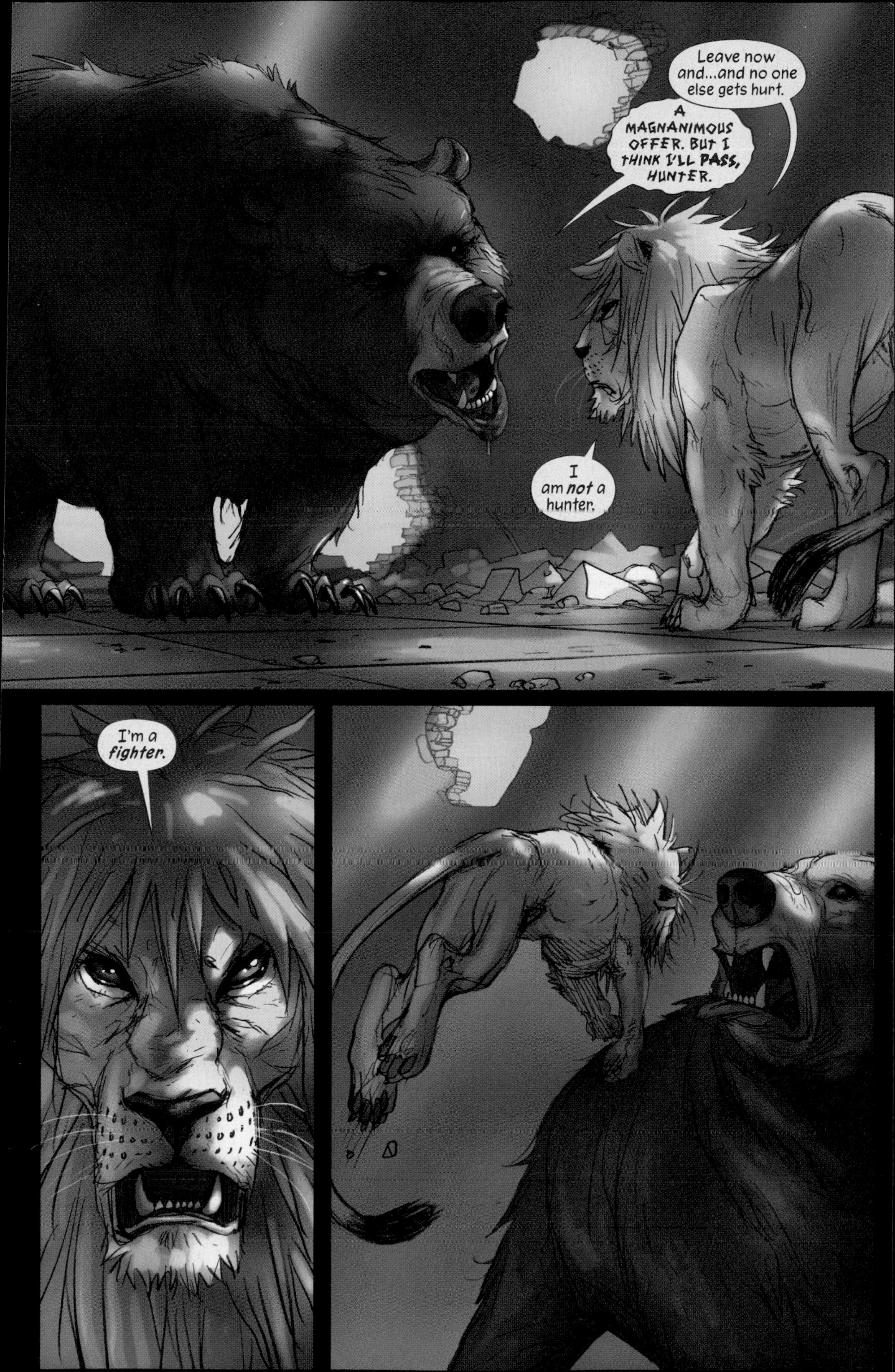
Leave now and...and no one else gets hurt.
A MAGNANIMOUS OFFER. BUT I THINK I'LL PASS, HUNTER.
I am *not* a hunter.
I'm a *fighter*.

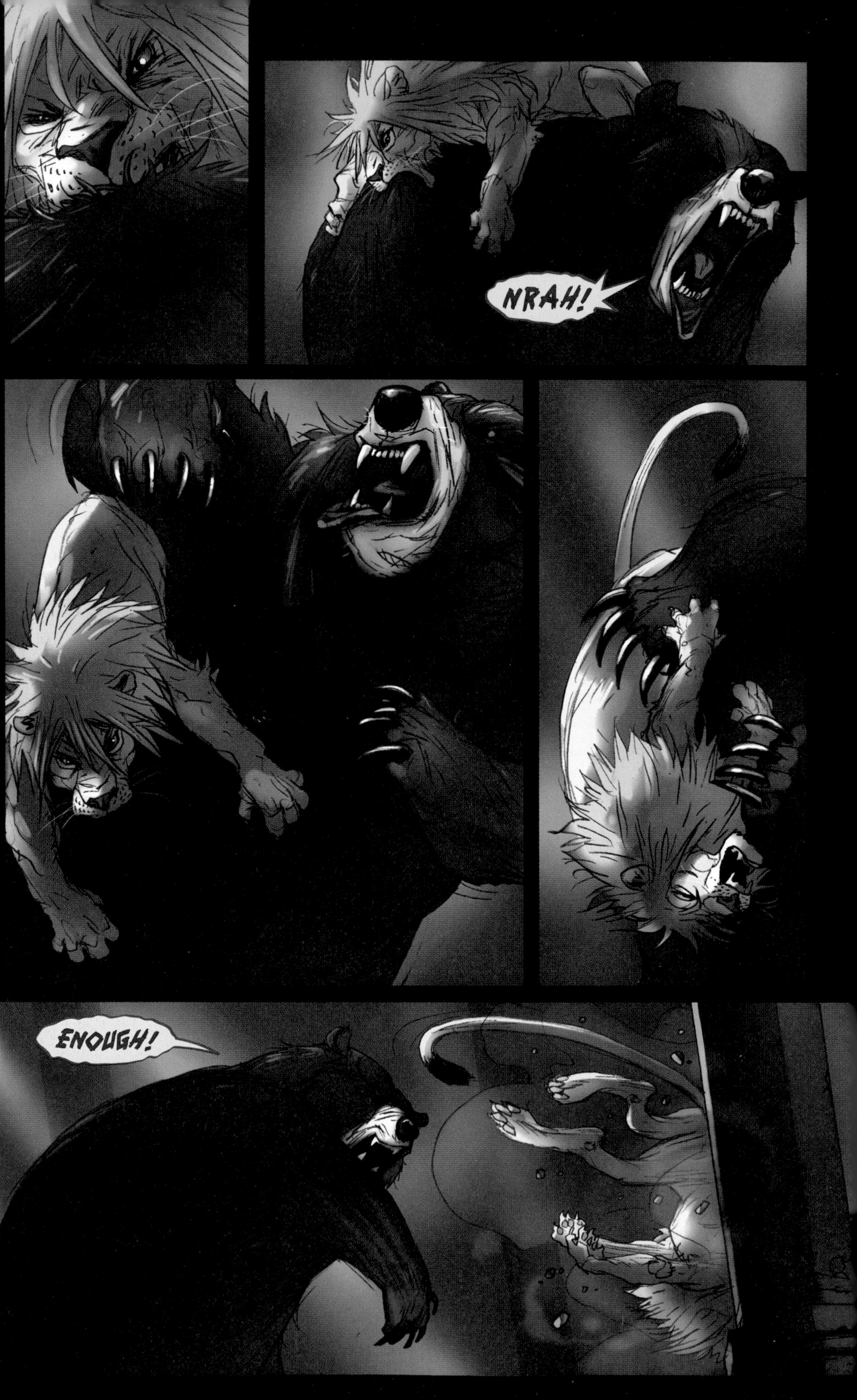
NRAH!
ENOUGH!

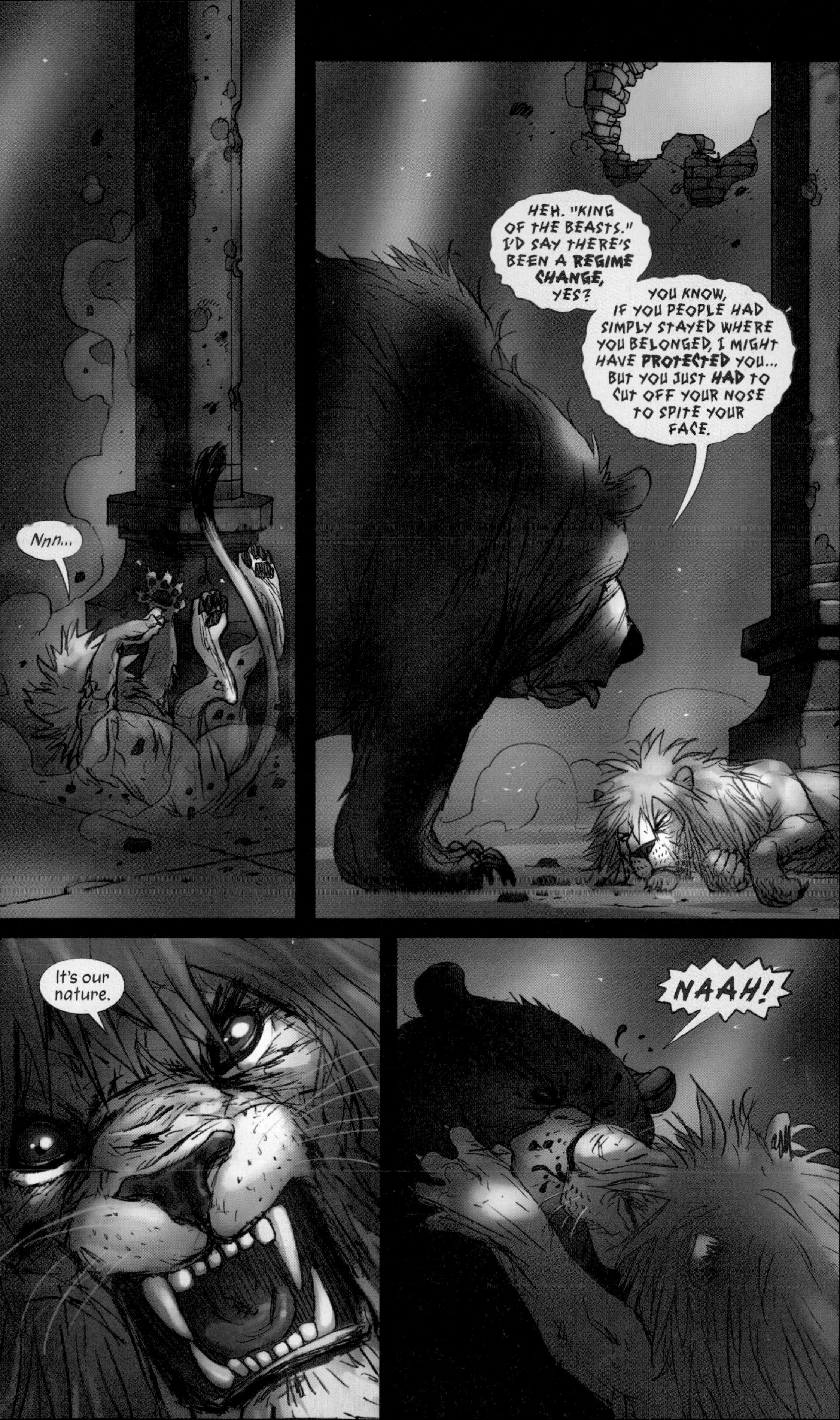
Nnn...
HEH. "KING OF THE BEASTS." I'D SAY THERE'S BEEN A **REGIME CHANGE,** YES?
YOU KNOW, IF YOU PEOPLE HAD SIMPLY STAYED WHERE YOU BELONGED, I MIGHT HAVE **PROTECTED** YOU... BUT YOU JUST **HAD** TO CUT OFF YOUR NOSE TO SPITE YOUR FACE.
It's our nature.
NAAH!

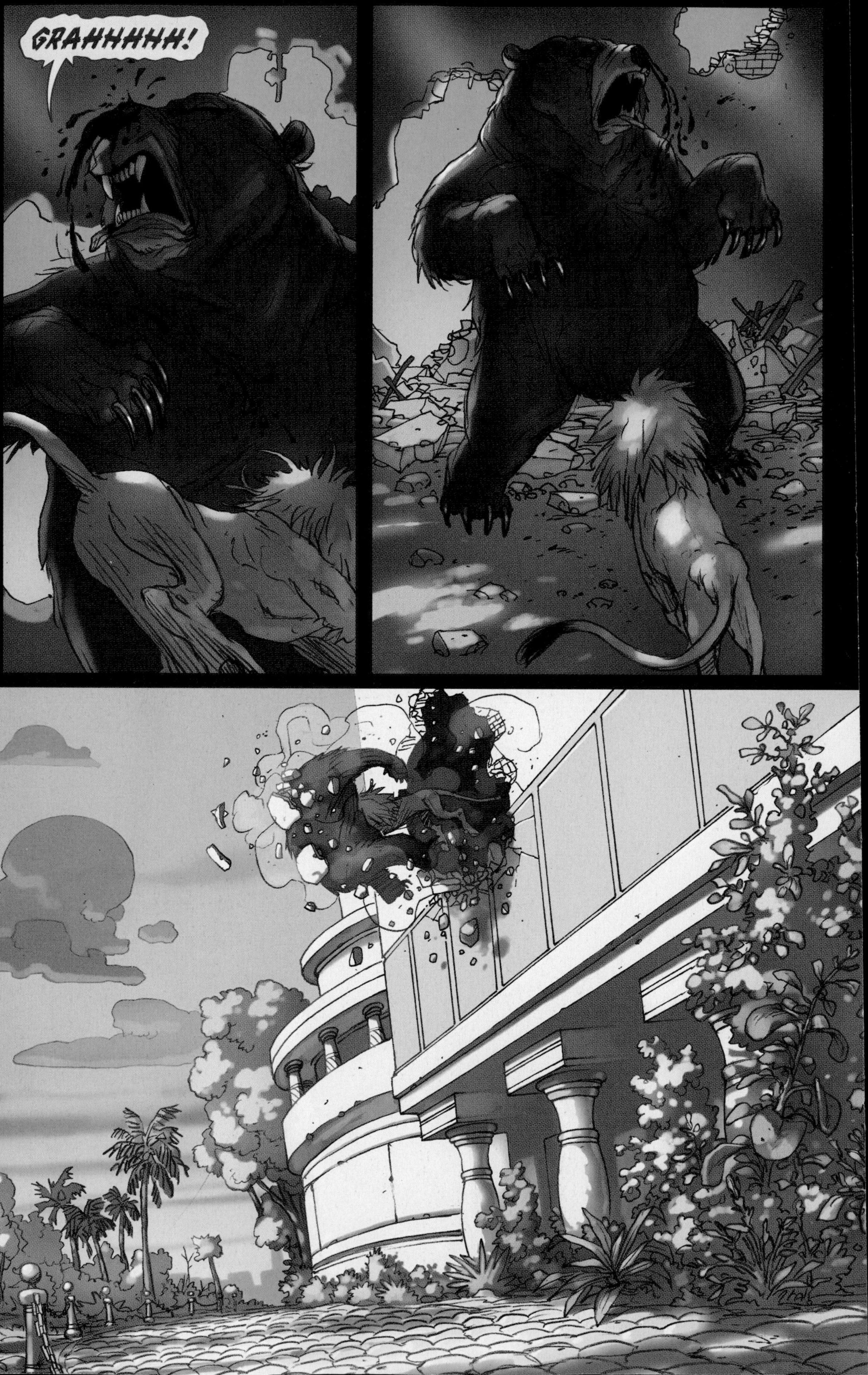
GRAHHHHH!

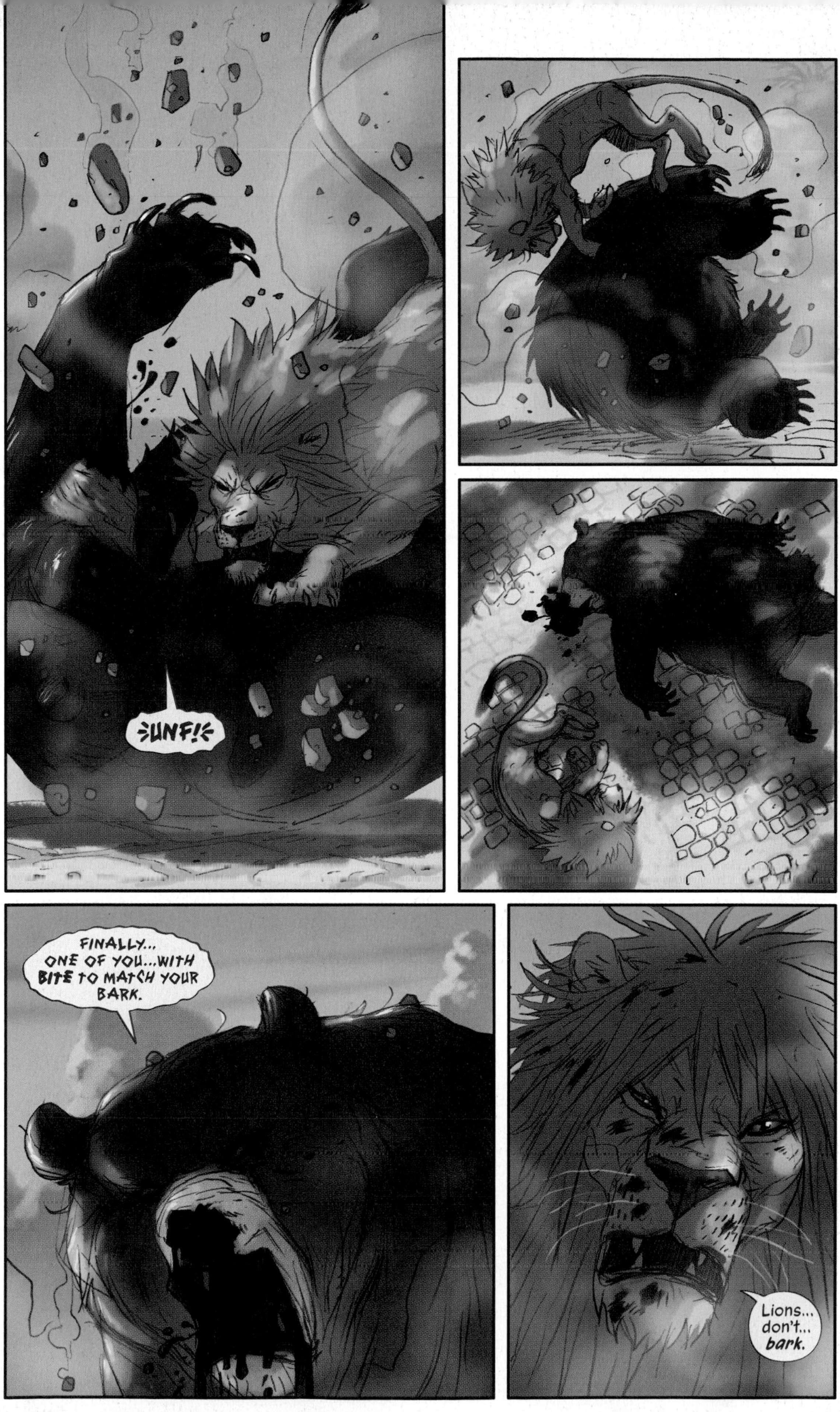
UNF!
FINALLY... ONE OF YOU...WITH BITE TO MATCH YOUR BARK.
Lions... don't... bark.

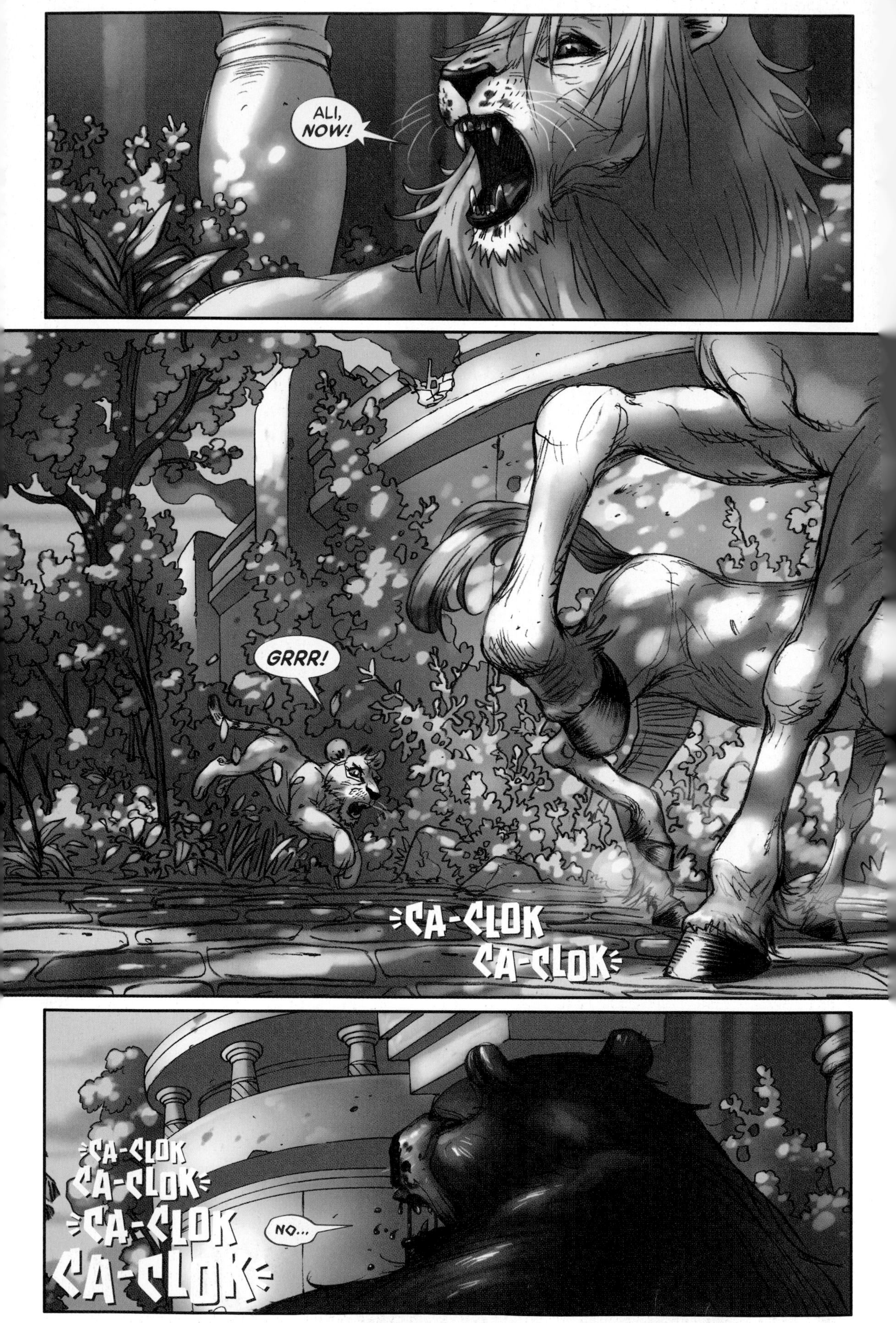

ALI, NOW!
GRRR!
CA-CLOK
CA-CLOK
CA-CLOK
CA-CLOK
CA-CLOK
CA-CLOK
NO...

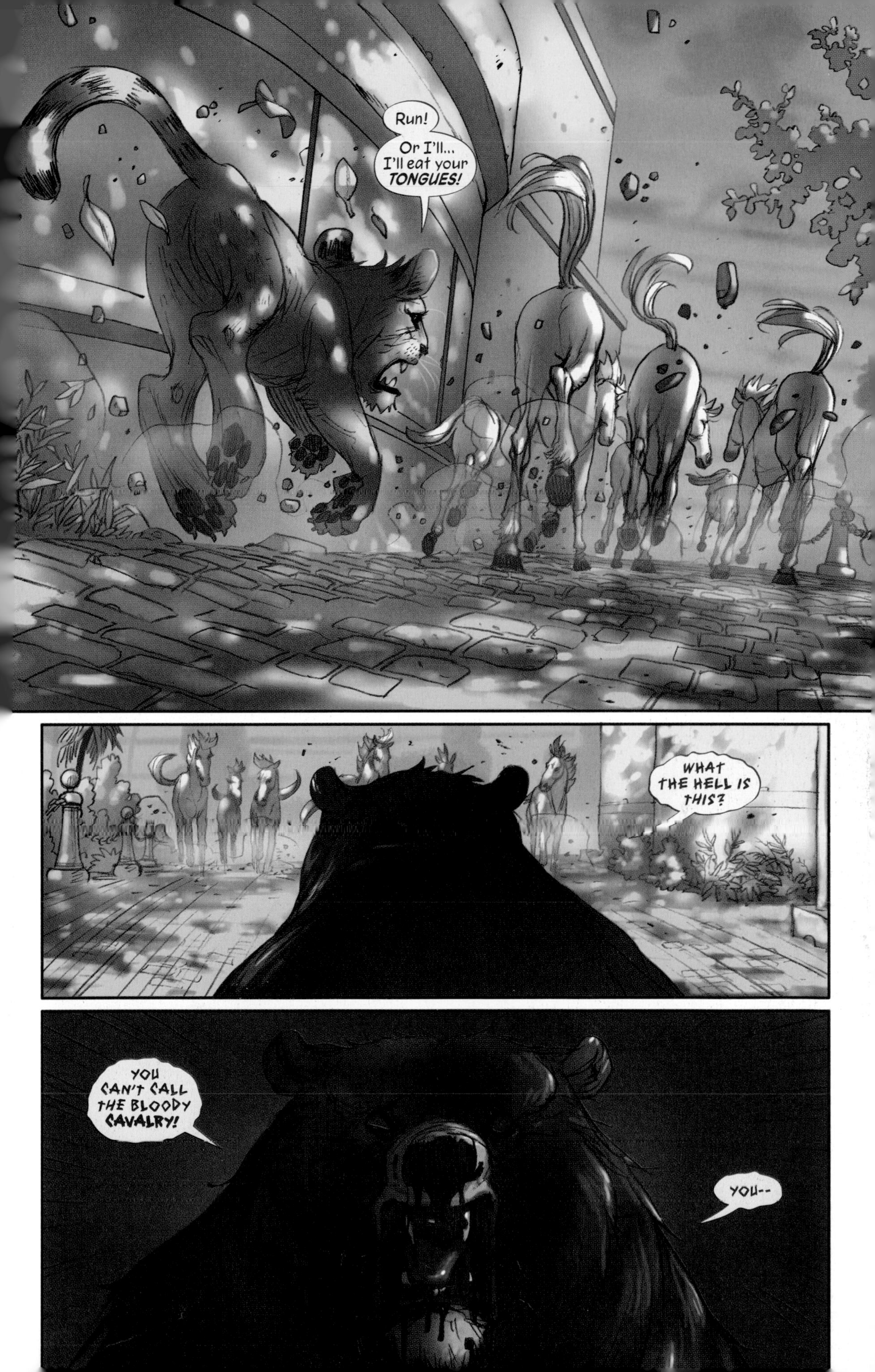
Run! Or I'll... I'll eat your TONGUES!
WHAT THE HELL IS THIS?
YOU CAN'T CALL THE BLOODY CAVALRY!
YOU--

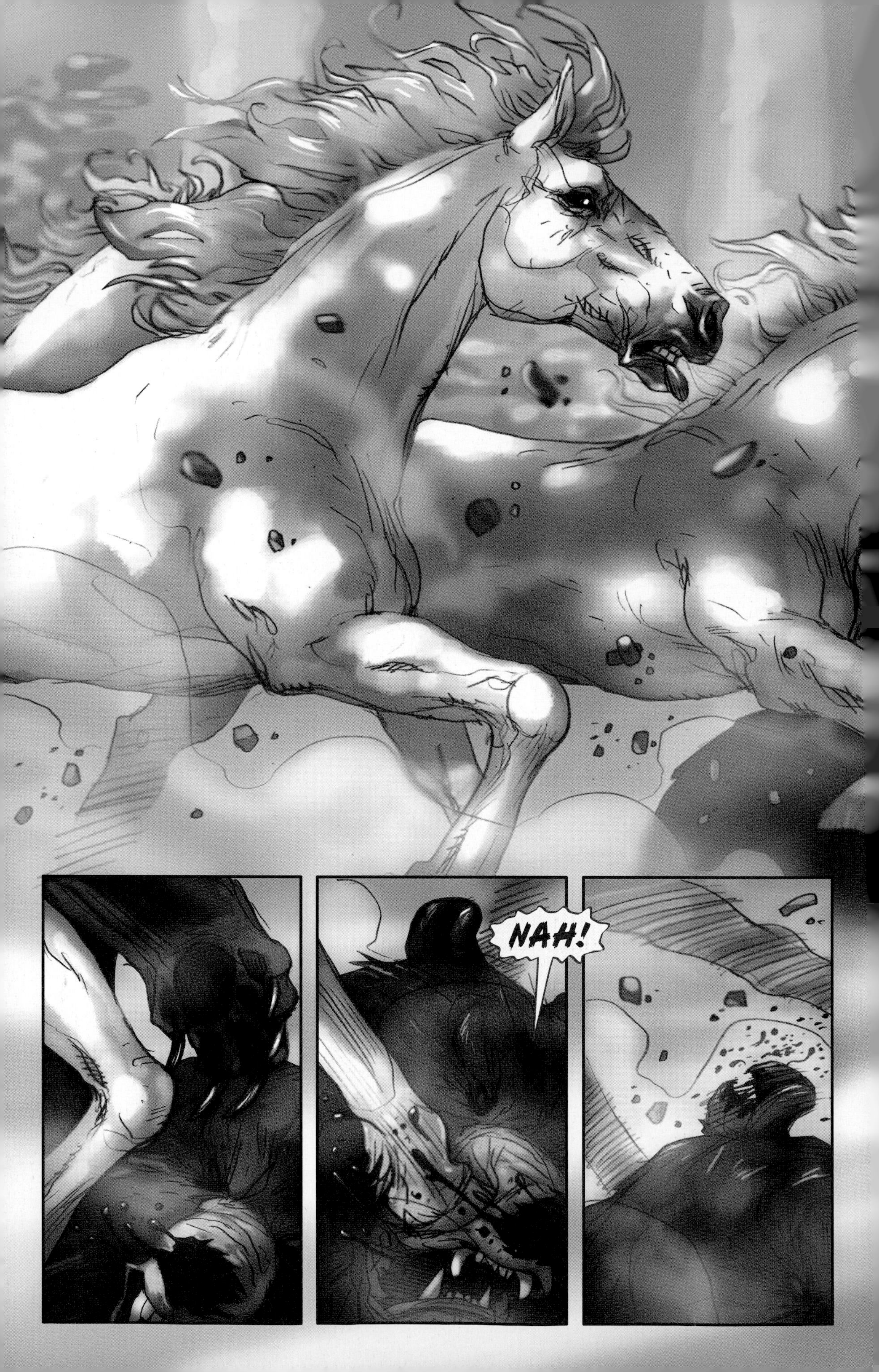
NAH!

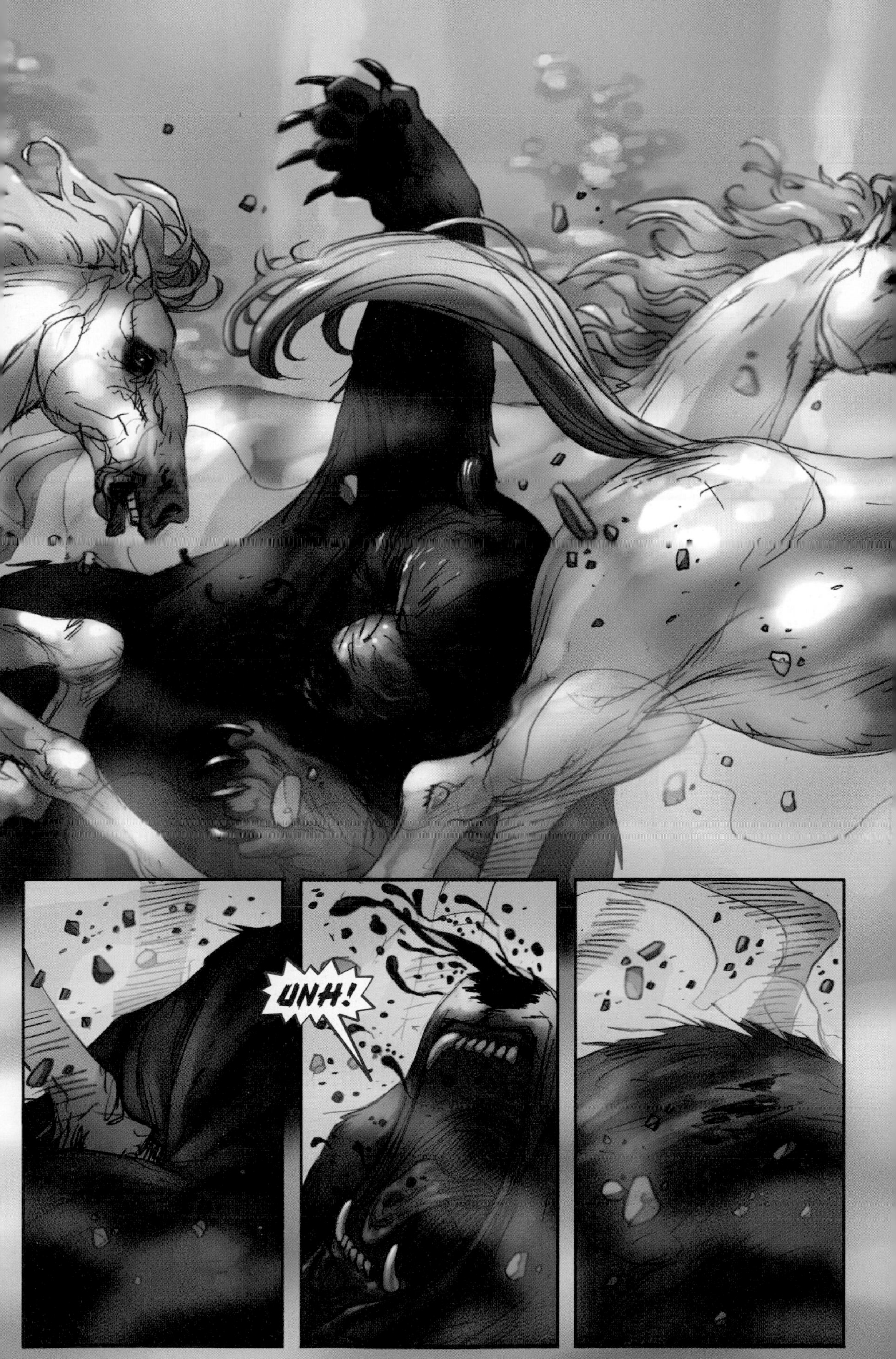
UNH!

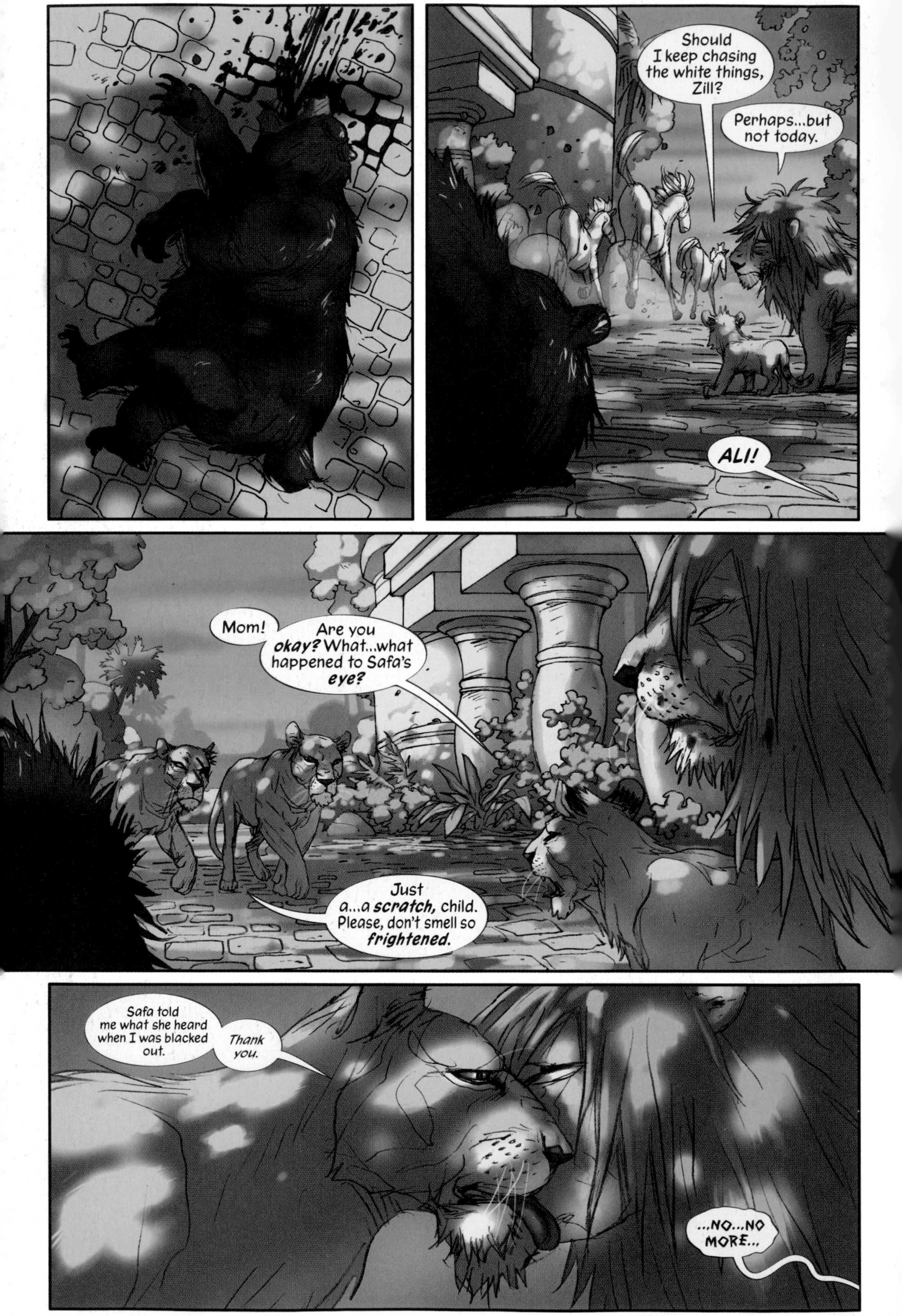
Should I keep chasing the white things, Zill?
Perhaps...but not today.
ALI!
Mom!
Are you okay? What...what happened to Safa's eye?
Just a...a scratch, child. Please, don't smell so frightened.
Safa told me what she heard when I was blacked out.
Thank you.
...NO...NO MORE...

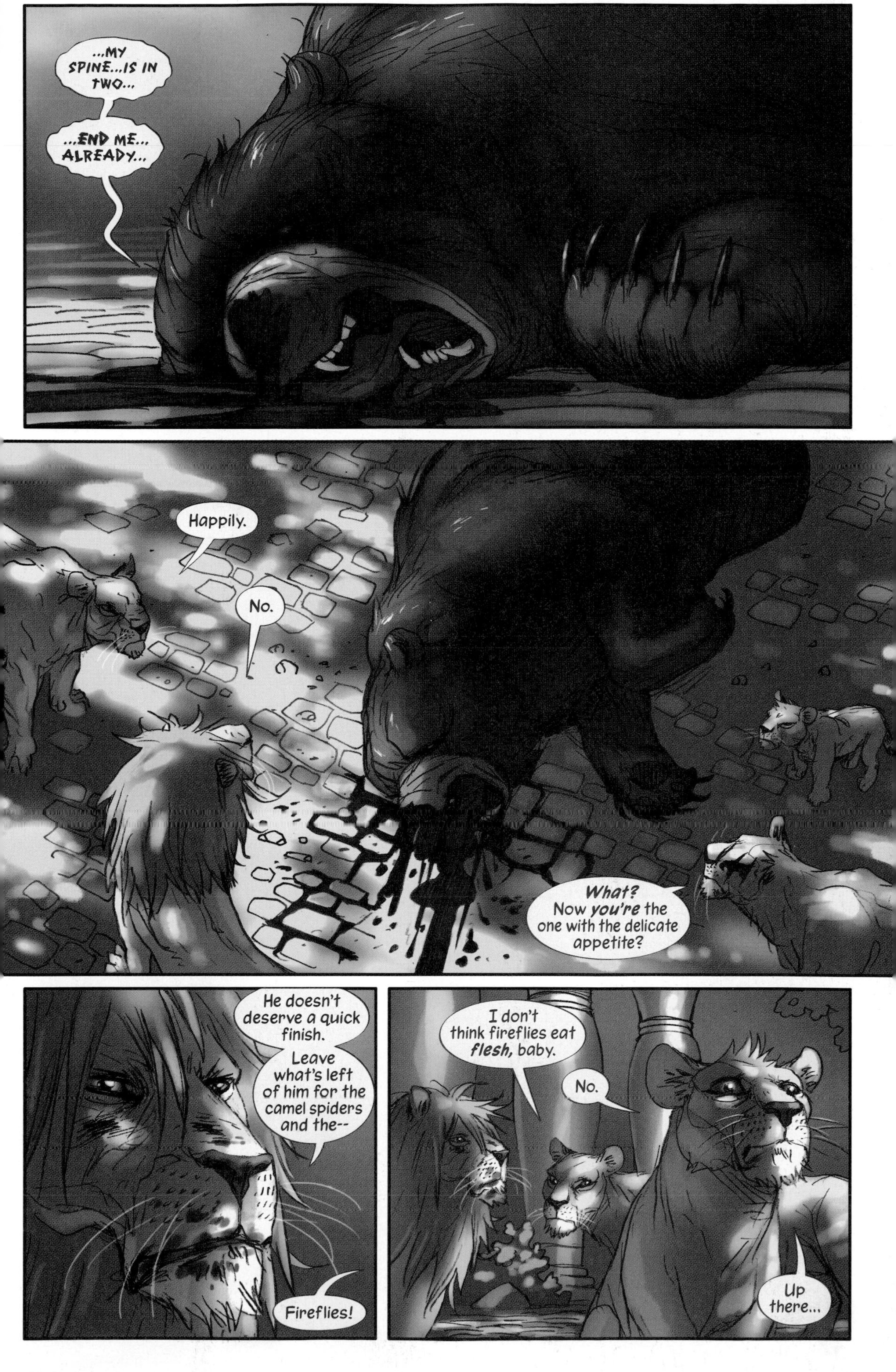
...MY SPINE...IS IN TWO...
...END ME... ALREADY...
Happily.
No.
What? Now *you're* the one with the delicate appetite?
He doesn't deserve a quick finish.
Leave what's left of him for the camel spiders and the--
Fireflies!
I don't think fireflies eat *flesh,* baby.
No.
Up there...

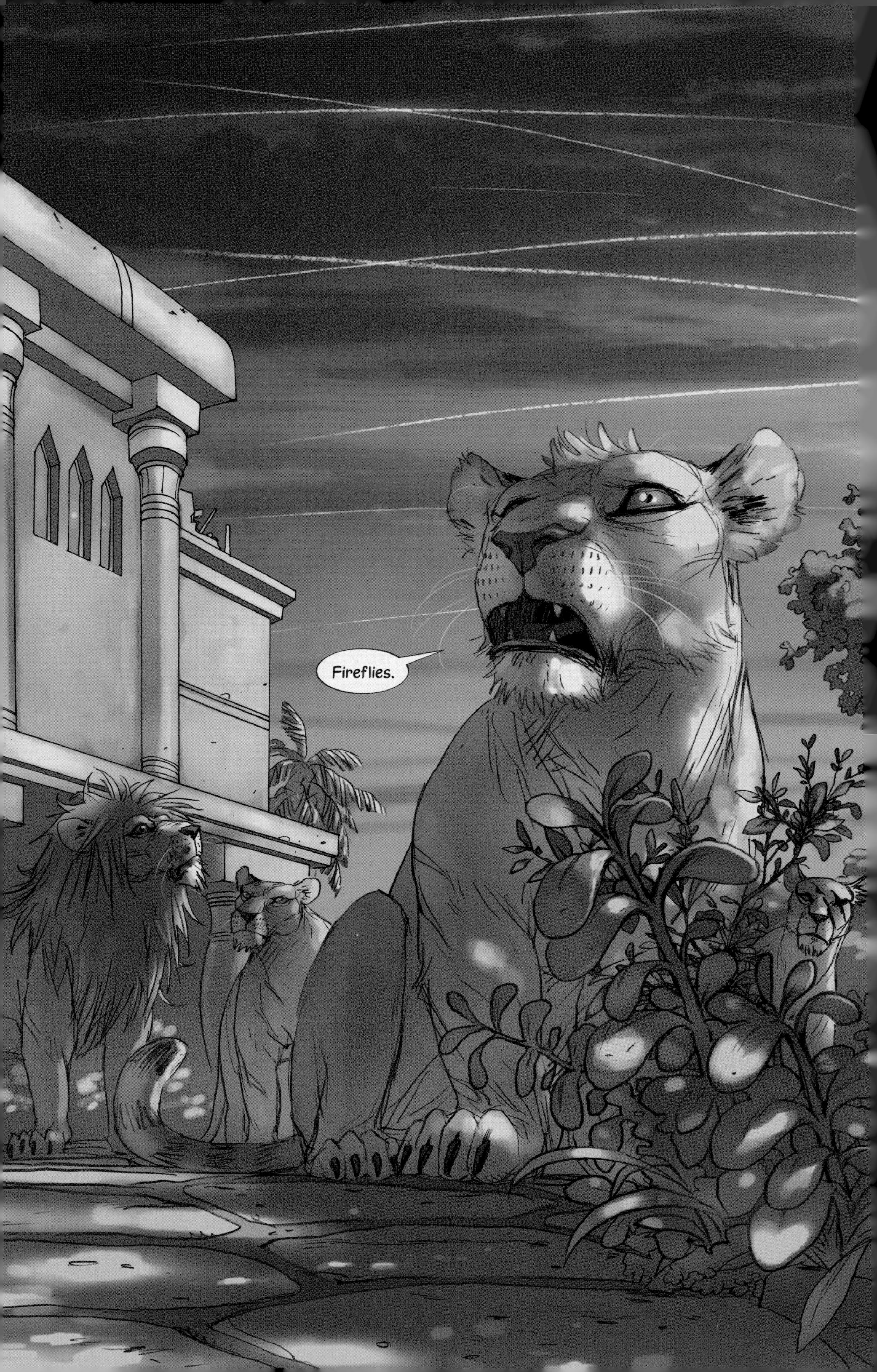
Fireflies.

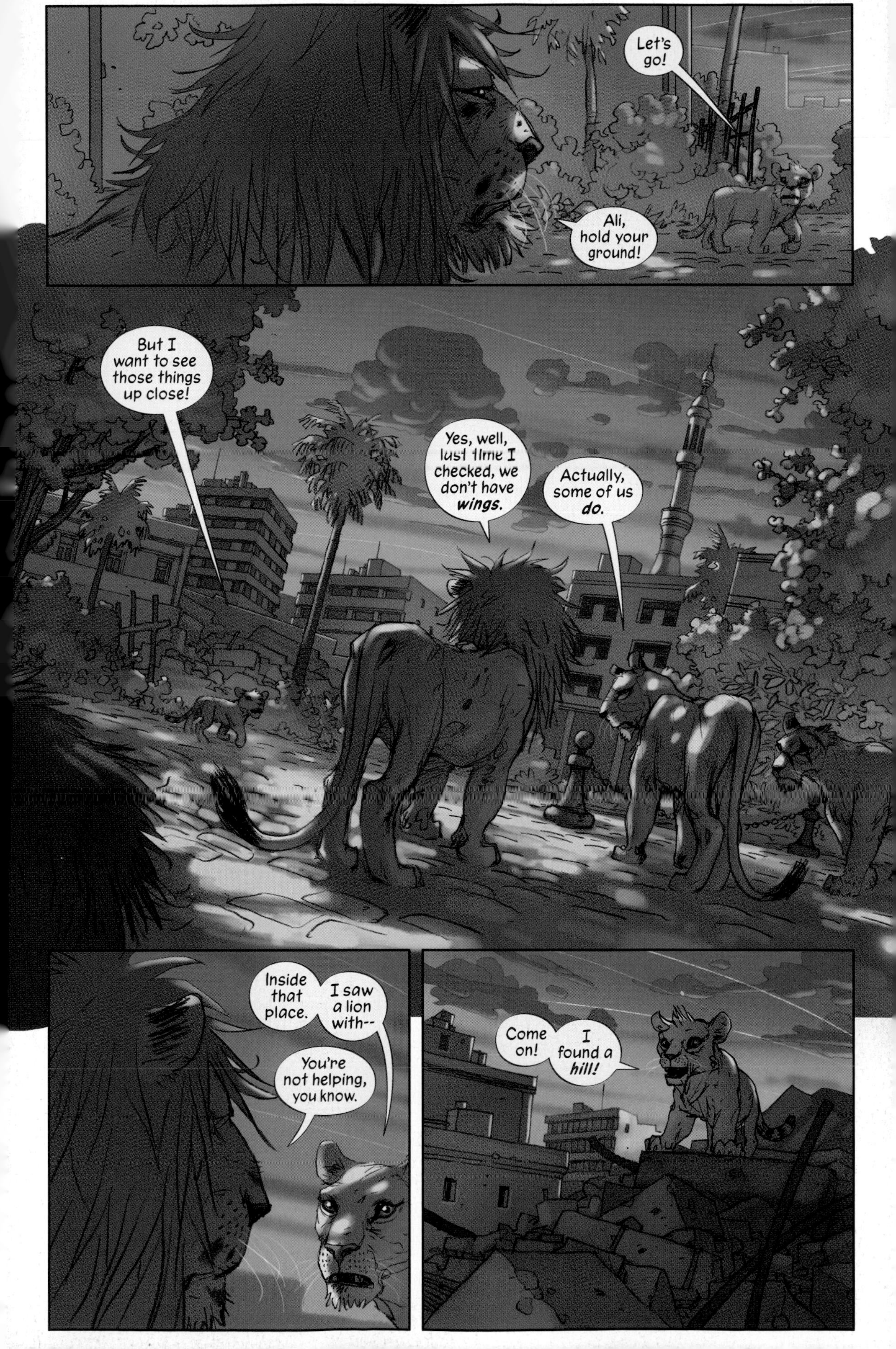
Let's go!
Ali, hold your ground!
But I want to see those things up close!
Yes, well, last time I checked, we don't have ***wings***.
Actually, some of us ***do***.
Inside that place.
I saw a lion with--
You're not helping, you know.
Come on!
I found a ***hill!***

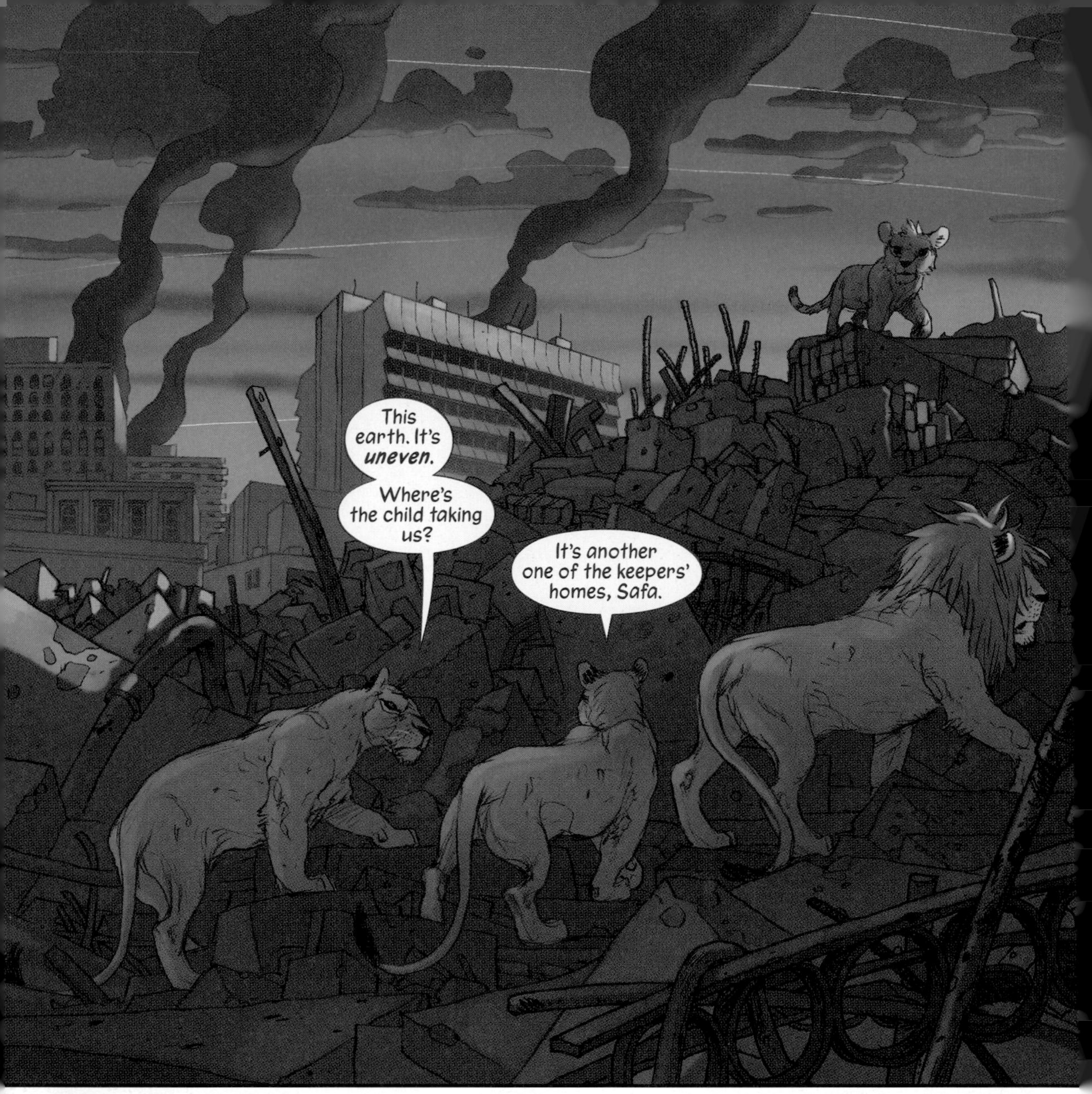
This earth. It's *uneven*.
Where's the child taking us?
It's another one of the keepers' homes, Safa.

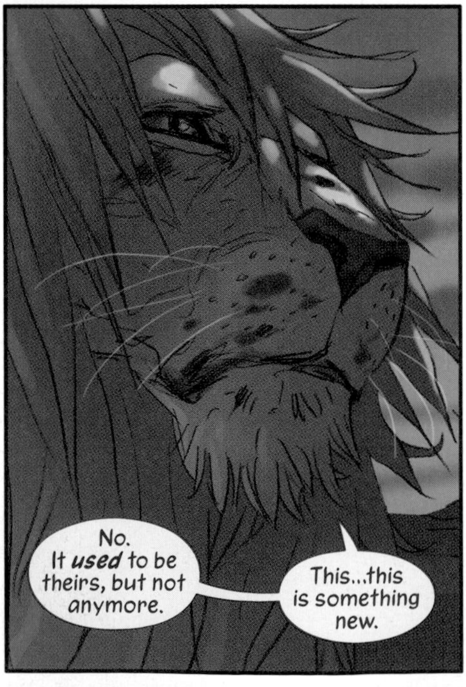
No. It *used* to be theirs, but not anymore.
This...this is something new.

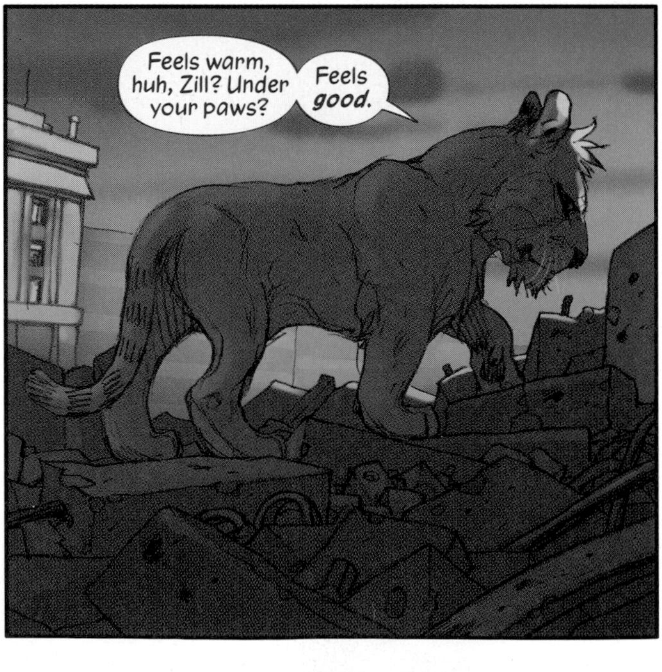
Feels warm, huh, Zill? Under your paws?
Feels *good*.

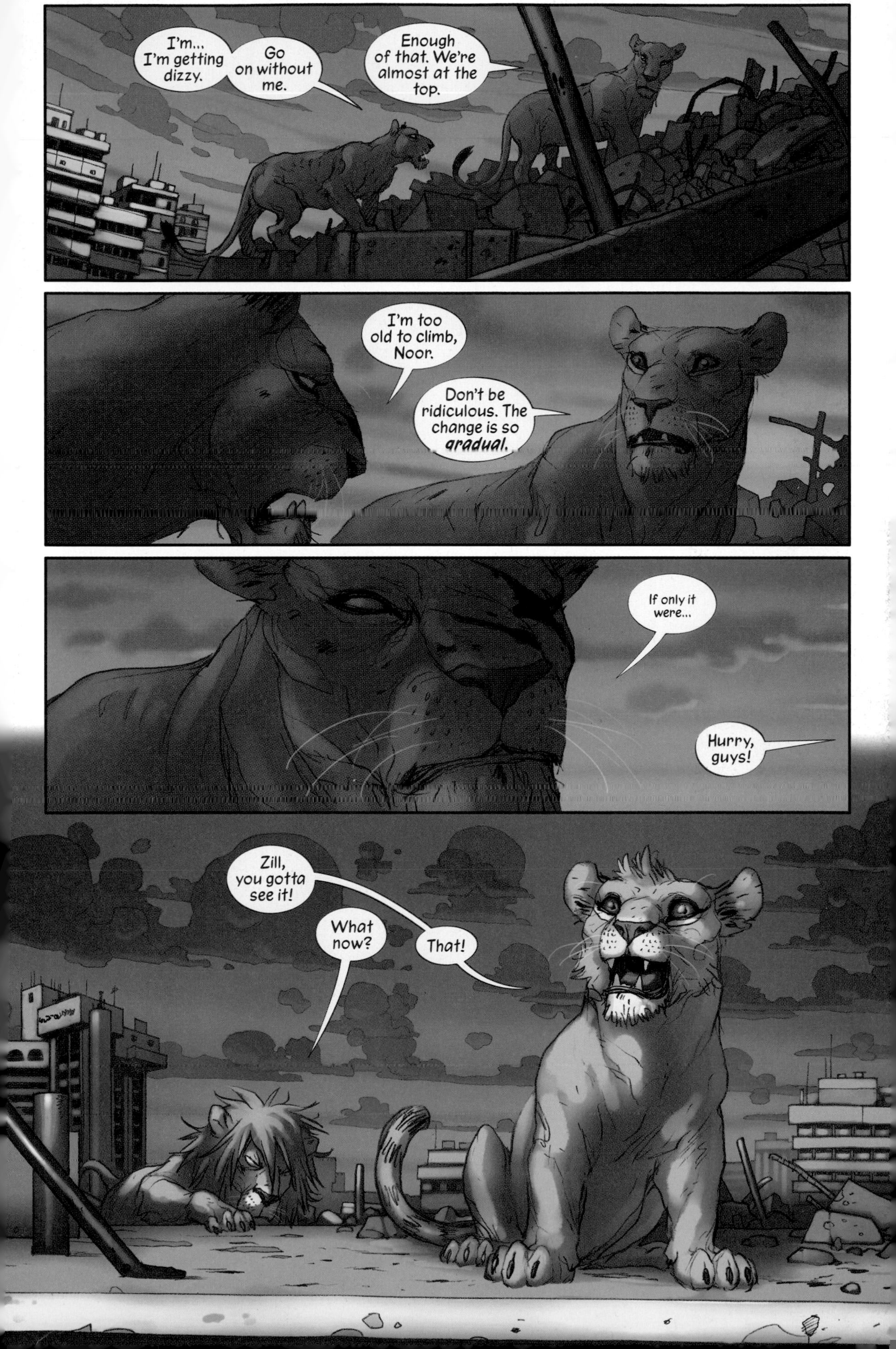
I'm... I'm getting dizzy.
Go on without me.
Enough of that. We're almost at the top.
I'm too old to climb, Noor.
Don't be ridiculous. The change is so *gradual.*
If only it were...
Hurry, guys!
Zill, you gotta see it!
What now?
That!

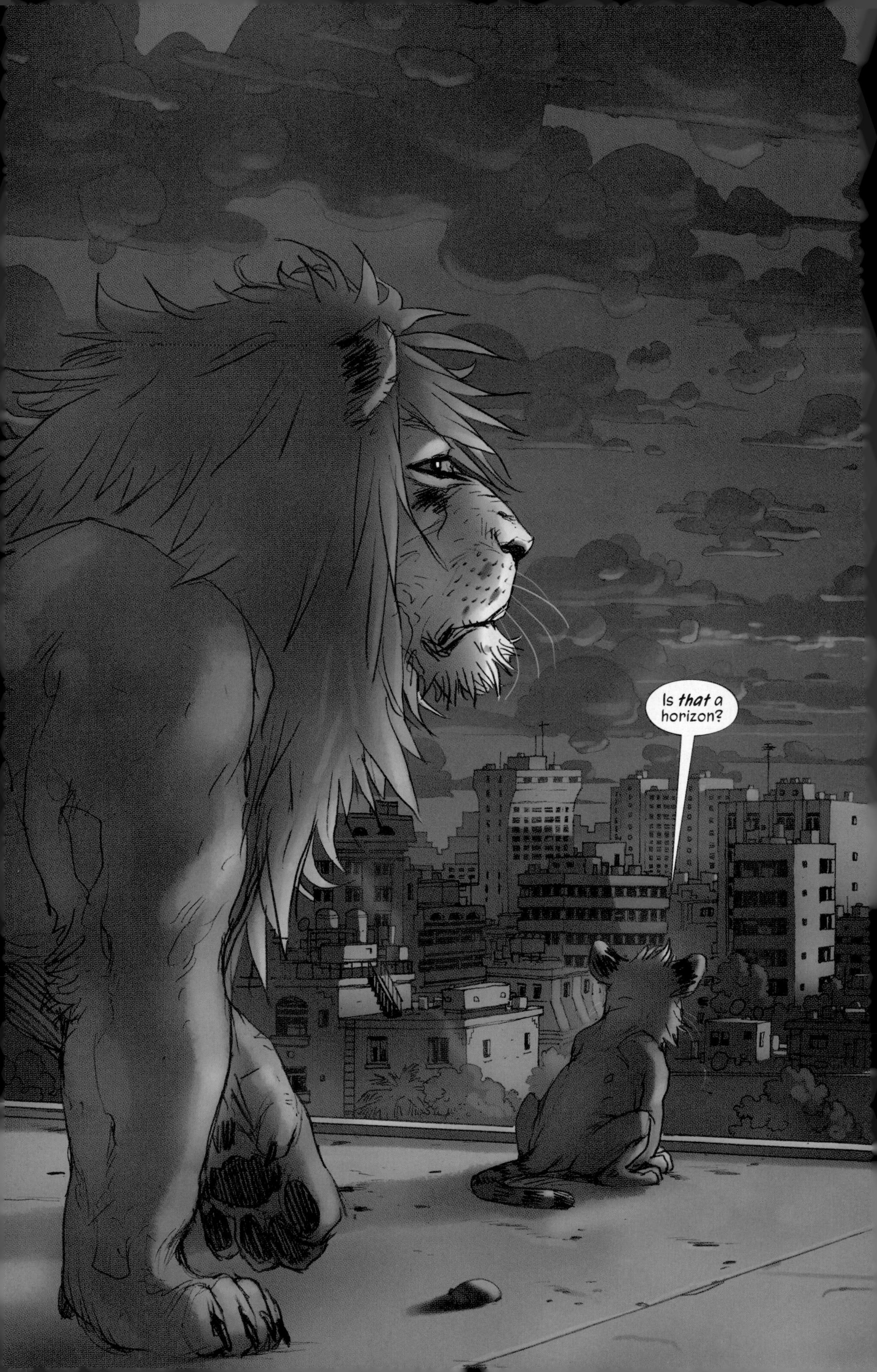
Is *that* a horizon?

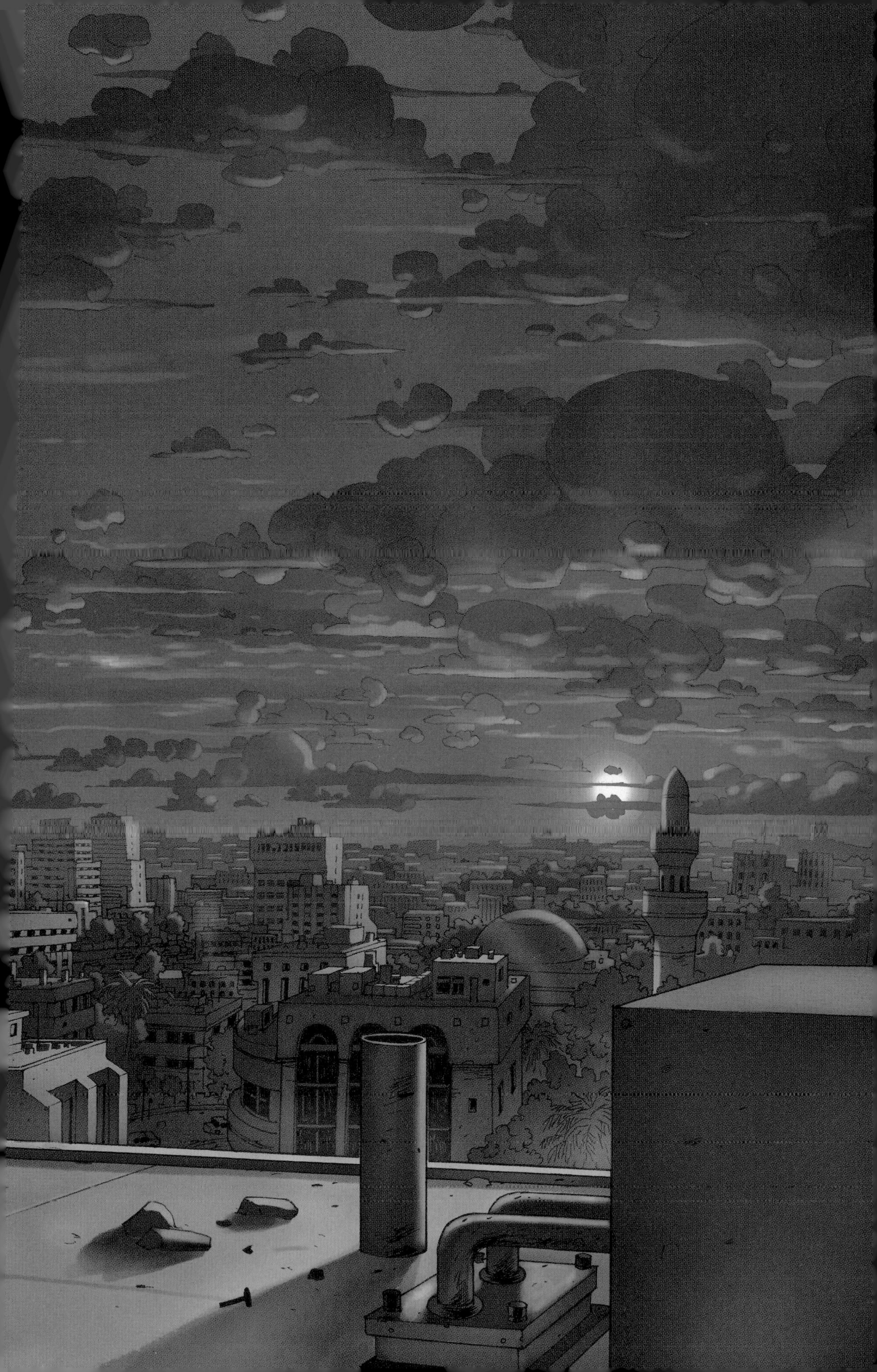

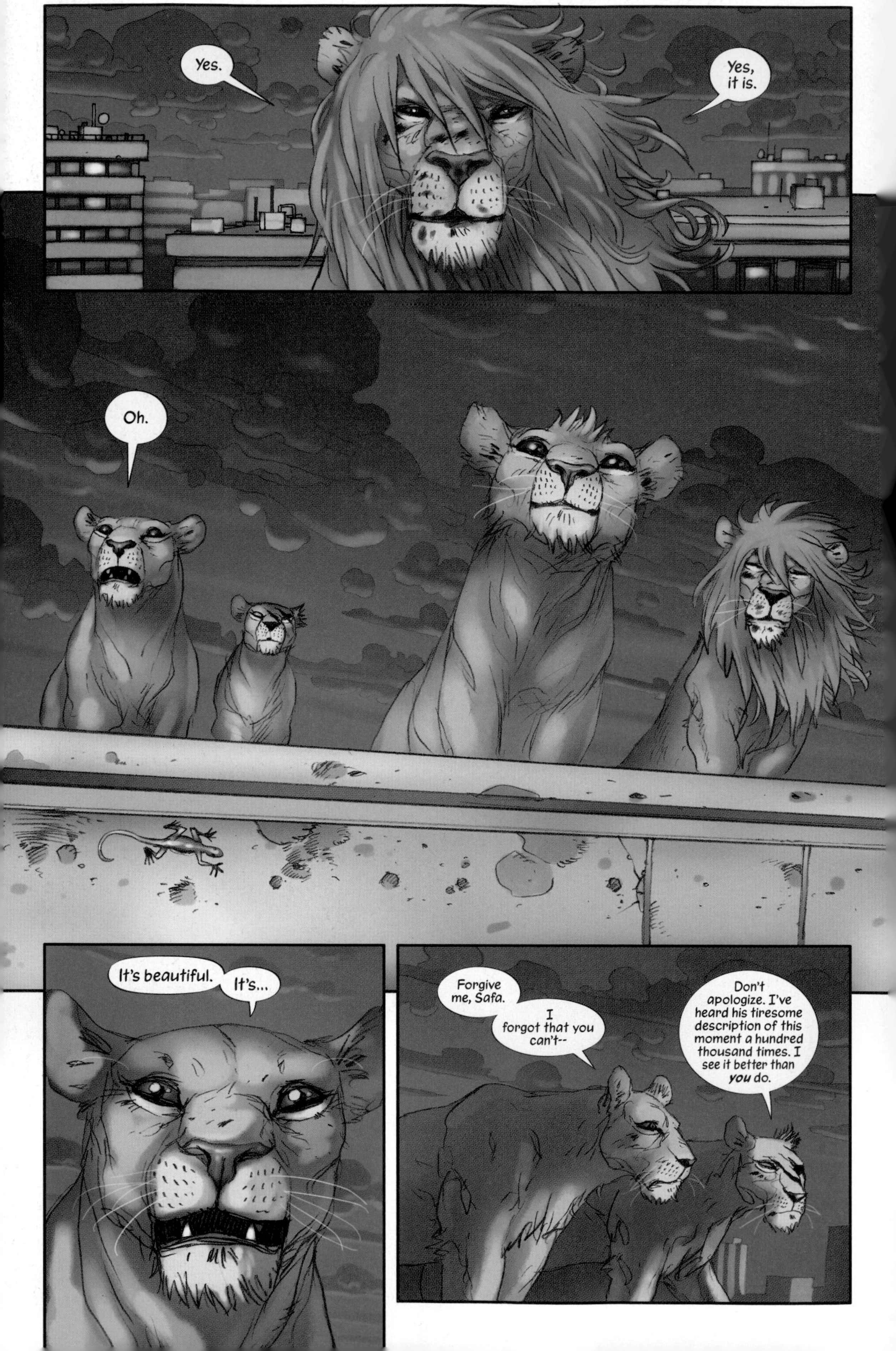
Yes.
Yes, it is.
Oh.
It's beautiful.
It's...
Forgive me, Safa.
I forgot that you can't--
Don't apologize. I've heard his tiresome description of this moment a hundred thousand times. I see it better than *you* do.

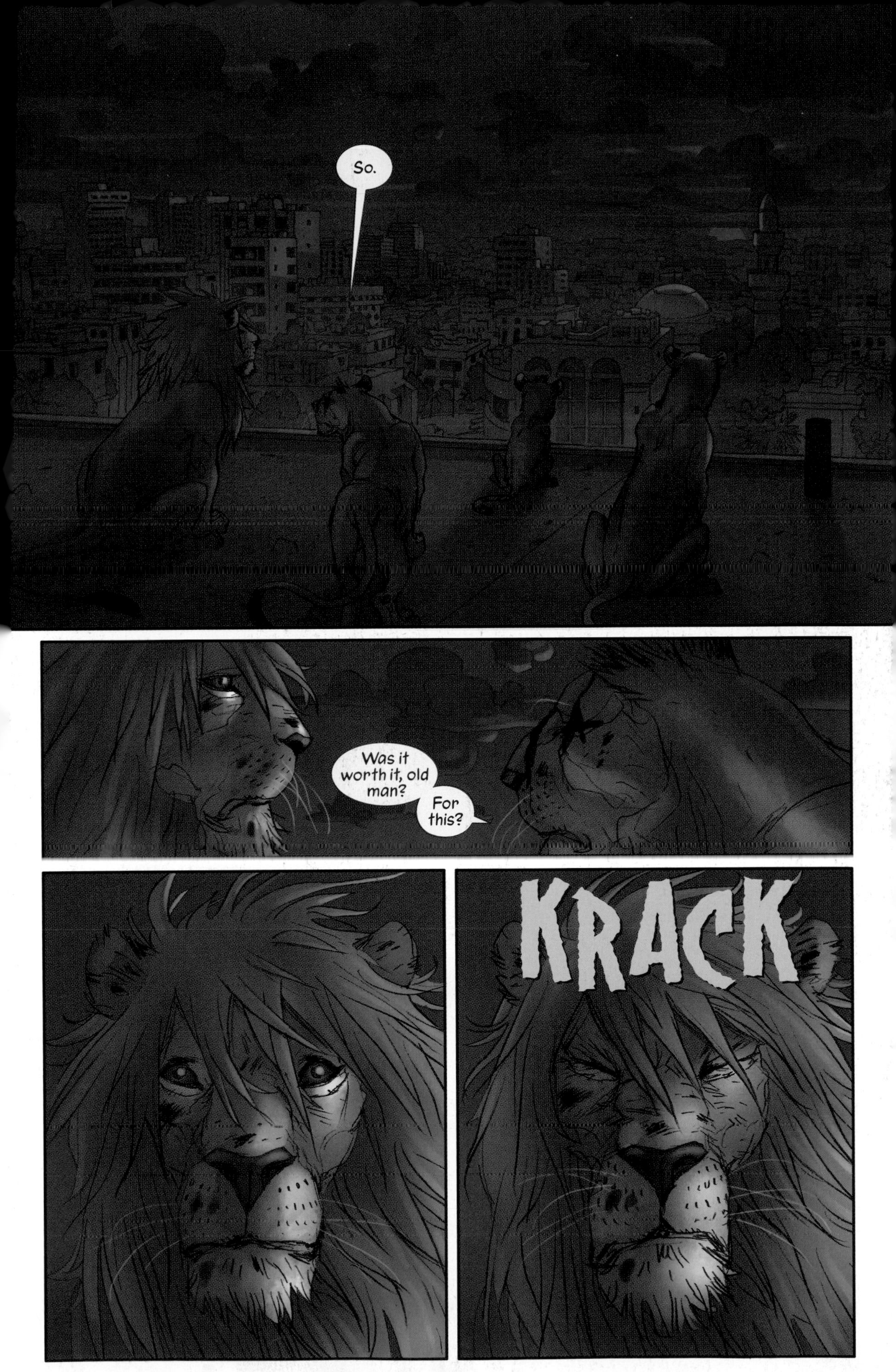
So.
Was it worth it, old man?
For this?
KRACK

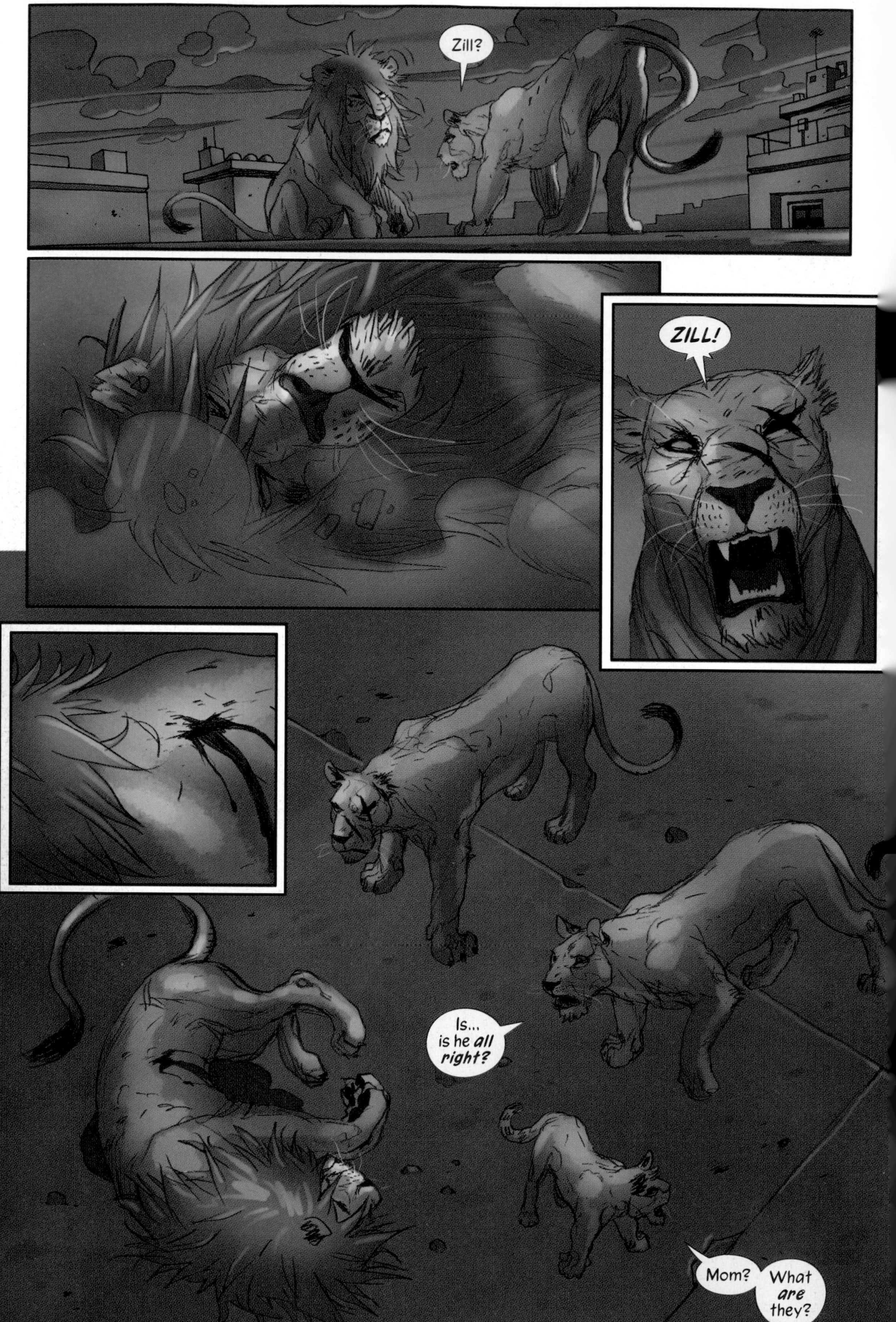
Zill?
ZILL!
Is... is he all right?
Mom?
What are they?

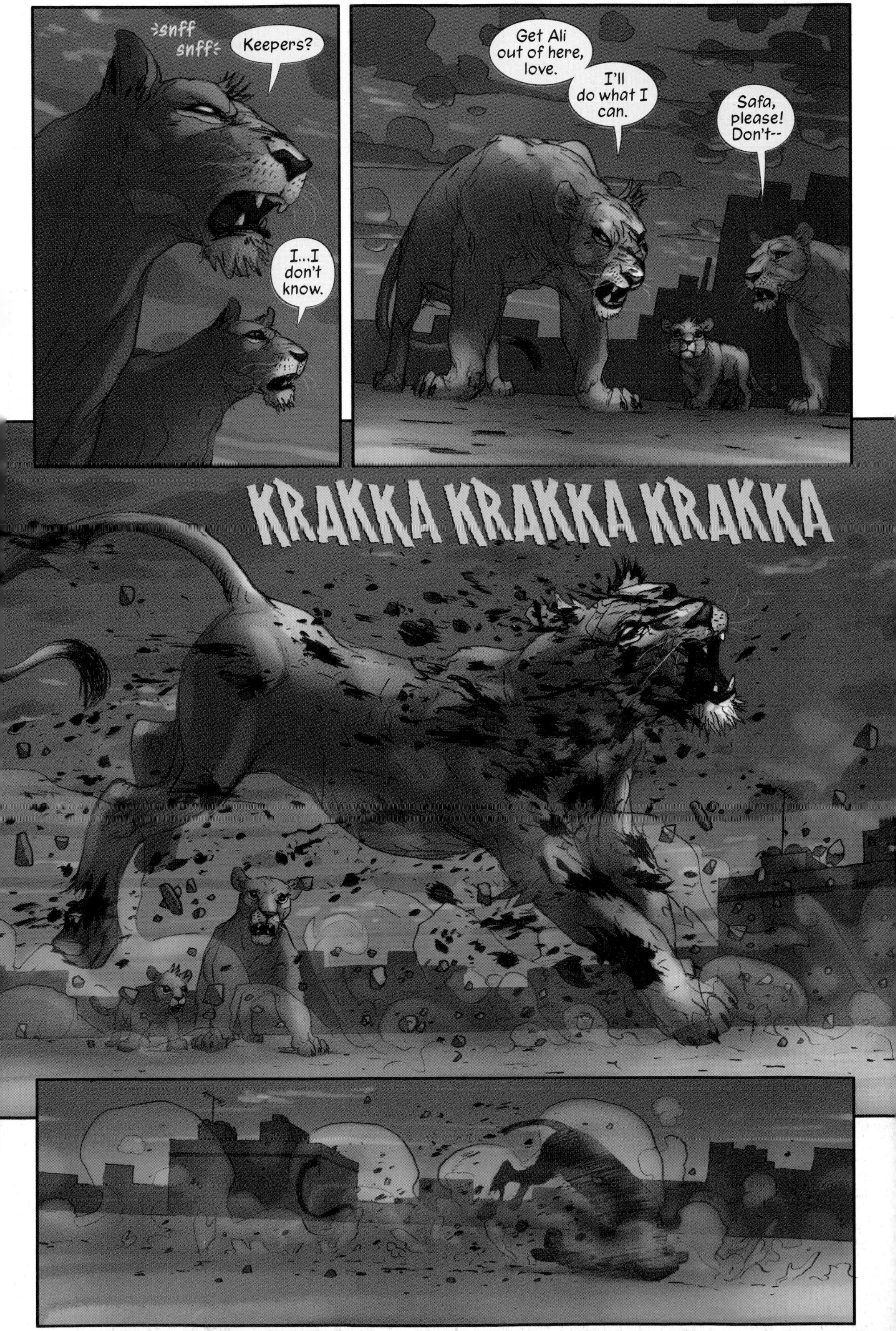

snff snff
Keepers?
I...I don't know.
Get Ali out of here, love.
I'll do what I can.
Safa, please! Don't--
KRAKKA KRAKKA KRAKKA

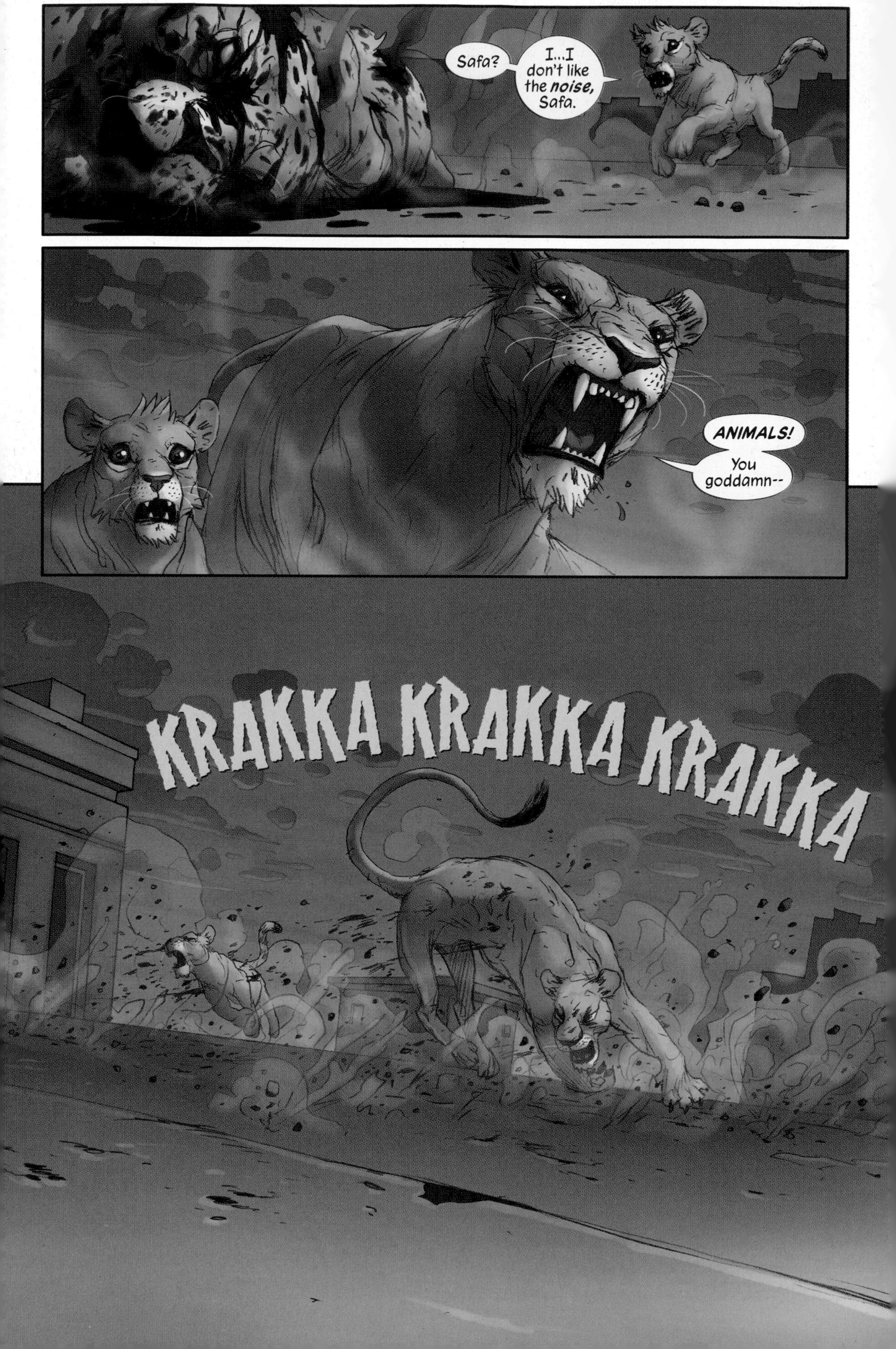
Safa?
I...I don't like the *noise,* Safa.
ANIMALS! You goddamn--
KRAKKA KRAKKA KRAKKA

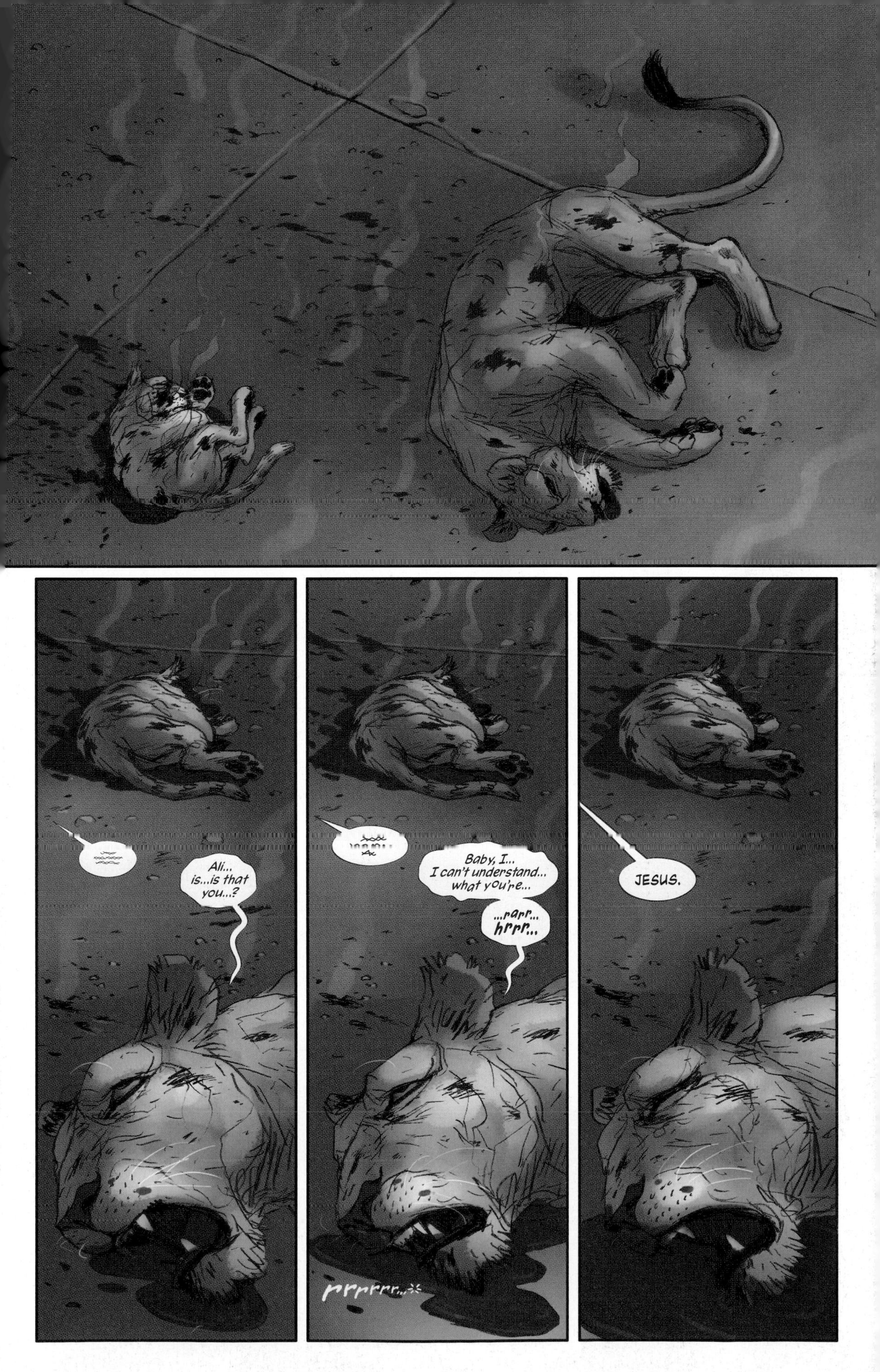
Ali... is...is that you...?
Baby, I... I can't understand... what you're...
...rarr... hrrr...
prprrrr...
JESUS.

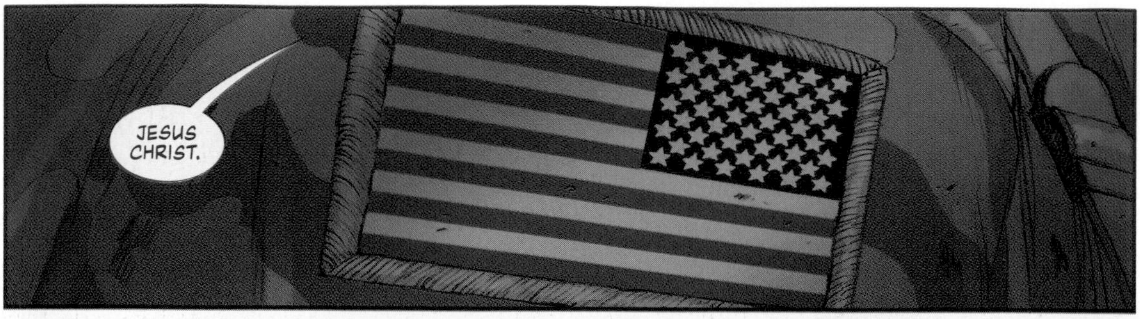
JESUS CHRIST.

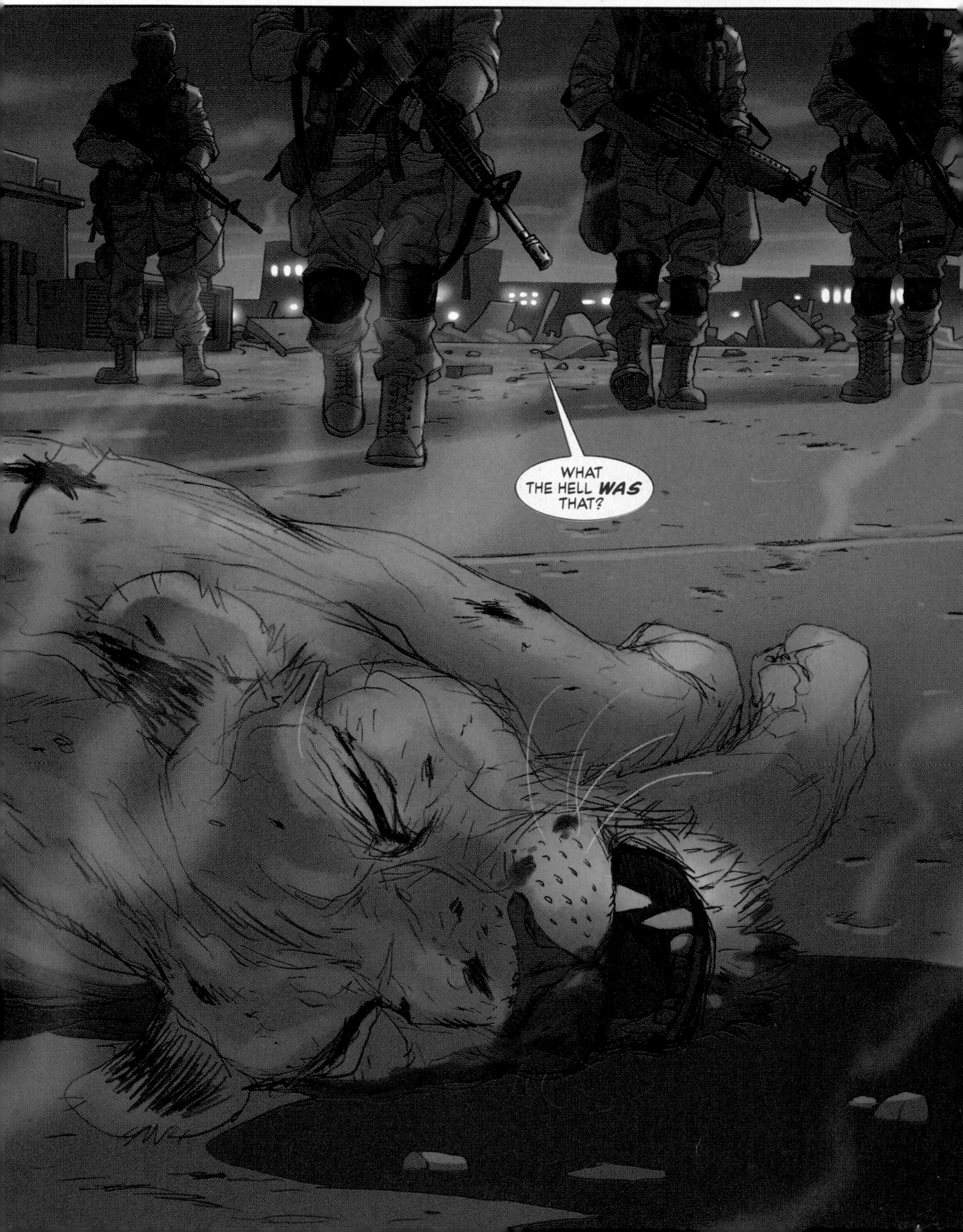
WHAT THE HELL WAS THAT?

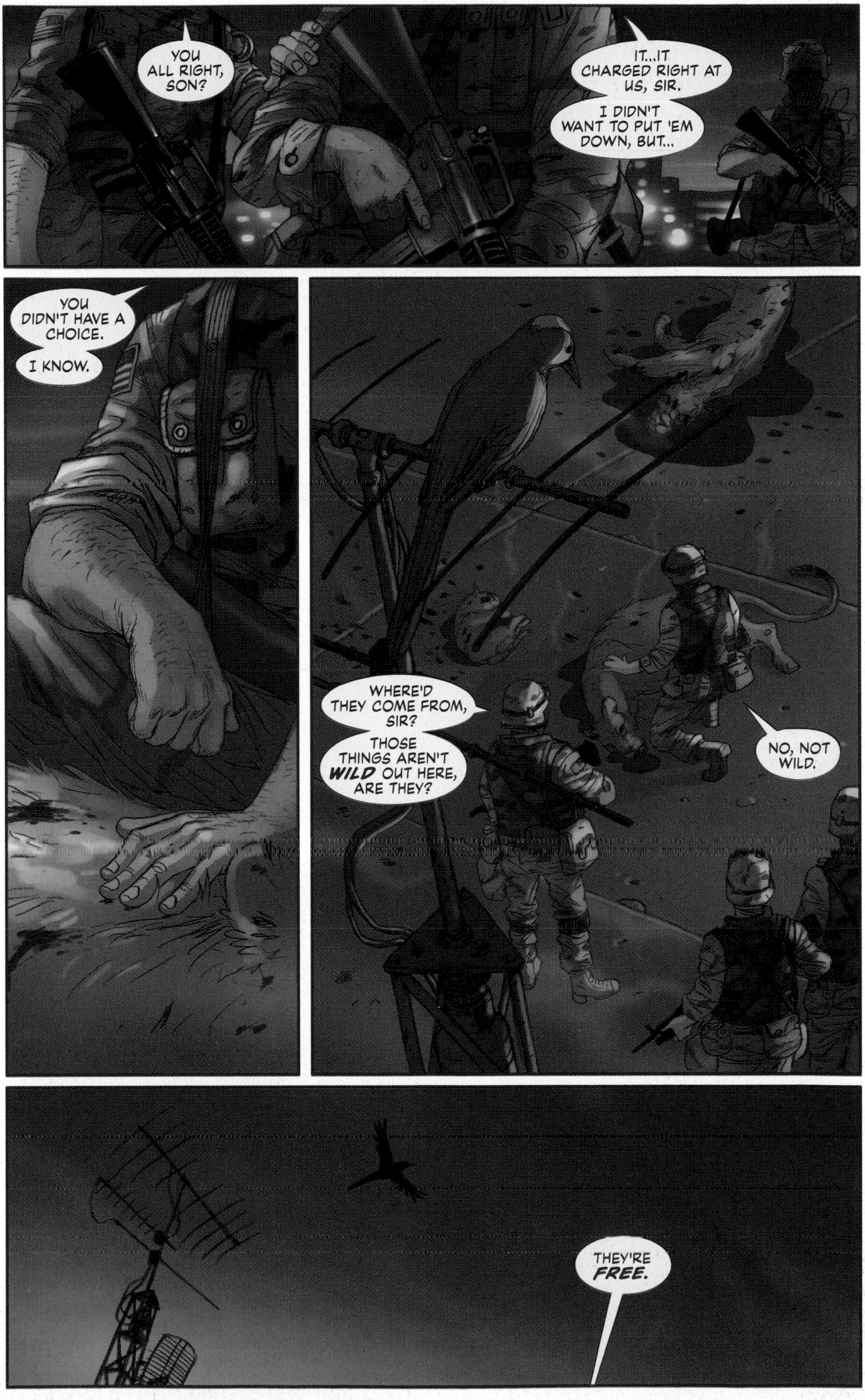

YOU ALL RIGHT, SON?
IT...IT CHARGED RIGHT AT US, SIR.
I DIDN'T WANT TO PUT 'EM DOWN, BUT...
YOU DIDN'T HAVE A CHOICE.
I KNOW.
WHERE'D THEY COME FROM, SIR?
THOSE THINGS AREN'T WILD OUT HERE, ARE THEY?
NO, NOT WILD.
THEY'RE FREE.

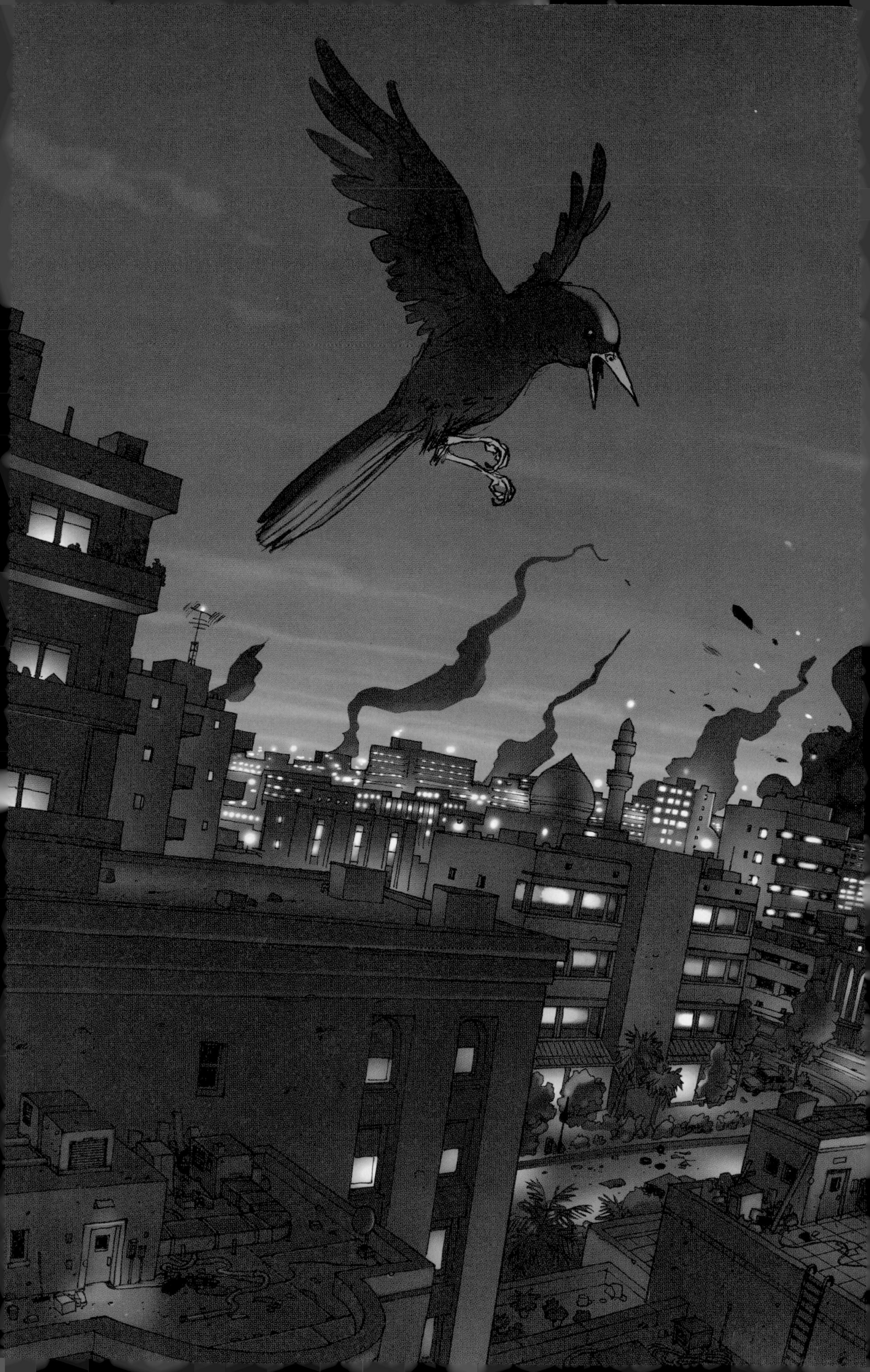

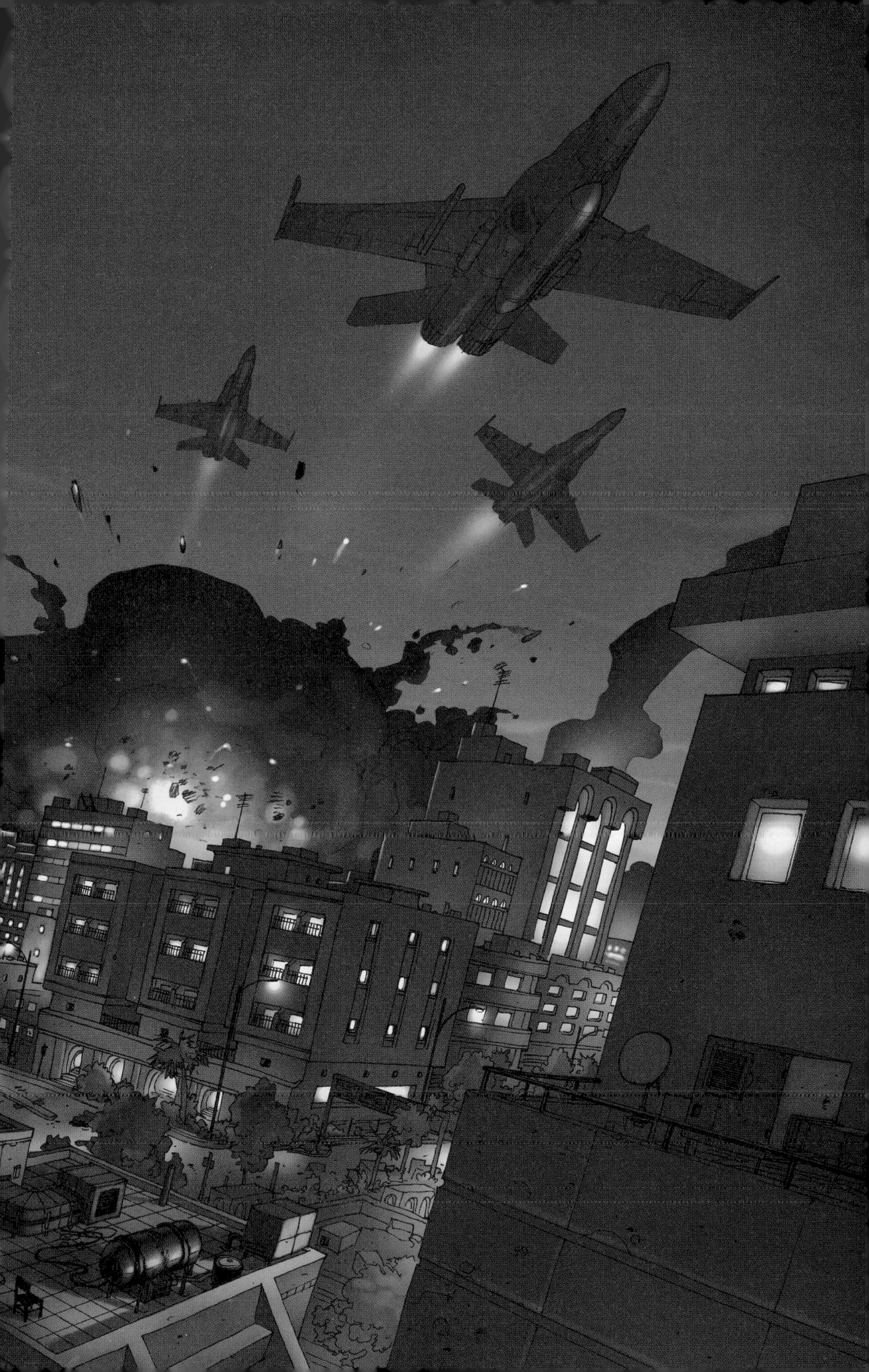

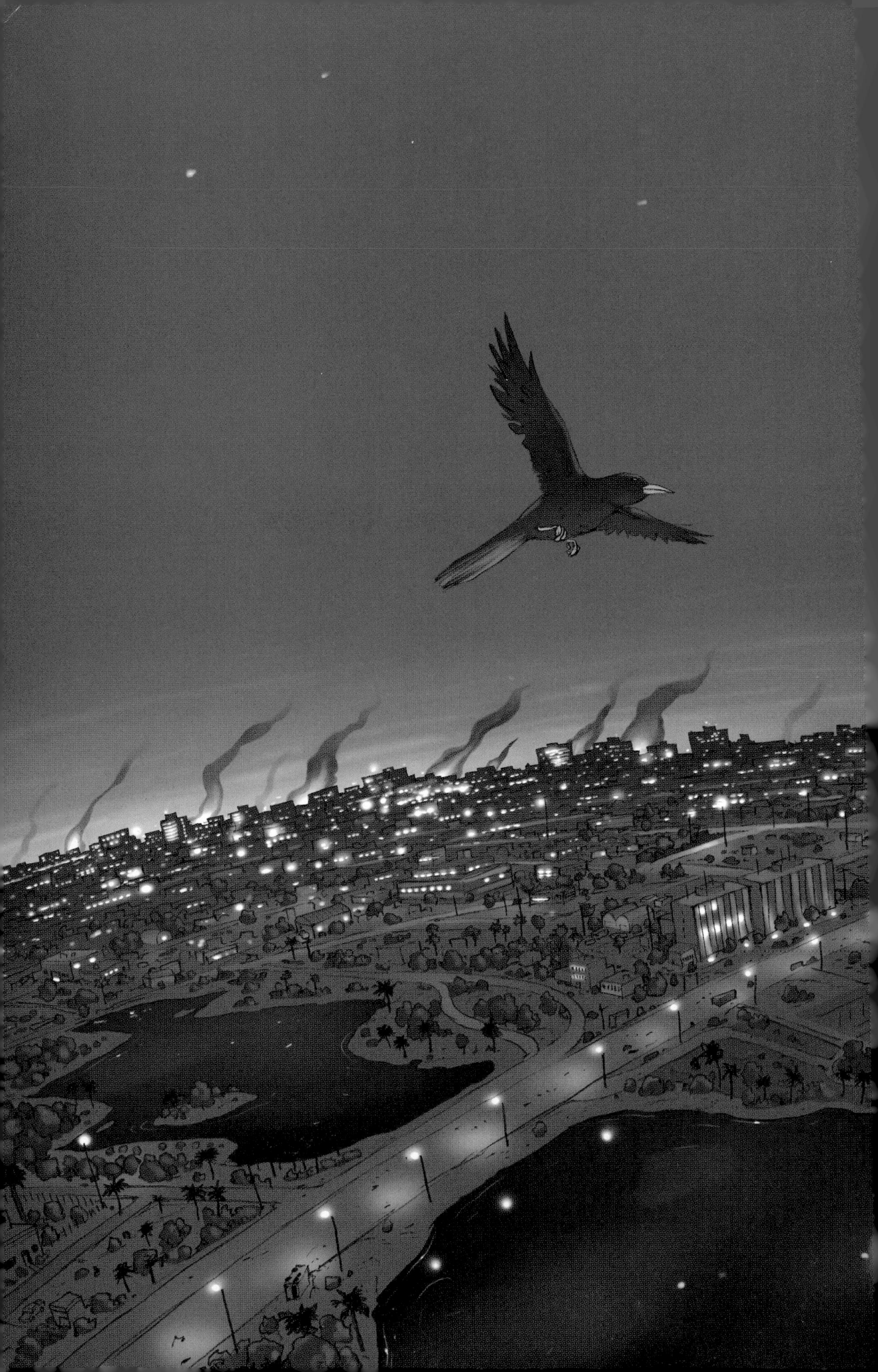

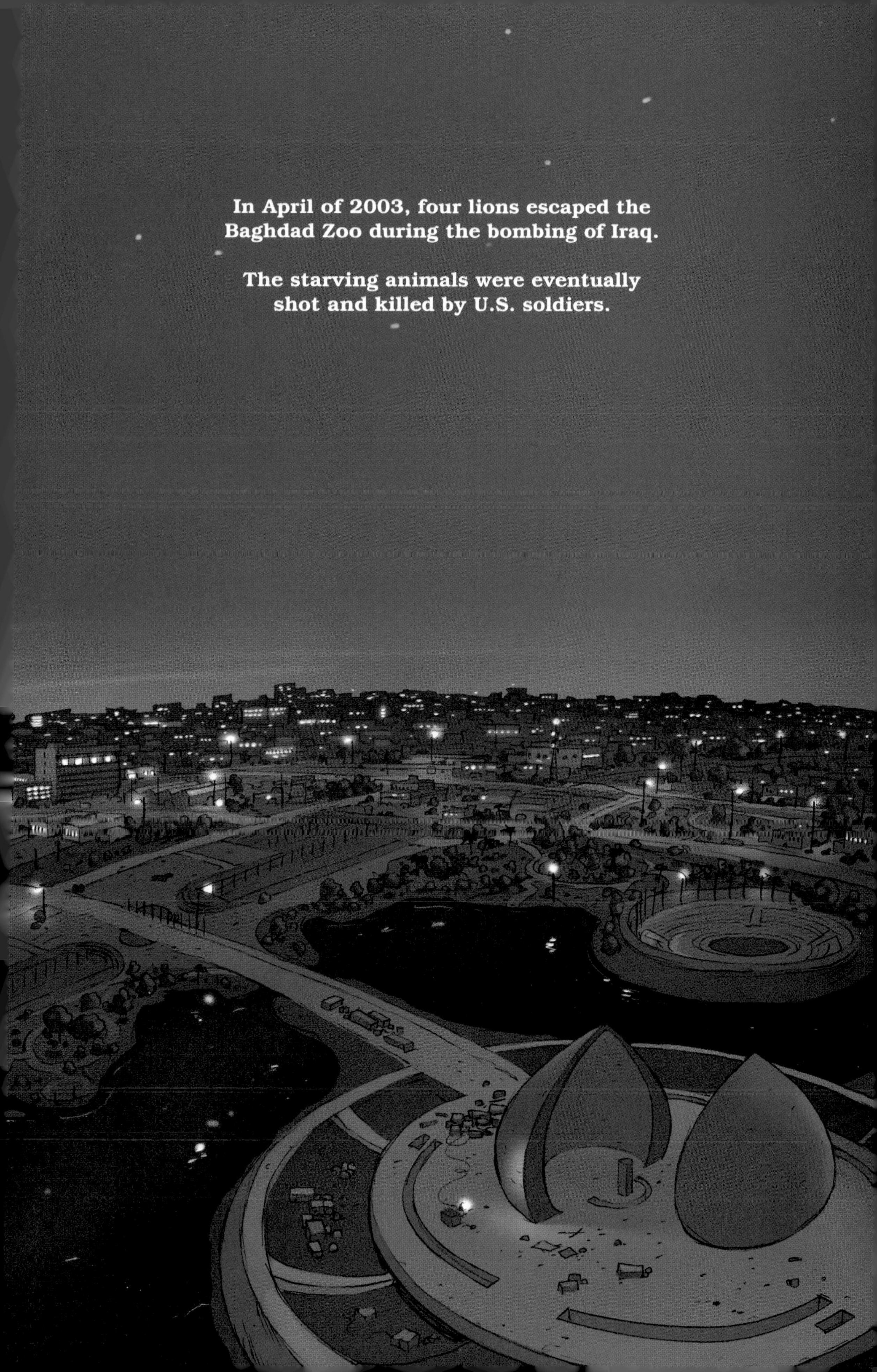
In April of 2003, four lions escaped the Baghdad Zoo during the bombing of Iraq.
The starving animals were eventually shot and killed by U.S. soldiers.

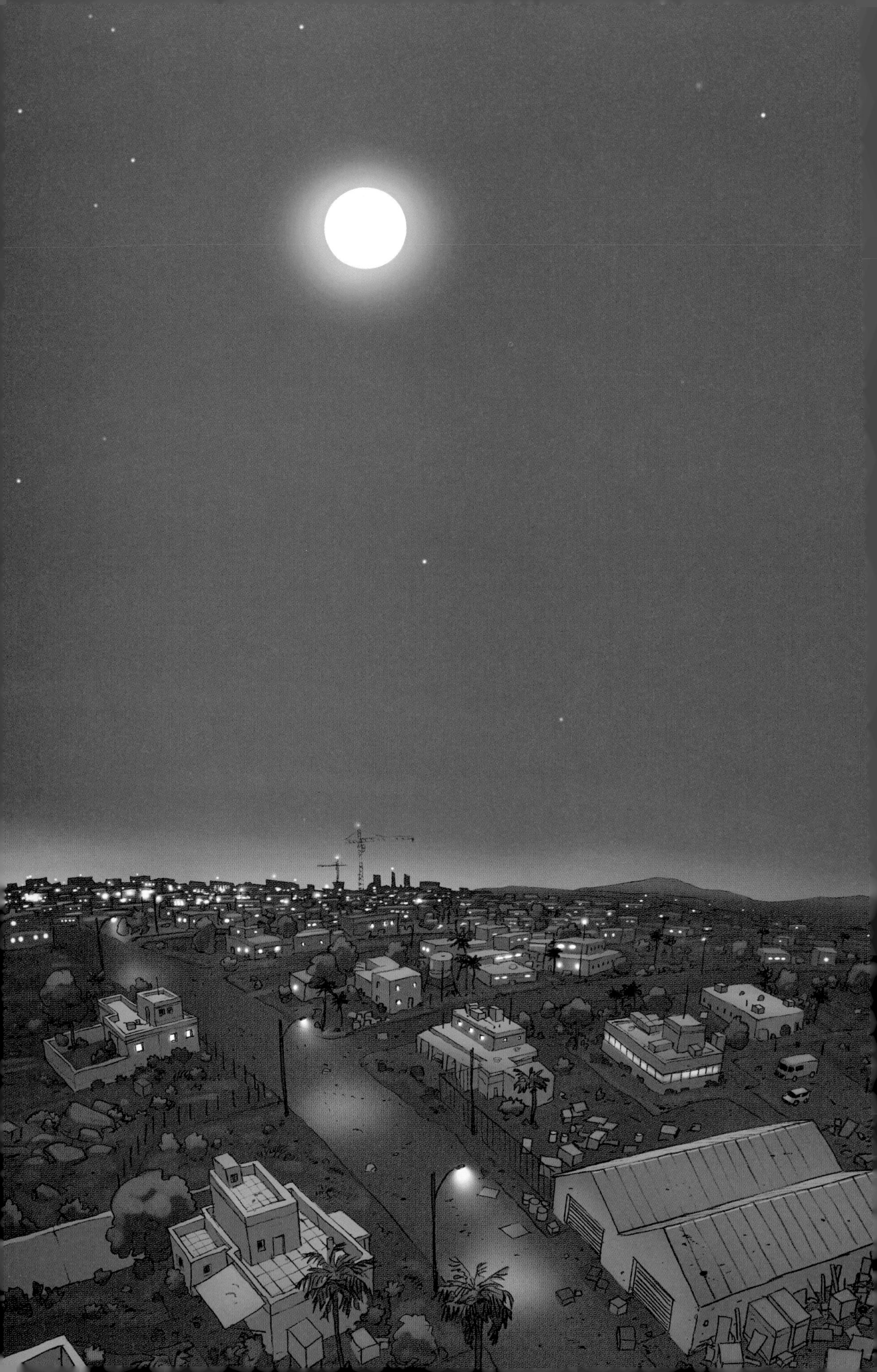

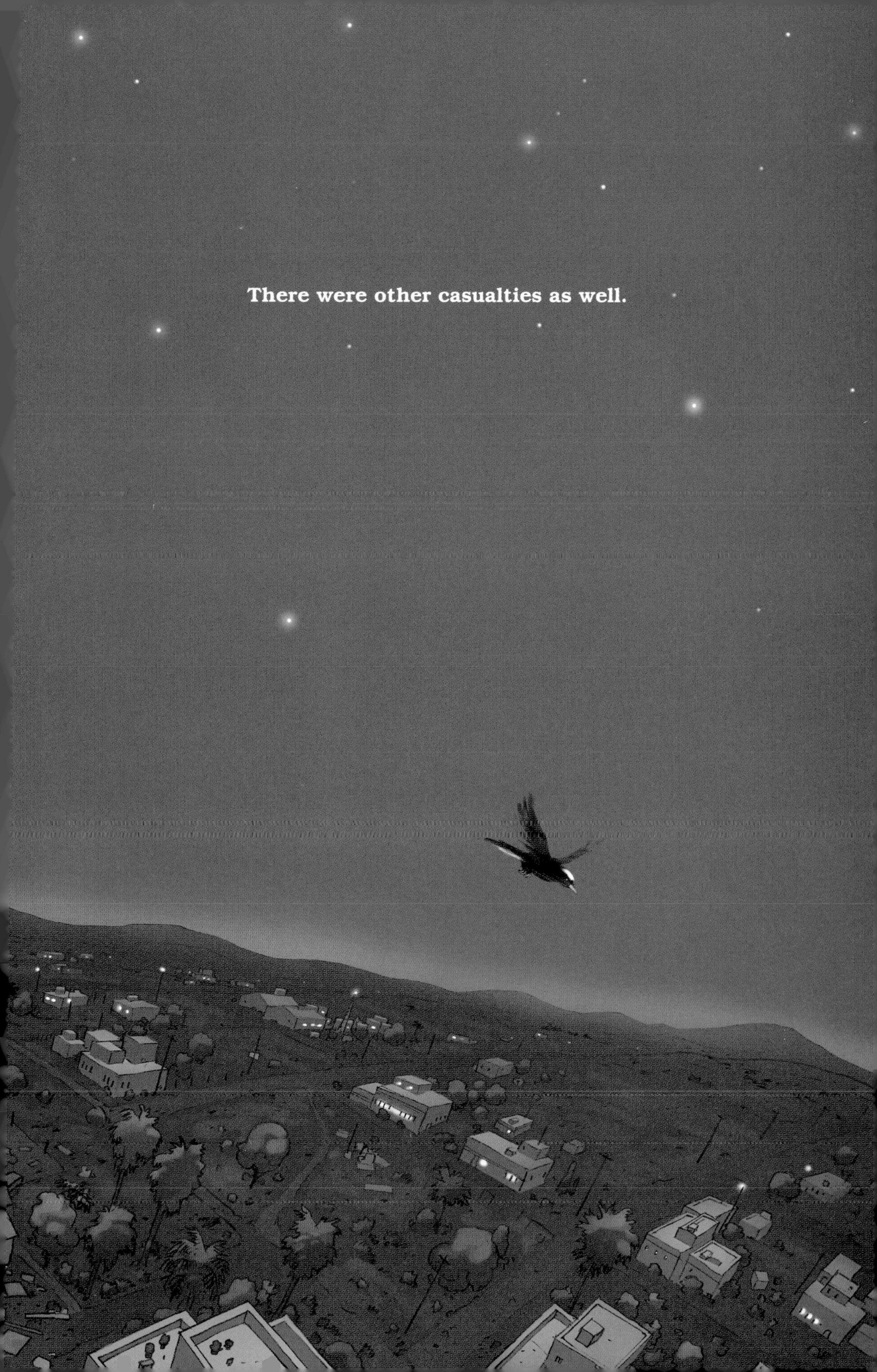
There were other casualties as well.

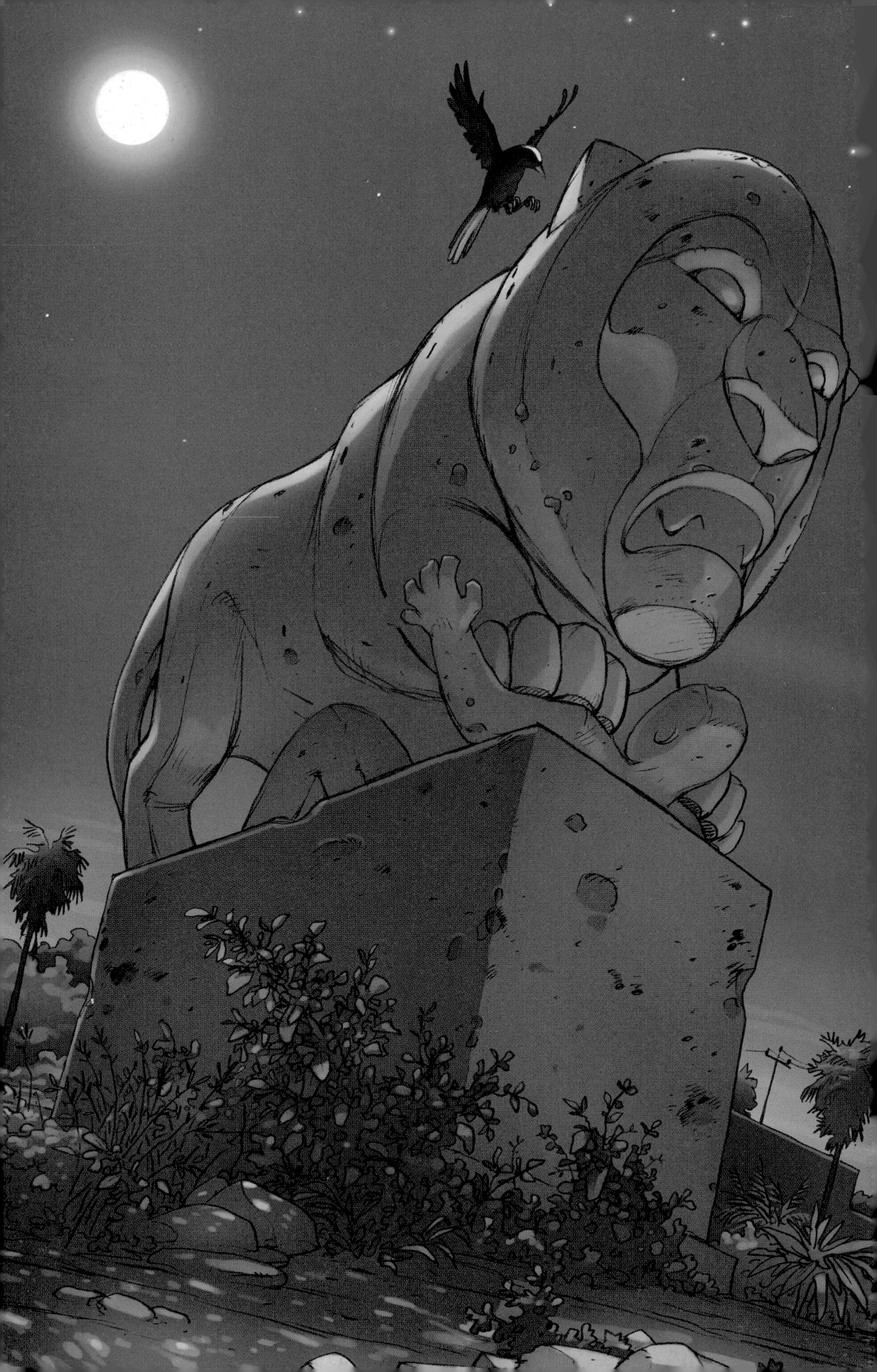